America: One Land, One People

AMERICA

ONE LAND · ONE PEOPLE

NOTED HISTORIANS LOOK AT AMERICA

EDITED AND INTRODUCED BY ROBERT C. BARON

HISTORY IS THE PATH TO OUR FUTURE

FULCRUM

Copyright ©1987
Fulcrum Incorporated

Book Design by Frederick R. Rinehart

LIBRARY OF CONGRESS CATALOGING-IN-PUBLICATION DATA
Baron, Robert C.
America, One Land, One People:
Historians Look at America

Bibliography: p.
1. United States — History. 2. Frontier and pioneer life —
United States. 3. United States — Territorial expansion.
I. Baron, Robert C.
E178.6.A392 1987 973 86-25670
SBN 1-5591-012-2

FULCRUM, INC.
GOLDEN, COLORADO

This book is dedicated, with gratitude, to:
Leo F. Baron, Marietta S. Baron,
Barry J. Holloway, and Jane H. Holloway

Publisher's Preface

The Fulcrum Christmas Series on American History

EACH YEAR, FULCRUM will publish a book about America specifically for the holiday season. The topic will be an important American historical or biographical work which may not be available to the general reader through other sources. The books will be made of the highest quality paper and cloth binding and will be produced as limited editions.

This year's book, *America — One Land, One People*, is about America and the American people and contains a dozen writings from some of the most thoughtful and readable historians and historical writers. America's story is one of expansion to new and unsettled lands, lands which have built America to what it is today. Many nations colonized the continent; people from over two hundred countries settled here, and yet America became one nation from sea to sea. This book includes sections on the settlement of the New World by France, Spain and England; the growth of the Northwest Territories, the Midwest and the South; the Westward migration; and the closing of the Frontier.

The 1987 Fulcrum Christmas Book will be Thomas Jefferson's *Garden and Farm Journals*. This book will be published in collaboration with the Massachusetts Historical Society.

We hope that you enjoy this year's selection.

Contents

About The Authors

CHARLES AUSTIN BEARD (1874-1948) was born near Knightston, Indiana and was educated at DePauw University and Oxford. He taught at Columbia University from 1907 to 1917 and at Johns Hopkins University beginning in 1940. One of the most influential historians during the early twentieth century, he later became disillusioned with Roosevelt and the New Deal and was a strong supporter of isolationism. His books include *An Economic Interpretation of the Constitution, The Economic Origins of Jeffersonian Democracy, American Citizenship, The Industrial Revolution, American Foreign Policy in the Making, American Government and Politics, President Roosevelt and the Coming of the War* and a series of books on American history written with his wife, Mary.

MARY RITTER BEARD (1876-1958) was an historian and writer. Her books include: *America Through Women's Eyes, The Force of Women in Japanese History,* and *The American Labor Movement.* Together with her husband she wrote: *The Rise of American Civilization, America in*

Midpassage, A Basic History of the United States, American Citizenship, and *The American Spirit: A Study of the Idea of Civilization in the United States.*

ROSCOE CARLYLE BULEY (1893-1968) was born in Georgetown, Indiana. Educated at Indiana University and the University of Wisconsin, he taught history in high school, at the University of Wisconsin and at Indiana University where he was a professor for more than forty years. He was a co-author of *The Midwest Pioneers* and wrote *The Indiana Home, The American Life Convention,* and *The Old Northwest: Pioneer Period 1815-1840* for which he won the Pulitzer Prize for History in 1951.

BRUCE CATTON (1899-1978) was born in Petosky, Michigan. For many years, he was a reporter for the Cleveland News, Boston American, and later the Cleveland Plain Dealer. From 1942 until 1952, he served in Washington as Director of Information, first for the War Production Board and later for the Departments of Commerce and the Interior. He was a co-founder of American Heritage magazine and served as editor and senior editor from 1954 until his death. He was the author of numerous books including *The War Lords of Washington, Mr. Lincoln's Army, Glory Road, This Hallowed Ground, Terrible Swift Sword, America Goes to War, Grant Takes Command, Grant Moves South,* and *Reflections on the Civil War.* In 1954, he won the Pulitzer Prize for History for his book *A Stillness at Appomattox* and in 1961, received a special Pulitzer Citation for *The American Heritage Picture History of the Civil War.*

WILLIAM BRUCE CATTON was born in 1926 in Cleveland, Ohio and educated at the University of Maryland and Northwestern University. He has taught history at the University of Maryland, Princeton and Middlebury College where he is now Professor Emeritus in History. His books include: *Two Roads to Sumter* and *The Bold and Magnificent Dream,* both co-authored with his father, Bruce Catton, and *American Epoch, 2nd Edition,* written with Arthur Link.

SIR WINSTON LEONARD SPENCER CHURCHILL (1874-1965) was the son of Lord Randolph Churchill and an American mother, Jennie Jerome Churchill. Educated at Sandhurst, he became an officer in 1894 and served in India and the Sudan. Resigning his commission, he was sent by an English newspaper in 1899 to cover the South Africa War. Captured and imprisoned by the Boers, he escaped and returned to a hero's welcome. First elected to parliament in 1900, he served in the cabinet as First Lord of the Admiralty prior to World War I. After spending time in the front lines in France, he returned to politics and served in the cabinet in a number of positions. As colonial secretary, Churchill negotiated the treaty that established the Irish Free State. When World War II broke out, he became Lord of the Admiralty and from May, 1940 to July, 1945, Churchill was Britain's Prime Minister. A stirring orator, he led Britain through its most difficult times. His books include: *Lord Randolph Churchill, First Journey, Marlborough: His Life and Times, My Early Life, The Island Race, A History of the English Speaking Peoples* (4 volumes), and the six volume *History of the Second World War.* In 1953, he received the Nobel Prize in Literature both for his writing and his oratory.

HENRY STEELE COMMAGER was born in 1902 in Pittsburgh. He obtained his degrees at the University of Chicago and did further work at Copenhagen, Cambridge and Oxford universities. He has taught at New York University, Columbia, and Amherst and has lectured at more than a score of foreign and American universities. He edited *Documents of American History,* and *Living Ideas in America.* His books include: *The Growth of the American Republic, Theodore Parker, America: The Story of a Free People, Majority Rule and Minority Rights, The American Mind: An Interpretation of American Thought and Character Since the 1880s, Freedom, Loyalty, Dissent, The Great Constitution, The Search for a Usable Past, The Empire of Reason,* and *Jefferson, Nationalism and The Enlightment.*

BERNARD A. DeVOTO (1897-1955) was born in Ogden, Utah. He taught English at Northwestern and Harvard. He once defined himself as a journalist, a novelist, a critic, an historian and an editor. He was the editor of The Saturday Review of Literature and for twenty years wrote the column "The Easy Chair" for Harper's magazine. He edited *The Portable Mark Twain,* and his books include *Mark Twain's America, Mark Twain at Work, The World of Fiction, The*

Easy Chair, the novels: *Chariot of Fire* and *Mountain Time,* and the three volume series of American history: *The Year of Decision: 1846, The Course of Empire* and *Across the Wide Missouri* for which he won the Pulitzer Prize for History in 1948.

ALEXIS DE TOCQUEVILLE (1805-1859) was born in France of a minor noble family. He studied law and was a junior magistrate at Versailles, when the French government sent him with an associate, Gustave de Beaumont, to study America. They arrived on May 9, 1831 in Newport, Rhode Island and stayed in America until February 20, 1832. America was then a country of 13 million people, mostly settled along the Atlantic coast. During the nine month visit, their travels took them not only to the east coast but as far west as a fort that became Green Bay, Wisconsin and as far south as New Orleans. During the trip, de Tocqueville filled fourteen notebooks with his observations and ideas about American democracy and social institutions. His analysis of America, *De La Démocratie en Amérique,* was published in two parts, in 1835 and 1840,, and established de Tocqueville's reputation. He was elected to the chamber of deputies in 1839 and served for ten years, becoming foreign minister for a short time. His second major work, *The Old Regime and the Revolution,* was published in 1856.

OSCAR HANDLIN was born in 1915 in New York City. He has taught at Harvard and Oxford. He is a major interpreter of the immigrant in America and won the Pulitzer Prize for History in 1952 for his book The Uprooted. He has received wide praise as a biographer and has edited The Library of American Biography. His books include: *Boston's Immigrants, Commonwealth, The American People in the Twentieth Century, Adventure in Freedom, Chance or Destiny, Al Smith and His America, The Dimensions of Liberty, The Americans, Race and Nationality in American Life, The Crisis in Civil Rights,* and *Abraham Lincoln and His America.*

SAMUEL ELIOT MORISON (1887-1976) was born in Boston and educated at Harvard. He taught history at the University of California, Oxford, New York University, Queen's University in Ontario, and for most of his life at Harvard University. He served in the United States Naval Reserves from 1942 until 1951, was historian of U.S. Naval Operations during World War II and retired as a rear admiral. He twice won the Pulitzer Prize for Biography — in 1943 for *Admiral of the Ocean Sea — A Life of Christopher Columbus* and in 1960 for *John Paul Jones — A Sailor's Biography.* Other books include: *The Maritime History of Massachusetts, The Oxford History of the United States, Builders of the Bay Colony, Three Centuries of Harvard,* the 15 volume *History of the United States Naval Operation in World War II, Strategy and Compromise, The Oxford History of the American People,* and *The European Discovery of America.*

JOSEPH ALLAN NEVINS (1890-1971) was born in Illinois. He was a journalist for The Nation magazine and was the literary editor for the New York Sun and the New York World. He taught at Cornell, Columbia and Oxford universities and in 1948, began the oral history project at Columbia. He was a founder of American Heritage magazine and the magazine's circulation grew to 300,000 before his death. A prolific author, Nevins wrote more than 70 books including: *Illinois, The American States During and After the Revolution (1775-1789), The Emergence of Modern America, Freemont — the West's Greatest Adventurer, The World of Eli Whitney, John D. Rockefeller, The United States in a Chaotic World, The Gateway to History* and was co-author of a three volume series on Ford. He won the Pulitzer Prize for Biography in 1933 for his book *Grover Cleveland: A Study in Courage* and in 1937 for *Hamilton Fish: The Inner History of the Grant Administration.*

FRANCIS PARKMAN (1823-1893) was born in Boston, the eldest son of Rev. Francis Parkman, a leader in the Universalist Church. In 1846, he took a trip west with his cousin, Quincy Shaw. The notes from that trip were published as *The California and Oregon Trail,* one of the most famous books of its time. Although plagued with poor health throughout his entire life, he became an important historian and writer. His books covered the struggle in North America between France and England and included: *History of the Conspiracy of Pontiac, Pioneers of France in the New World, The Jesuits in North America in the Seventeenth Century, La Salle and the Discovery of the Great West, Montcalm and*

Wolfe, The Old Regime in Canada, and *A Half Century of Conflict.*

FREDERICK JACKSON TURNER (1861-1932) was born in Portage, Wisconsin and was educated at the University of Wisconsin and Johns Hopkins. He taught at the University of Wisconsin, Harvard, and the Carnegie Institute. An influential and innovative teacher, at Wisconsin he became the first professor in the United States to offer a course on the American West, and his department was also the first to offer a course on diplomatic history. His paper *The Significance of the Frontier in American History,* presented at the Columbian Exposition in Chicago in 1893, is one of the most influential papers ever presented by an American historian. His books include: *The Significance of Sections in American History,* for which he won a Publitzer Prize for History in 1933, *Rise of the New West, The Frontier in American History,* and *Frederick Jackson Turner's Legacy,* which was published posthumously.

Robert C. Baron

INTRODUCTION

W̲HY STUDY HISTORY? Because history is the study of ourselves — what has occurred to our ancestors, our people,
our region, our nation and our world. Those who study the
past can begin to understand the present and make educated
guesses and plans for the future.

In an address to the Society of American Historians,
Bruce Catton said:

> "As the world grows more and more complex,
> and as its complexities come to conceal an in-
> creasing number of pitfalls which can drop the
> whole human race straight down into the starless
> dark if they are not noticed in time, it becomes
> more and more important for men to understand
> their own history, to see how former trials were
> met, to learn how some of these pitfalls develop,
> and to get the knowledge they must have if they
> are to make their way through the perplexing and
> ominous twentieth century. Above all things,
> they need to know the story of their own past, and
> if they don't get it from the historian they won't

get it from anybody – not, at least, in a form that will be of any use to them.

"If our (historians') work has any final value, that value must depend very largely on our ability to see the essential truth beyond the darkness and the error, and to create a faithful picture out of something that never makes itself explicit – on our ability, in short, to perform the historian's difficult task not only with the the historian's competence but also with the skill, the insight, and the demanding conscience of the literary artist. In the end we can do no more than draw the thing as we see it, knowing that we cannot possibly see all of it. If we succeed, the history we write takes its place as literature. Good history is literature."[1]

In this book, twelve selections, by fourteen historians, tell the story of America. Reading these selections, as well as other works by these writers, provides the knowledge about the past which Catton refers to, and gives a sense of how to deal with the political, economic and personal opportunities and challenges of the present and the plans and dreams of the future. These selections trace the history of this country from the initial explorations and territorial claims through the first settlements, three centuries of westward migration and into the beginnings of the twentieth century.

The selections also demonstrate how enjoyable the reading of history can be, for these authors are not only outstanding historians, they are excellent writers and their stories of the American experience are good literature. They write not only about the people but also for the people of this country. Among them, they have won ten Pulitzer prizes for History and Biography and one Nobel Prize for Literature.

THE WRITERS, THE SELECTIONS, THE TIMES

It would be foolhardy to try to add to the words and ideas of these wonderful writers. Perhaps the discrete thing is to get out of the way and let the reader instantly begin to enjoy the following selections. For those who wish to begin immediately with the main meal, you are excused.

But perhaps some readers may wish to think about the selections. Why these historians? Why these selections? The answer to the first question is easy. The selections that follow are written by some of the best historians and writers. They stand at or near the apex of their profession in their writing about America. They think and write clearly. They deserve to be read. A major goal of Fulcrum's Christmas Series is to introduce our readers to the best of American historical writing.

History written by good writers may be the most enjoyable of all reading. There is little in literature that is more pleasurable or more instructive than to read Bruce Catton's *A Stillness at Appomattox* or Dumas Malone's biography of Thomas Jefferson or Bernard DeVoto's *The Course of Empire* or Samuel Eliot Morison's *Admiral of the Ocean Sea*.

Why these selections? Perhaps they offer answers to the myriad of questions we ask about four centuries of the American experience. How did America become one from sea to sea — unified in government, language, and people? Why wasn't America "Balkanized" into many different nations, as were Eastern Europe, Africa, South America and Central America? What has made America become what it is today?

An unknown continent was explored by people from Spain, England, France and many other countries. Land now within the American borders was claimed by England, France, Holland, Mexico, Russia, Spain and Sweden, and was already occupied by hundreds of Indian tribes. This country had received immigrants from more than two hundred countries; in fact, every country in the world may have had citizens emigrate to the United States.

Yet, from the beginning, the American people have shared the feeling of being in a very special place, a place unlike any other. Listen to the words of three of the founding fathers, America's first three presidents.

". . . The citizens of America, placed the most enviable condition as the sole Lords and Proprietors of a vast tract of Continent, comprehending all the various Soils and climates of the World, and abounding with all the necessaries and conveniences of life, are now, by the late satisfactory pacification, acknowledged to be possessed of absolute freedom and Independency. They are from this period to be considered as the Actors on a most conspicuous theatre, which seems to be peculiarly designated by Providence for the display of human greatness and felicity. Here they are not only surrounded with every thing which can contribute to the completion of private and domestic enjoyment, but Heaven has crowned all its other blessings, by giving a fairer Opportunity for political happiness, than any other Nature has ever been favored with . . ."[2]

George Washington

"I always consider the settlement of America with reverence and wonder, as the opening of a grand scene and design in providence, for the illumination of the ignorant and the emancipation of the slavish part of mankind all over the earth."[3]

John Adams

"We hold these truths to be self-evident; that all men are created equal; that they are endowed by their creator with certain unalienable rights; that among these are life, liberty, and the pursuit of happiness; that to secure these rights, governments are instituted among men, deriving their just powers from the consent of the governed..."[4]

Thomas Jefferson

America was truly blessed as a country. The selected historians write about the events, actions and people that have made this country. Perhaps the major factors in the development of America were the American land, the flow of immigration and the American character.

THE AMERICAN LAND

Another Fulcrum book, *Of Discovery and Destiny*, notes that the American character was forged from our learning about and contending with the vastness of the land that makes up this country.[5] During the four centuries of the American people, there was never a limit to the land, just to our imaginations and our strength. This is a very large country and it must have seemed infinite to the first settlers huddled along the Atlantic coast.

Experiences with the vast amounts of land that exist in the North American continent defined America's ideas about ourselves and our perceptions of limitation, boundary, possibility and opportunity. Americans have looked to the land to draw and form our independent character as a people and as a country.

Land was available to all who would take it. Settlers could move west, clear the land, start farming and achieve a degree of personal independence. They needed no approval from a king, a lord, an absentee land owner or the church. Land was there for the taking. In this country, a family could feed themselves if they would but work. The land and the opportunity were there.

The Northwest Ordinance, passed in July 1787, was one of the most important and enlightened laws ever passed. It provided for the orderly and speedy organization of Western territories into states and for the admission of these states, with full equality, into the union. Unlike other parts of the world, American territories were not to be held for the benefit of the central government but were to become full and equal partners with the existing states. This principle applied to all states as the country expanded to the Pacific. Thus, not only could a person own his own land, he could be a full and equal citizen with those who had come before.

In 1802, Thomas Jefferson saw the importance of the Mississippi River Valley to America and was able to acquire the Louisiana Territory. No longer was there a powerful European country owning land to the west and hindering westward migration. By bringing political unity to the country from the Atlantic to the Mississippi Valley, America was free to expand and grow. The history of America, in large part, became the history of the migration west.

The Homestead Act was approved May 20, 1862, granting land to settlers for family farms. The country accelerated its westward rush. Frederick Jackson Turner wrote that between

1880 and 1900, a territory equal to the area of France, Germany, England and Wales combined was added to the farmland of America.[6]

As long as land was available to all who wanted it and were prepared to settle on and work the land, the country continued to expand. For most members of a frontier community, there were no hierarchies — any man was as good as any other. Performance was what mattered, not family background or social status. And anyone dissatisfied with his situation had the opportunity to move west and start again.

In 1890, the director of the Census declared that a continuous frontier (a line between wilderness and settled land) no longer existed. By the turn of the nineteenth century, the opportunity for migration to unsettled lands had disappeared. The passage of the Taylor Grazing Act in 1934 regulated government range land and provided for the withdrawal of all public lands for homesteading in ten western states. A four hundred year era in American history had come to an end.

AMERICA AND THE IMMIGRANTS

> "Once I thought to write a history of the immigrants in America. Then I discovered that the immigrants were American history."[7]

> Oscar Handlin

America is a country of immigrants and descendents of immigrants. Table 1 shows immigration during every ten year period from 1820 to 1980. In four decades, the 1840s, the 1850s, the 1880s, and the 1900s, the number of people immigrating into this country each decade was a number greater than ten percent of the country's population as registered by the census starting the decade. In every decade for eighty years, the number of immigrants was at least five percent of the people listed in the prior census.[8]

Immigrants supplied the farmers, merchants and workers to run the factories and build the railroads, roads and canals. In 1820, the population of the United States was 9,638,453. In the following century, over 33 and a half million men, women and children immigrated to the United States. In the 165 years since 1820, more than 52 million people immigrated to this country.

In his book *The Atlantic Migration,* Marcus Lee Hansen stated:

> "Though the thirteen American colonies owed their growth and prosperity largely to the recurrent additions of population from Europe, the century from 1815 to 1914 marked the most significant period in the peopling of the United States. The years from the fall of Napoleon to the outbreak of the (1st) World War spanned exactly one hundred seasons of migration in which a great flood of humanity rolled westward across the Atlantic and swept over the waiting continent. To that flood every nation, every province, almost every neighborhood, contributed its stream. Beginning in Ireland and the valley of the Rhine, the fever of emigration extended toward the north and east, gripping the English midlands, the Scandinavian countries and the north of Germany, spread southward through the Baltic provinces, Poland and Austria into Italy and, before it finally ran its course, afflicted the Balkans and the Near East. Only France and Spain proved immune so far as the United States was concerned. It is clear that the cause of so vast an exodus was wider than race or nationality and deeper than legislation or politics. It was not the mania of a single generation, nor of ideas that prevailed for a mere decade or two. The cause was as universal as the movement itself."[9]

Overpopulation, famine, war, poverty, laws regulating the poor, unsuccessful political revolutions and the desire for religious or political freedom drove the rural peasants from their land to the nearby market towns, to industrial centers and then across the Atlantic. The United States is but one of the nations populated by immigrants. So too are Australia, Canada, New Zealand, Southern Africa, Argentina, Brazil and other parts of Central and South America. The nineteenth century was a time of great and prolonged migrations of people.

One concept of America and immigration was stated by

Israel Zangwill: "America is God's crucible, the great melting pot where all the races of Europe are melting and reforming."[10] Consider the mixture of the Irish, Welsh, Prussians, Lithuanians, Norwegians, Swedes, British, Poles, Ukranians, Armenians, Germans, Czechs, Austrians, Hungarians, Italians, Greeks, Scots, Russians, Jews, Arabs, people from the West Indies, Chinese, Turks, Japanese, Mexicans, Canadians, Africans, Koreans, Phillipinos, Vietnamese, Cubans, and Latin-Americans — all becoming Americans.

Emma Lazarus wrote the famous statement on immigration which is inscribed on the base of the Statue of Liberty.

THE NEW COLOSSUS

> Not like the brazen giant of Greek fame,
> With conquering limbs astride from land to land;
> Here at our sea-washed, sunset gates shall stand
> A mighty woman with a torch, whose flame
> Is the imprisoned lightning, and her name
> Mother of Exiles. From her beacon-hand
> Glows world-wide welcome; her mild eyes command
> The air-bridged harbor that twin cities frame
> "Keep, ancient lands, your storied pomp!" cries she
>
> With silent lips. "Give me your tired, your poor,
> Your huddled masses yearning to breathe free,
> The wretched refuse of your teeming shore.
> Send these, the homeless, tempest-tost to me,
> I lift my lamp beside the golden door!"[11]

Immigration has made America rich and dynamic. It has also provided the base for America's industrial and agricultural expansion throughout its history. Oscar Handlin wrote:

> "Immigration had so long been a familiar aspect of American development that it was not until the end of the nineteenth century that any question was raised as to the propriety of its continuance. The whole history of the peopling of the continent had been one of immigration. The seventeenth century movement of population had brought the first settlements to the Atlantic seacoast. The eighteenth century newcomers had

pushed those beyond the Alleghenys. And in the nineteenth century, a continued flow of new Americans had helped open the West and, at the same time, had contributed to the development of urban life and the growth of an industrial economy." [12]

In the late nineteenth century, pressures developed to keep out or restrict new immigration. In 1917, over the second veto of President Wilson, the Immigration Act became law on February 5, ending the open door to immigration. This law restricted the flow of immigrants, required a literacy test and established a quota system by which each country was restricted to a certain number of admissions per year, except for Orientals who were barred completely. The quota law of 1921 restricted the number of aliens of any nationality to three percent of the number of foreign born of that nationality resident in the United States in 1910. These laws were modified in 1924, 1952, 1965, 1968 and again in 1980, first to set numerical limitations by foreign state and later to eliminate national quotas and set preferences for immigrants, including their professions and their relationship to American citizens.

With America's continued inability to resolve the problems of illegal aliens and to reevaluate the total immigration numbers, we continue to wrestle with the immigration situation. Meanwhile, as can be seen from Table 1, immigration, as a percent of population, remains at historically low levels.

THE AMERICAN CHARACTER

> "I agree with you that there is a natural aristocracy among men. The grounds of this are virtue and talent." Thomas Jefferson, Letter to John Adams Oct. 28, 1813.

America has always been a land where performance is more important than talk, where mobility is more important than stability, where what one does is more important than who one is and where the future is more important than the past. It is a country without an aristocracy, or a self-

9

appointed group of leaders, a country where the self-made man is an important individual and where anyone has the potential to achieve anything, even to become president.

What made an American? Perhaps because of the chalenges and opportunities in dealing with the vastness of the land as well as the challenges presented to the new immigrants, the major characteristics might be said to be independence, self-reliance and optimism. Americans relied on themselves, their families and their neighbors. They had little reason to expect help from the national government and they would have looked with displeasure on any interference in their lives from the federal government.

Henry Steele Commager, in his excellent book *The American Mind* , wrote the following about the nineteenth century American:

> "Nothing in all history had ever succeeded like America, and every American knew it. Nowhere else on the globe had nature been at once so rich and so generous, and her riches were available to all who had the enterprise to take them and the good fortune to be white. As nature and experience justified optimism, the American was incurably optimistic. Collectively, he had never known defeat, grinding poverty, or oppression, and he thought these misfortunes peculiar to the Old World. Progress was not, to him, a philosophical idea but a commonplace of experience: he saw it daily in the transformation of wilderness into farm land, in the growth of villages into cities, in the steady rise of community and nation to wealth and power.
>
> "To the disgust of Europeans, who lived so much in the past, he lived in the future, caring little for what the day might bring but much for the dreams — and profits — of the morrow. He planned ambitiously and was used to seeing even his most visionary plans surpassed; he came at last to believe that nothing was beyond his power and to be impatient with any success that was less than triumph.

"With optimism went a sense of power and of vast reserves of energy. The American had spacious ideas, his imagination roamed a continent, and he was impatient with petty transactions, hesitations, and timidities. To carve out a farm of a square mile or a ranch of a hundred square miles, to educate millions of children, to feed the western world with his wheat and his corn, did not appear to him remarkable."[13]

America is a country born of an idea. In the nearly five centuries since Columbus and his ships sailed to a new world, in the more than four centuries since the founding of our oldest city, St. Augustine, Florida, in the two centuries since Jefferson's immortal words proclaimed our independence, America has marched on. From the villages and towns of Europe and Asia, immigrants sailed and steamed across the ocean to reach America's shores. And once in the new world, they walked and rode across the continent, heading west, toward new opportunities, jobs and the open land — marching on to the leadership of the free people of the world.

It is this story — of America and America's people — that this book and these historians tell. For in knowing our past, our nation's and our ancestor's dreams, beliefs and history, we begin to know ourselves.

ENDNOTES

1. Bruce Catton, *Prefaces to History* (Garden City: Doubleday & Company, 1970).

2. George Washington, "Letter to Governor William Livingston," June 12, 1783.

3. John Adams, Notes for "A Dissertation on the Canon and Feudal Law," 1765.

4. Thomas Jefferson, "Declaration of Independence," July 4, 1776.

5. Robert C. Baron and Elizabeth Darby Junkin, *Of Discovery and Destiny* (Golden: Fulcrum, Inc., 1986).

6. Frederick Jackson Turner, "Social Forces in American History," *American Historical Review*, January, 1911.

7. Oscar Handlin, *The Uprooted* (Boston: Atlantic Monthly Press, 1951.)

8.Table 1. Immigration to the U.S. from all Countries per Decade.

Decade	Immigration In Decade	Immigration As % of Population At The Beginning of Decade
1821-1830	143,439	1.5%
1831-1840	599,125	4.7%
1841-1850	1,713,251	10.0%
1851-1860	2,598,214	11.2%
1861-1870	2,314,824	7.4%
1871-1880	2,812,191	7.3%
1881-1890	5,246,613	10.5%
1891-1900	3,687,564	5.9%
1901-1910	8,795,386	11.5%
1911-1920	5,735,811	6.2%
1921-1930	4,107,209	3.9%
1931-1940	528,431	0.4%
1941-1950	1,035,039	0.8%
1951-1960	2,515,479	1.7%
1961-1970	3,321,677	1.9%
1971-1980	4,389,639	2.2%

Source: U.S. Bureau of the Census

9. Marcus Lee Hansen, *The Atlantic Migration, 1607-1860* (Cambridge: Harvard University Press, 1940).

10. Israel Zangwill, *The Melting Pot*, Act I, 1908.

11. Emma Lazarus, "The New Colossus," 1883.

12. Oscar Handlin, "Immigration as a Factor In American History," *The Uprooted* (Boston: Atlantic Monthly Press, 1951).

13. Henry Steele Commager, *The American Mind* (New Haven: Yale University Press, 1950).

I

Charles A. Beard and Mary R. Beard

EXPLORATION, TERRITORIAL CLAIMS, AND COLONIZING AGENCIES

IMPELLING CURIOSITY WAS one of the prime forces that drove adventuresome Europeans to sail westward across the uncharted Atlantic, centuries ago, to come by surprise upon the great wilderness later called America. Impelling curiosity, too, induced European settlers in America and their descendants to investigate with growing success the complex laws of the physical world about them. Finally, impelling curiosity led Americans, enriched with the new accumulation of knowledge, to undertake the ultimate in exploration — the probing of the vastnesses of the mighty universe itself. In 1959 a device built and launched in the United States shot past the moon into permanent orbit around the Sun, millions of miles from the Earth. It was followed by an American electronic complex that observed the planet Venus, and by a later probe that flashed photographs of Mars back to Earth by radio. Work has begun on vehicles to carry men to the moon, perhaps to be followed by human visits to Mars. Once the solar system has been conquered, what will stand in the way of going even deeper into the dim immensities of space?

Plunging into this great stream of exploration near its source, where the details of our story may properly begin, we find Europeans of the late fifteenth century contemplating a daring project. It was that of sailing westward across the Atlantic, defying unknown hazards, in quest of new routes to old lands, and perhaps finding hitherto unsuspected regions along the way. Then as now, major exploratory projects were expensive. Like the space probes of our own times, they were government-financed, and considered by many as important to the maintenance of national prestige.

While it has been claimed that Leif Ericson might have reached North America around the year 1000, the first major exploratory expedition westward across the Atlantic to produce lasting results was that of Christopher Columbus, financed largely by the Spanish royal treasury and actively backed by Queen Isabella, who saw the possibilities of the enterprise. With her good wishes and a small fleet Columbus and a motley crew left Spain and came upon islands well off the southeastern coast of what is now the United States. The year was 1492.

Within a short time, other European nations entered the exploratory race, in quest of fame and fortune. Of particular interest to Americans was the project of King Henry VII of England, which assigned to John Cabot, an Italian navigator, and his three sons, the task of seeking hitherto unknown heathen lands to the west, on the way to Cipango (Japan) and China via the Atlantic.

In carrying out his orders, Cabot reached the shores of what is now Canada, in the region where the mighty St. Lawrence River pours forth into the sea. There, in 1497, he landed and planted the banner of the English king, claiming for his sponsor what he supposed was the east coast of Asia. With news of his labors, he went back to England. The next year Cabot was sent out again. This time he sighted the east coast of Greenland but his sailors mutinied against pushing north into the strange, icy seas that interested him. To satisfy the crew, he headed southward, coming to the continent of North America and following its shores to a point in the neighborhood of what is now called Chesapeake Bay. Unable to find a rich people with goods for profitable trade, he returned to England deeply disappointed.

14

On the basis of Cabot's discoveries, the King laid claim to a domain of unknown size and character in North America on which the history of the United States was to unfold. By this simple act, he opened for the English the greatest real estate and investment opportunity in the history of Western civilization.

But nearly a century passed before the English began to take full advantage of that opportunity. In the interval numerous and wide voyages by Portuguese, Italian, Spanish, French, and English explorers led to mapping, if roughly, the contours of a large part of the two Americas. And as an outcome Spanish, Portuguese, and French rulers also laid claims to large shares of land in the Western Hemisphere.

Intrepid explorers under the flag of Spain, by innumerable journeys, were the first to penetrate the mainlands. Spanish conquerors led by Hernando Cortes and Francisco Pizarro invaded Mexico and Peru, robbed them of gold, silver, and precious stones, and excited all Europe by reports of wealth in the New World. Between 1539 and 1542 Hernando de Soto traveled overland from the coast of Florida, with his mounted companions, to the Mississippi River and some distance beyond. During those years Francisco Vásquez de Coronado, with an armed band of horsemen, toiled his way northward from Mexico into the heart of the region lying west of the Mississippi, looking for more treasure in the rumored Indian cities of Cibola. In 1565 the Spanish planted the settlement of St. Augustine in Florida.

By the middle of the sixteenth century the Spaniards seemed about to take possession of the newly discovered world. Though they had not found more gold and silver in regions above Mexico or the elixir of youth sought in Florida by Ponce de Leon, by 1550 the ruler of Spain, Charles V, could claim as his property many islands in the Caribbean; Mexico by right of conquest; all of South America except Brazil, which the Portuguese had seized; and an immense area, if indefinite as to boundaries, north of the Gulf of Mexico and the Rio Grande. To back up his claim he had at his command a big navy, a large merchant marine, and many hardy soldiers. With his conquering hosts were associated dauntless Catholic priests to aid in establishing a New Spain in the New World — a state, church, and feudal aristocracy all resting on the labor of subject peoples.

Before the English government began to develop its territorial rights by occupation the monarchs of France had also become interested in the New World. Francis I laughed at Spain and Portugal for pretending to own so much of it, and declared that he wanted to see the will of Father Adam, the first proprietor, bequeathing to them the inheritance they claimed. In 1524, while Henry VIII, who had succeeded his father in 1509, was neglecting the patrimony won by Cabot's voyages, Francis sent an .Italian seaman, John Verrazano, across the Atlantic to hunt for a northwest passage to the Orient. Verrazano did not find the passage, but he did sail along the coast of North America and gave Francis good grounds for asserting that he too owned a big share of the new continent. Several years later Francis sent Jacques Cartier forth on two successive voyages. They resulted in explorations of the St. Lawrence River region, the bestowal of the name Montreal on an Indian village, and a more definite claim to a huge area in that neighborhood.

Such were the rights asserted by England, Spain, and France to enormous masses of land in the New World when Queen Elizabeth came to the throne of England in 1558. Her father, Henry VIII, had done nothing to develop the real estate nominally acquired through the voyages of Cabot. Busy with intrigues on the continent of Europe, his marital troubles, and his quarrels with the Pope, he had continued to neglect his opportunities in the New World. During the reigns of his son Edward VI and his daughter Mary, England had been torn by religious disputes, and the exploitation of land over the sea had been slighted by English statesmen.

With the accession of Queen Elizabeth, however, many things incited English enterprisers to develop the real estate and investment opportunity opened to them by the voyages of Cabot under Henry VII. Elizabeth was high-spirited, well educated in the secular learning of the Renaissance, and greatly interested in adding to the riches and power of her realm. She was determined that her people should be kept Protestant in religion under the Church of England, firmly united, and strong enough to break the dominion of her Catholic rival, the King of Spain, in the Atlantic Ocean. Elizabeth gathered around her Protestant statesmen of the same mind, fostered the growth of the English navy, and encouraged her sea captains to plunder Spanish ships and colonies wherever they could.

The new temper of the Elizabethan age was imperiously displayed in 1577-80 when the English "sea dog," Francis Drake, sailed around the world plundering cities and Spanish ships laden with treasure as he went — down along the east coast of South America, up along the west coast, to the shores of California, and all the way home.

From this exploit English capitalists got an inkling of the investment opportunity before them, on and across the seas. Money for Drake's expedition had been supplied by a corporation in which Elizabeth held shares. The company's original investment was £5000. In return for the stockholders' risk, Drake's treasure ships brought them £600,000 in profits — enough to satisfy the most expectant investor. As a prudent ruler Elizabeth used her portion of the proceeds to pay off the debts owed by the Crown. According to careful estimates, the numerous raids on Spanish ships and colonies during Elizabeth's reign netted the handsome sum of £12,000,000.

With news of splendid returns on investment undertakings at sea ringing in their ears, English merchant capitalists, including investors among fair ladies, began to take a serious interest in the real estate of the English Crown in the New World. Since it was undeveloped real estate — not land occupied by peoples abounding in wealth — its exploitation demanded colonization by the English people themselves and the founding of a "New England" under the Crown of the old England. Having this project in view, Queen Elizabeth gave Sir Walter Raleigh, one of the favorites of her court, a patent to all the territory he might colonize, on condition that he pay to the Crown one fifth of the returns from the mining of precious metals.

Under this patent Raleigh sent out in 1584 an expedition which visited the island of Roanoke off the coast of North Carolina and brought back reports of a favorable climate and country — "the most plentiful, sweet, fruitful, and wholesome of all the world." The next year Raleigh dispatched seven ships and 108 colonists to Roanoke, but the colonial experiment was a failure. Raleigh made another attempt in 1587, only to fail again. The colonists who shared in that venture utterly disappeared from the scene, leaving behind them not even a clue to their fate. The sixteenth century came to a close without the creation of a single permanent English settlement in America.

But the century did not close until the English navy, aided by a terrible storm at sea, had destroyed in 1588 the Spanish Armada, a mighty fleet sent by the King of Spain to crush the rising power of England. Though this victory, by eliminating powerful enemy forces, would have facilitated the settlement of America, the English did not immediately follow up their advantage with a wave of colonization.

While the English rested, three rival powers made the most of the lull to strengthen their positions in America. Following Hudson's trip in 1609, up the river now bearing his name, his Dutch employers laid claim to the surrounding territory. As "New Netherland" this holding became an important farming and trading community with what is now New York City as its chief port. Farther to the North, in Canada, French fur traders set up temporary quarters which were followed, in 1608, by the establishment of Canada's oldest permanent community — Quebec. From this base, French missionaries journeyed westward, creating missions all the way to the Great Lakes by 1616. Meanwhile Spain expanded from her Florida base to build posts and missions along the Atlantic Coast as far north as what is now the State of South Carolina. On the other side of the Mississippi River, Spaniards went from Mexico northward into what is now the State of New Mexico, in 1598. By 1610 their settlements were being governed from a capital at Santa Fe, a community that has come down to our own times to serve as the capital of a modern State.

By the time the English finally got around to exploiting in earnest the territory nominally under the English Crown, the French, Spanish and Dutch already had good footholds in the New World. To cope with these established rivals, England now most urgently needed large, permanent, and prosperous colonies, something new to British experience. Beside this complicated undertaking the spectacular dispatch of Drake on a voyage of exploration and the sensational robbery of Spanish vessels were mere theatrical displays of power and daring. To arm a few ships, shoot up Spanish galleons, loot them, and send them to the bottom of the ocean was an operation that required little money — mainly skill in navigation and the fighting spirit.

Qualities and courage of a different sort were necessary to create large and orderly societies in a wilderness. This business demanded huge capital. It was more than men's work: women in great numbers had to be associated with it. All the ideals, arts, and sciences of civilization were involved in it.

Not fully aware of all that colonization implied but eager to exploit the real estate in America, English merchant capitalists sought that privilege from the Crown at the beginning of the seventeenth century. They had already formed trading companies to engage in commerce with Russia, the Levant, and the East Indies. In corporate enterprises of that type they had demonstrated their ingenuity. Besides they had accumulated much capital for investment. This capital they now proposed to use in colonial enterprise, about which they knew so little. Only one aspect of it was clear to them: individual farmers, merchants, artisans, and their families, with small savings or none at all, could not embark unaided on any such undertaking as large-scale colonization.

Under English law all the territory claimed in America belonged to the Crown. The monarch could withhold it from use, keep any part of it as a royal domain, or grant it, by charter or patent, in large or small blocks, to privileged companies or private persons. It was to the Crown, therefore, that English enterprisers bent on colonizing America turned for grants of land and powers of government. And in making such grants by charter or patent, the Crown created two types of legal agencies for colonization: the corporation and the proprietary.

The corporate type of colonizing agency was the company, or group of individuals merged into a single "person" at law by a royal charter. The charter named the original members of the company and gave them the right to elect officers, frame bylaws, raise money, and act as a body. It granted to the company an area of territory and conferred upon it certain powers: to transport emigrants, govern its settlements, dispose of its land and other resources, and carry on commerce, subject to the laws of England. Such a corporation was akin to the modern joint-stock company organized for profit-making purposes.

The proprietary agency for colonizing consisted of one or more persons to whom were given a grant of territory and various powers of government by the Crown. The proprietor or proprietors thus endowed with special privileges had authority to found a particular colony and enjoy property, commercial, governing, and other rights similar in character to those vested in a company by royal charter.

Companies and proprietors did not, however, have a completely free hand in managing their colonial affairs. They were limited by the terms of their charters or patents and were compelled to confer upon free settlers certain liberties and immunities enjoyed by English people at home, including a share in the making of local laws.

Various motives inspired English leaders to form companies or embark on careers as proprietors in America. Among the motives was the desire to extend English power, to make money out of trading privileges and land sales, and to convert the Indians to Christianity. For some companies and proprietors the idea of establishing religious liberty in America for members of persecuted sects was also among the primary considerations in their colonizing activities. Still another purpose entering into the plans of companies of proprietors was that of giving poor and otherwise unfortunate persons in England a chance to work and live better in a new country so open to opportunity. In other words, political, economic, religious, and charitable motives induced English leaders to devote their energies to the business of colonization.

The systematic beginnings of all the American colonies were made by companies or proprietors or under their jurisdiction. By 1733, the year in which the last colony, Georgia, was started at Savannah, there were thirteen colonies under the Crown at London, legally known as the British Crown after the Union of England and Scotland in 1707. These colonies, taken arbitrarily in geographical order, with references to origins, were:

New Hampshire — partly an offshoot of Massachusetts, given a separate status in 1679.

Massachusetts — founded in 1630 by Puritans under the Massachusetts Bay company; with it became associated in 1691 the colony of Plymouth, established by the Pilgrims in 1620 on land belonging to the Plymouth Company chartered by James I in 1606.

Rhode Island — incorporating two offshoots from Massachusetts, Rhode Island and Providence Plantations, to which as a single colony, a royal charter was given in 1663.

Connecticut — originating partly in offshoots from Massachusetts planted in the Connecticut River valley in 1635 and partly in settlements on the shore, united under a royal charter in 1662.

New York — founded as New Netherland under the Dutch West India Company in 1624; seized by the English in 1664 and given the name of New York.

New Jersey — founded under Dutch auspices, seized by the English in 1664, and afterward named New Jersey.

Delaware — first settled by the Dutch under the Dutch West India Company and by Swedes under the Swedish South Company; taken by the English in 1664 and placed under the proprietorship of William Penn in 1682.

Pennsylvania — granted to William Penn as proprietary by Charles II in 1681; first settlement at Philadelphia in 1682.

Maryland — granted to Lord Baltimore as proprietary in 1632 and started by settlements on Chesapeake Bay in 1634.

Virginia — founded by settlement at Jamestown in 1607, made under the London Company chartered by James I in 1606.

North Carolina — early settlements made by pioneers from other colonies; passed under an association of proprietors in 1665 by a royal grant covering all the Carolina region, formerly within the jurisdiction of the Virginia Company; given a separate status as the royal province of North

Carolina in 1729.

South Carolina — granted to proprietors in 1665; settlements made at Albemarle Point in 1670 and near Charleston in 1672; an independent royal province after 1729.

Georgia — granted to a board of trustees, or company, by George II in 1732; Savannah founded in 1733.

This listing of some of the corporate and proprietary agencies under which English colonization took place, does not give an adequate impression of the amount of free movement by individuals and groups in America, especially after the first settlements had been planted. Nothing less than an encyclopedia could do that.

Take for example North Carolina. Virginians had made a permanent settlement in that region at least five years before it was granted to proprietors in 1665, and other pioneers, mainly Scotch, Scotch-Irish, and Germans from Pennsylvania, went down into North Carolina on their own motion.

Again, take New Hampshire in the far north. An independent settlement was established there as early as 1623 under a royal grant. Other beginnings in New Hampshire had been made before the Puritans came to Massachusetts Bay in 1630. When Puritans pushed over into the New Hampshire region and claimed it as a part of their grant, they encountered stout opposition from the forerunners. Only after many disputes was a final separation from Massachusetts effected by New Hampshire in 1679.

But independent undertakings and individual or group migrations from colony to colony, significant as they were in colonial beginnings had relatively little influence on the rise of self-governing colonies. It was under companies and proprietors holding grants of land subject to the English Crown that systematic colonization on a large scale was made possible. It was under companies and proprietors that the foundations of all the colonies were securely laid. Crown, companies, and proprietors — their work in colonization was to have from the outset a profound influence on the course of affairs which eventuated in the formation of the continental United States.

Bruce Catton and William B. Catton

CHOICE GRAIN TO WILDERNESS

By THE EARLY years of the eighteenth century an identifiable American society had emerged, still recognizably English yet unmistakably different. Many of the leading strands in the complex fabric that was British North America already pointed clearly toward Lexington and Concord and Yorktown; some pointed only a little less clearly, toward the longer-range future — toward the Age of Jackson and continental expansion, Manifest Destiny and sectional controversy, civil war and the rise of industry.

Of prime importance was the sheer fact of population growth. In 1650 there were perhaps 50,000 English-speaking settlers in North America, centered almost entirely in the coastal regions of Chesapeake Bay and southern New England. By 1700 this population had grown to about a quarter of a million, still heavily concentrated in those two regions but with smaller bridgeheads established and pushing inland from such newer centers as New York, Philadelphia, and Charles Town. The eighteenth century was the spectacular growing time for Great Britain's mainland colonies. The figures are little more than educated guesses, the best of which suggest that there were over 600,000 colonists by 1730, well over 1,000,000 by 1750, and something close to 2,000,000 by 1770.

By the latter date, although there were still sizable blocks, of sparsely settled land here and there, even near the coast, the edge of settlement had pushed well inland and begun penetrating the foothills of the Appalachians. One advance guard ·was already moving into the upper Ohio Valley, another through the Cumberland Gap along Daniel Boone's trail to Kentucky. The major seaports — Boston, Newport, New York, Philadelphia, Charleston — had achieved the status of small cities; Philadelphia, then the leader with a population of perhaps 35,000, had become one of the largest urban centers in the British empire.

After 1700, in short, the beginning-time, the period of struggle merely to survive and maintain a precarious foothold in the New World, was well past. The seaboard colonies were going concerns, and rapid population growth, with all of its benefits and problems, had become a leading fact in American colonial life.

This fast-growing society displayed a well defined class structure, varying somewhat from place to place but having enough common characteristics to make possible a general description. Three classes, loosely defined in the terminology of the day as "better sorts," "middling sorts," and "meaner sorts," had emerged in every colony.

At the top stood a fairly distinct colonial aristocracy. It lacked the titles, most of the pretensions, and nearly all of the privileges of its counterparts in England and Europe; it was self-made rather than hereditary; it had arisen, often quite recently, from modest middle-class circumstances; and it was not rich by European standards. Nevertheless, each colony's politics, society, and economy were led and dominated by a small group of landed or mercantile families, who had come to occupy most of the key positions and won recognition and deference from the classes below them.

The middling sort, the most important element in colonial society, was composed primarily of independent landowning farmers, together with the equally independent, equally property-conscious artisans, shopkeepers, and tradesmen in the villages and towns. Shading imperceptibly off below the middling sort was a large and fluctuating group of tenant farmers and journeymen who in prosperous times might climb upward into the middle class and in depressed times might slide as easily downward into the ranks of the meaner sort.

These, in town and country, were much like the poor in Europe — farm hands, dependent artisans, free servants, apprentices, day laborers, sailors. In the very lowest ranks, at least temporarily, were the indentured servants, and, more permanently, those drifters and improvident marginal types who existed to a greater or lesser extent in every town and on the fringes of every rural community — folk whose lack of skill, incentive, health, or luck had mired them at the bottom of the heap.

By the eighteenth century the American heap had acquired a large and formidable layer even beneath the lowest classes, and here all resemblance to the European class structure ceased. For under the poorest, humblest, and most debased of white settlers, of which every colony had its share, lay the institution of slavery — African slavery, composed entirely of blacks and based frankly and explicitly upon the fact of color difference.

Blacks were brought to mainland North America within a dozen years of the establishment of the first permanent settlement at Jamestown, but they were negligible, in numbers or importance, until around 1700. By then, however, and increasingly thereafter, slavery was firmly established, especially in the Southern colonies, and the black population grew every bit as spectacularly as the white. Toward the end of the seventeenth century, when the institution began its real period of growth, perhaps 8 per cent of the colonial population were slaves. By the 1760s this proportion had climbed beyond 20 per cent. Nine out of ten of them were in the Southern colonies, with perhaps a third concentrated in Virginia alone. Only in South Carolina had blacks become a majority but they comprised 40 per cent of the inhabitants of Virginia and about one third in Maryland, North Carolina, and Georgia.

Despite this concentration in the staple-producing South, slavery was established by law in all of the colonies, questioned in none, and more than marginally present in parts of the North. In New York, where a pre-emptive overlay of great landed estates had acted to discourage white settlement, blacks in the 1760s made up no less than 13 per cent of the population. They exceeded 7 per cent in Rhode Island, approached 7 per cent in New Jersey, and stood at around 5 per cent in Delaware. Only in New England and Pennsylvania, where as occasional seamen, artisans, and house servants they composed about 2 per cent of the total inhabitants, were blacks a negligible quantity.

An infinitesimal minority of blacks, mostly in the North, had achieved freedom, although the term had a special and qualified meaning. It was an uneasy, precarious, ill-defined halfway house between slavery and the full citizenship to which only people with white skins could aspire. But fenced in as it was by the enduring suspicion and hostility of the white community, those slaves who knew about freedom wanted it desperately. It was at least a step upward.

In any case a caste system based on color lay underneath the European class system, and nearly every generalization that can be made about the transatlantic society is in one way or another dependent on that fact. The forced immigrant from Africa and the voluntary immigrant from Europe were becoming Americans together; not least among the many factors making for "Americanness" was the presence of the two races and the challenge posed by their co-existence.

A brief regional review of the colonial class structure displays variations in detail but no important difference in the prevailing pattern. In the New England colonies the aristocracy was primarily urban, based upon commercial wealth and allied or auxiliary professions and skills, a few fortunes in Rhode Island also derived from large estates devoted to the raising of horses and livestock for export to the West Indies. Below the prosperous first families of Boston, Newport, and a few smaller towns was the largest and most stable middle-class element in all of British North America. Each of the townships that constituted the basic political unit in New England contained its own substantial families and local elites, yet wealth and land were distributed more equitably in most New England communities and shared in by a higher percentage of the total male population than anywhere else on the planet. This stable, orderly region also had its quota, in village, town, and city alike, of landless and dependent poor.

The situation in Pennsylvania and New Jersey resembled that in New England. Philadelphia occupied the role of Boston as chief distributing and marketing center, with wealthy Quaker and Anglican merchants exhibiting much the same diligence and self-assurance as their Puritan counterparts to the northeast. The ethnic composition of the Middle Colonies were more heterogeneous, and farms tended to be larger; but they were like New England in the size and preponderance of their middle-class farming element, in the general prosperity of that element, and in the relatively equitable distribution of wealth.

The same could not be said for New York, which contained one of the most powerful groups of great landed families to be found anywhere in America, and correspondingly fewer opportunities for enterprising yeoman farmers. The colony had some of these, to be sure; it also had a mercantile element based on the Manhattan seaport and an influential fur-trading element based on Albany. But New York had a more uneven distribution of wealth, a smaller middle class, a larger tenant population, more slaves, and a higher incidence of poor and disaffected sorts than any other Northern province.

Below Pennsylvania lay the South, already distinguishable from the Northern settlements in tone, social composition, and outlook. Slavery and a high proportion of blacks, staple-crop agriculture with large landholding units, and a more decidedly rural society gave the South its regional identity. Yet even here the variations were considerable.

The Chesapeake colonies, where tobacco dominated the economy and bulked large in men's thoughts, contained a well-entrenched, energetic, tightly knit aristocracy of great planters, no towns worthy of the name, and a substantial number of degraded poor whites. Yet both Virginia and Maryland also possessed a middle class of yeoman farmers and small planters, prosperous and enterprising in the best colonial tradition. If this middling element was smaller than in Pennsylvania or New England, it was of greater consequence than the traditional Southern stereotype would indicate.

North Carolina, though slavery was firmly rooted and one third of the inhabitants were black, was the least Southern of the Southern colonies. There were big tobacco plantations with their first families in the northeast, adjoining Virginia, and big rice plantations with their first families in the Cape Fear region adjoining South Carolina, but for the province as a whole the American norm of small and middle-sized farms was more in evidence than elsewhere in the South. The towns were few and small, barely more than villages; the general level of prosperity was lower, the incidence of poverty and bare self-sufficiency somewhat higher, than in the North. But North Carolina represented a distinct modification of the standard Southern image.

South Carolina had the newest and wealthiest of the colonial aristocracies. The second quarter of the eighteenth century was a boom period there: sustained high prices for rice and indigo, and plenty of good land on which both crops could be grown. The result was rapid expansion, rapid accumulation of wealth, a rapid importation of slaves until they outnumbered the white population by a ratio of three to two, and a pattern of life (at the top) more frankly given over to the pursuit of pleasure than anywhere else in British North America. The big South Carolina planters owned more land and more slaves than the first families of Virginia and Maryland. Unlike the Chesapeake planters, the South Carolinians divided their vast holdings into manageable units, placed each in the hands of a resident overseer, and avoided the rural plantation life with its English gentry overtones in favor of stately town houses, cooling Atlantic breezes, and the urban pleasures of Charleston — the one town of any consequence south of Philadelphia. In no mainland colony was wealth more unevenly distributed or plantation slavery more predominant. Though not without its quota of small farmers, small planters, and townsfolk catering to Charles-

ton's elite or serving the rice and indigo trade, South Carolina had strayed conspicuously farthest from the colonial
middle-class norm.

As for Georgia, the southernmost colony and much the
youngest, less than a generation old at the middle of the
eighteenth century, important changes were afoot. These
changes offered an instructive lesson, by which the entire
colonial experience might be read. It added up to this: what
the majority of settlers wanted, especially if they wanted it
badly enough, was sooner or later going to prevail over anything to the contrary that planners or founders might have
had in mind.

Philanthropic and imperial interests had conjoined to
prepare a well-planned blueprint for Georgia. It was to be a
haven for England's debtors and other sturdy unfortunates,
who would receive small but workable tracts of free land in
the unsettled country below the Savannah River and who
would be available, in their sturdy and rugged independence, as a ready-made citizen soldiery protecting the more
settled British colonies from the incursions of hostile Spaniards and Indians operating out of Florida. The blueprint
was duly tried out. Assorted felons, debtors, and other pris-
oners were recruited, brought over, and given their fifty
acres, with the careful stipulation, written into law, that all
such grants without a male heir would revert to the trustees.
The other stipulations, equally in the interest of maintaining
a stable force of border guards, forbade rum and slavery.

This was eighteenth-century philanthropy at its best, and
no set of rules could have gone more completely against the
colonial grain. Fifty acres permitted no more than bare self-
sufficiency. Rum, here as in most of the New World, was regarded as little less than a necessity of life. And the ban on
slavery, well intentioned and healthy though it was, ran into
unfortunate timing: Georgia was founded and the settlers arrived just when neighboring South Carolina entered upon its
boom years, with fortunes being made in the cultivation of
rice and indigo on large plantations by slave labor. Geor-
gians could see all of this happening, not only across the Savannah but right under their noses; a few South Carolinians
took up large tracts in Georgia and brought their slaves with
them in order to take advantage of the boom, in casual defi-

ance of the new colony's rules.

Public pressure against these rules mounted steadily, and not long after the middle of the century the whole blueprint collapsed. Large holdings, entailable with or without a male heir, were permitted; so was rum; so was slavery. And in the generation just preceding the Revolution, Georgia began its first period of growth and development as a thoroughly Southern colony, importing blacks and creating a plantation system as fast as it could.

West of the towns and settled farming regions along the coast lay an irregular and ill-defined area known simply as the back country; by the mid-eighteenth century this region had begun to exhibit certain social patterns of its own. For the Northern colonies, the westward movement had gone about as far as it could then go. The best and most accessible land in western Massachusetts and Connecticut was pretty well taken up. New Englanders had also begun moving northward into New Hampshire, Vermont, and southern Maine, but this expansive thrust paused uncertainly at mid-century in the face of the continuous threat posed by imperial France and her Indian allies. The influence of landed proprietors and Albany fur traders combined to curb the flow of migration into frontier New York; in Pennsylvania, where the tide of settlement had reached the Susquehanna and in a few places crossed it, the same cloudy danger zone that New Englanders faced farther north, beyond which hostile French and Indians lurked, acted to stem or divert the westward movement until after the Seven Years' War. The most active area of back-country migration during the second quarter of the eighteenth century was in the southern colonies — into the Piedmont regions of Maryland, Virginia, and the Carolinas. The farm country was good here, in places excellent; the Indian menace, if it still existed, was much reduced by the comparative inaccessibility of the area to the prodding efforts of imperial France.

Much of the bustle, energy, confusion, and hectic pace that later generations of Americans would experience accompanied this process of settling the back country. With regional variations, the same sort of thing was observable all along the frontier, from New England on down. Order was at a discount. Land titles tended to be cloudy, and disputes, at law and sometimes at gunpoint, correspondingly more frequent and more bitter. Rude cabins were thrown up and trees were girdled in a hurry. Many individuals and families eked out a squalid, precarious existence in conditions that travelers from the more settled regions could only regard as barbarous; nearby, in contrast, newcomers might establish prosperous farmsteads that struck outside observers as positively idyllic.

The former condition was observed, for example, among recent Scotch-Irish arrivals in interior North Carolina. "The clothes of the people consist of deerskins, their food of johnnycakes, deer and bear meat. A kind of white people are found here who live like savages. Hunting is their chief occupation." The idyllic contrast was noted at about the same time by an observer of some new German settlers in the Shenandoah Valley in the 1760s: "They know no wants and are acquainted with but few vices. Their inexperience of the elegancies of life precludes any regret that they have not the means of enjoying them; but they possess what many princes would give half their dominions for — health, contentment, and tranquility of mind."

As Richard Hofstadter has pointed out, both of these pictures are true enough, yet neither accurately describes what was really going on when settlers streamed into the back country. Crude savagery and idyllic self-sufficiency were phases that most colonists sought to escape as soon as they could clear enough acres to grow a marketable surplus. In much of the back country there were rivers providing avenues of sorts to the seaboard markets, and in most new communities the crude egalitarianism usually associated with the frontier soon gave way to the kind of haphazard inequality that variable combinations of luck, incentive, and enterprise acted to bring about.

A prime mover in this process of back-country settlement was the land speculator — a far more representative and important character in the building of America, for better and for worse, than is sometimes recognized. Mark them well, these speculators. They are ubiquitous if sometimes sha-

dowy figures, present whenever a boom or the promise of a
boom or the chance of persuading someone else of the promise of a boom exists. Their predecessors helped organize
the first companies and the first movements by which the
first Englishmen crossed the Atlantic. We shall meet them
again during the early national years, and again during the
railroad heyday, and in the mining towns of the Far West,
on the Great Plains, and always on the urban frontiers, from
seventeenth-century Manhattan to twentieth-century Levit-
town — drawing up maps and prospectuses, organizing companies, staking out claims, buttonholing legislators, hiring
agents to circulate among prospective customers. The speculator was composed of varying quantities of dreamer, sales-
man, patriot, and con artist, on a scale that ranged from
penny-ante pitchman to continental empire builder. He
tended to know his way around in politics, and he had a
quick tongue, a quick imagination, and a keen eye for the
main chance. In all of this he was thoroughly American, whether of the seventeenth, eighteenth, nineteenth, or twentieth century. More often than not, he provided the agencies,
printed material, organization, and machinery whereby individuals, families, and groups were induced to pull up
stakes and brought to this or that portion of America.

These speculator-adventurers were hard at work during
the settling of the back country before the Revolutionary
War. Their efforts undoubtedly added to the confusion and
the conflicting land titles, the inequities in distribution and
price of land; they also contributed greatly to the speed with
which this hitherto uncharted region was peopled and built
up.

With equal speed, the crude, isolated, hastily thrown together settlements were transformed into back-country rep-
licas of the older societies whence these folk had come.
Hard on the heels of the pioneer farmers came a scattering
of artisans, ministers, lawyers, merchants, rootless vaga-
bonds and ne'er-do-wells, desperate men a step ahead of
the law, and sundry other types that went into the making of
a colonial community. In the Southern colonies, too, came
planters or would-be-planters, sometimes with a slave or a
handful of slaves. Buzzing energetically to and fro with all

these newcomers were some of the speculator-adventurers whose schemes and political connections and prospectuses had helped set the tide in motion in the first place. And from this motley assortment not merely farms but villages and small towns and a class structure emerged in a few short years, as roughhewn and recent as the new buildings and the trails that led there, yet consisting of the same identifiable hierarchy of better sort, middling sort, and meaner sort that characterized the social structure of British North America as a whole.

Two items distinguished American colonial society most sharply from those of Western Europe. It was more fluid, and the middle class was proportionally larger and more important.

Class lines were drawn, of course, and the established social hierarchy was never seriously questioned. But these lines were undeniably easier to cross than in Europe, even than in England, and this difference was widely recognized. The degree of mobility in any society is a relative matter, depending upon the object of comparison. Europeans, especially of the upper class, tended to view the fluidity in colonial America as bordering on anarchy; they were impressed chiefly by the greater ease with which the social ladder was mounted — or descended — than in the Old World. Yet by the standards of nineteenth-century America the situation in the colonies seems far more stable, the mobility more circumscribed.

There is scattered evidence to indicate that class lines in America were hardening somewhat and that mobility, especially into the upper ranks, was becoming more difficult at about the middle of the eighteenth century. This change was to prove relevant to the tangle of thoughts and reactions that Americans began having as the controversy with the mother country assumed revolutionary proportions. But until this counter trend set in, and for most of the first half of the eighteenth century, when due allowance is made for the exaggerations of shocked conservatives and Old World aristocrats, the mainland colonies offered a degree of social mobility unknown anywhere else on earth.

This mobility operated into and out of a middling element that was both larger and more influential than in other Western societies. (The Dutch and the Swiss afforded possible exceptions to this statement, but the circumstances in both cases were so different that meaningful comparisons are difficult to make.) The American colonies struck many observers, foreign and domestic, as consisting almost entirely of a huge, spread-eagle middle class. This was noted despairingly or admiringly, depending on the observer's politics. It was noted most frequently, of course, in those colonies where middle-class dominance was most evident. As a writer in 'the *Pennsylvania Journal* in 1756 put it: "The people of this province are generally of the middling sort, and at present pretty much upon a level. They are chiefly industrious farmers, artificers, or men in trade; they enjoy and are fond of freedom, and *the meanest among them* thinks he has a right to civility from the greatest."

This was an exaggeration, even in the eighteenth-century Pennsylvania of Benjamin Franklin, but it was inspired by a fundamental truth. Notwithstanding the power, wealth, and influence of the upper classes and the deference generally accorded them, notwithstanding the widespread existence of poverty, colonial America was first and last a middle-class society. The norms, standards, and values were set here, and even before the democratizing influences of the revolutionary, Jeffersonian, and Jacksonian eras had been felt, ultimate power resided here, and nearly everyone knew it.

In every colony the better sort led, but most of them knew or sensed that the freeholding farmers and property-owning townsfolk who were generally content to follow their lead would withhold this support when the leadership tried to move in directions the middling sort found unacceptable — as had been the case, for example, in Georgia. The middling sort had the franchise, which gave them a potential majority in provincial legislatures and New England town meetings. They also exercised the more subtle, less tangible, but ultimately more compelling influence of public opinion — the weight of community sentiment. When this opinion was largely of one mind about something, that was the way things were going to move, as James Oglethorpe and many other lords proprietor had already learned, and as the British king and Parliament and their cadre of officials would find out in their turn.

For most colonial elites, the matter of arranging to lead where the middling sort wanted to go was seldom very difficult. Partly this derived from political sensitivity, an awareness of where the votes and the decisive political power resided. But mainly it stemmed from the simple fact that, almost without exception these colonial elites were of middle-class origin themselves — if not self-made, then only a generation or two back. Only a negligible handful of the English upper classes came to America; Crown officials and their retinues to one side, colonial leadership was home-grown and self-made. Some Southern planters, New York patroons, and Yankee merchants, as their holdings expanded, might come to feel enormously superior to the ordinary farming folk; they might surround themselves as completely as possible with the trappings of Old World aristocracy — in their clothing, equipages, homes and furnishings, the education of their children, in their manners and what a later generation would call their life style. But the great majority of these colonial aristocrats never really transcended the pervasive middle-class values that have lain so consistently at the center of the American experiment.

These values have been noticed before, innumerable times. They have been invoked so frequently, and usually in such reverent and admiring tones, that the invocation has become a kind of litany, a stylized cliché. But certain concepts become clichés, after all, because they contain a truth, and few things were truer in colonial America than the fact that bourgeois values reigned supreme.

Put as briefly as possible, these values revolved around the work ethic, which made cardinal virtues out of industry, frugality, honesty, and self-reliance. The colonist's religion also made virtues of these qualities, as did his experience on the frontier. And of course his European origins had bequeathed them, well developed and in working order. The bourgeois mentality had been emerging in Western Europe, and above all in Holland and England, for some time before the first English ships and colonists set sail.

What made the crucial difference in America was that there were almost no competing values to offset this bourgeois emphasis. The wilderness did not contain, nor was it possible to transplant, a titled hereditary nobility, a crown and court, a living legacy of armored knights and turreted castles, a truly established church that was everywhere accepted, with a tradition centuries old and all the pomp and panoply of cathedral orders and episcopal hierarchy.

The result was that the work ethic flourished in the mainland colonies like the green bay tree. Few vices were subject to as much condemnation as those connected with indolence. The class distinctions accepted by the colonists rested not upon pedigree, coat of arms, or title but upon personal achievement, measured chiefly in material terms. Acceptance of class differences, and of corresponding differences in wealth and property, was accompanied and tempered by a growing conviction that people should rise or fall according to their talents and virtues. Attempts to duplicate the manners and customs of the English gentry or nobility could only be made within this context.

Hence the colonial elites, whatever their pretensions or pipe dreams, were a *working* aristocracy, imbued with a bourgeois sense of responsibility that betrayed their bourgeois origins. Except for the pleasure-hunting rice planters who had got rich so quickly in eighteenth-century South Carolina — men who let overseers run their plantations and provincial government atrophy almost to the vanishing point — the folk at the top of the colonial hierarchy minded both their own affairs and those of their provinces with an energy and dedication that did much to explain the general success of colonial governments and the essential harmony that prevailed between the middle and upper classes.

This harmony was further enhanced by the fact that what the upper classes had, the more ambitious members of the middle class might get, either in their own lifetime or in that of their children. By the same token, there was a general disposition on the part of the "meaner sorts" to accept the system and work within it. For the poor man with ambition and energy — and the colonial era contained thousands of such

— it was clear that he could "better himself" more easily here than anywhere else on earth. And for that sizable portion of the lower classes who were permanently mired in their low estate, there was no real disposition to question the system or do more with one's frustrations than brood or toil or drink or idle the waking hours away.

All of this helped to explain the unremitting energy with which colonial society went about its tasks. It also had an enormously stabilizing effect. There were strong counter tendencies at work, but the emphasis upon diligence and self-reliance made for a sensible, steady, disciplined people. Unless deeply challenged, they would prefer the moderate approach. The middle-class consensus had a built-in stability that even revolutionary times, when they came, could not seriously impair.

The bourgeois motif struck yet another chord. Stable and steady though they might be, colonial Americans were nonetheless a society of climbers — acquisitive, materialistic, assertive folk who looked hungrily upward and contemptuously downward. They had a way of measuring merit and value in monetary terms, and they operated with a powerful conviction, which little in their own experience did anything but strengthen, that those who failed to make it — that is, poor folk — had failed because of some grave moral defect or congenital inferiority, and hence were deserving of neither sympathy nor assistance. The middle-class temperament contained a hard and calculating quality, and it, too, was operating in an environment with few offsetting forces.

Obviously the colonists were considerably more and considerably less than one large happy family working industriously together toward a single goal. Each colony offered a wide range of political disputes and antagonisms. The settlers did not learn the ways of representative government merely by solemn play acting. They learned their politics well, and thoroughly, in the only way that it can be learned — by hashing out their differences in the political arena.

These differences were inevitable, arising from the welter of conflicting needs and demands of people living in a growing and increasingly sophisticated society. Continual political battles occurred in each colony over the basic questions of land, currency, religion, representation, taxation, the role of government, Indian policy, and the like. Class antagonism frequently entered these disputes, and it would be fatuous to assume that colonists of middling or low estate were uniformly content with the leadership of the better sort, or that the better sort consistently governed in the best interests of all. Many of the disputes were sectional — protracted and sometimes bitter conflicts between the eastern and western areas of a colony, in which frontiersmen demanded fairer representation and a higher allocation of tax moneys for roads, defense, and so forth than the older, well-entrenched eastern sections were willing to grant. These disputes were often further complicated by the role of the English government, which tended to have firm ideas of its own about Indian, land, and currency policies, the treatment of dissenting religions, and other matters. Except for a few brief instances, however, clashes between colony and mother country were of secondary importance until after 1760; the colonists gained most of their political experience battling one another.

Some of these disputes were fairly rugged. Middle-class stability and moderation did not prevent colonial Americans from losing their tempers and occasionally resorting to more robust methods than those of debate, petition, and majority vote. There were several serious rent riots in New York, sparked by the bitter resentment of struggling tenants on the large estates of the patroons. Proprietary New Jersey experienced a similar clash. Examples of armed struggles between the eastern and western sections of a colony ranged from Nathaniel Bacon's rebellious movement in Virginia in the 1670s to those of the Paxton Boys in Pennsylvania and the Carolina Regulators ninety years later.

Sectional and class antagonisms existed, but they were less important over the long run than harsh factional disputes between rival groups of upper-class leaders. Indeed, it was in these quarrels between competing factions of the colonial elite that people of middling and low degree often became more active and more aware. Ignored by his leaders in quiet times, the ordinary colonist found politics coming in search of him during the long factional contests. (The normal process whereby a ruling group courted the favor and sought the support of lesser folk, in the interest of beating out a rival faction, was a vital early step toward greater mass participation in politics. Other steps would follow.)

A complex range of political disputes was not the only disruptive force at work. One of the outstanding features of colonial development was the high proportion of those who came here in some form of bondage. This had numerous consequences and implications — beginning, of course, with the brute fact of slavery; a distressingly large portion of the colonial structure was being built on the forced labor of human chattels.

And while the wealth piled by the black bondsman's unrequited toil began to accumulate, with an unseeen rate of interest compounding itself silently and inexorably on the debit side of the ledger, the white bondsman, too, came and helped build America. It has been estimated that as many as half — and outside of New England, where the process never really took hold, considerably more than half — of all the white immigrants during the colonial period came as indentured servants.

This is neither as simple nor as attractive a story as it is often made out to be, although the picture had its brighter side. Some of these bonded immigrants were redemptioners — Europeans of some little substance who often came with their families and a modest store of tools and personal possessions. Usually they were able to pay a portion of their passage money and bonded themselves to redeem the unpaid portion by laboring for someone else for a specified term of years: one or two, or perhaps as many as four, depending upon the amount of passage money they had had to borrow. A far larger number were indentures, people with no money at all and no possessions beyond the clothes on their backs, coming under a contract that could be bought and sold (as could the bearer, while working out its terms) and called for a specified number of years of labor in return for passage and board and keep. A great many, too, were convicts, at least in the sense that they came from English prisons — debtors, perhaps, or those found guilty of one of the innumerable petty crimes which carried heavy prison sentences under the harsh penal code of the times. A few in this final category had committed or been convicted of more serious offenses, and not a few, whatever the extent or reality of their guilt, had become more or less hardened criminals simply by too long association in the brutalizing confines of an unenlightened prison system.

The brighter side of this picture, and the one that receives most attention, is the happy ending that a beneficent system had in store for many of these newcomers once they had worked out their terms. It was the first version of the great American success story — or perhaps the second, if the survival and achievements of those initial settlements in Virginia and Massachusetts be accounted the first. America was here being the fabled land of opportunity from the very start, permitting thousands of penniless folk to come over, labor awhile in servitude, and then achieve independence and success by their own efforts once they could begin working for themselves.

And many thousands did just this; the large colonial middle class included a substantial number of people who came out of poverty in this fashion, and even more who were descended from that element. Certainly the redemptioners, most of whom were from continental Europe rather than from England, and whose origins were a shade less humble than those of the indentures, often moved rapidly from their period of servitude into the ranks of the independent landowning farmer. Many indentures and ex-convicts were also able to do this.

But the success story is only part of the story. One of the most careful studies of indentured servitude in America has estimated that some 10 per cent of the bondservants went on to become freeholding farmers; another 10 per cent achieved comparable status as artisans, overseers, and the like. The rest — eight out of ten — flouted the traditional success story by failing to make it. Some died during their servitude; others drifted back to the Old World; the majority simply took up permanent residence, as it were, in the ranks of the American lower class — sufficiently beaten down by their experiences in either the Old World or the New, or both, to be unable to take advantage of the opportunities America offered. Many indentures, including some of the very poorest and not a few of the convicts, were sold for the term of their contract to Southern plantations, where most were assigned the arduous, endless chores of manual labor required by tobacco or rice culture. Paupers from the London slums were ill prepared for field work in the hot Southern climate. It is hardly surprising that most of them failed to survive this experience or make a go of it afterward.

This is worth a comment or two. The law governing indentures, and the mere possession of a white skin, gave the white bondsman several large advantages over his black counterpart toiling beside him or on the next plantation; only a willful misreading or ignoring of the total evidence can lead one away from the bedrock conclusion that nobody's lot in colonial America was as bad as that endured by the black man. The psychic adjustments demanded of the black slave and the white bondsman in, say, the Virginia tobacco country were basically different in that the slave had no hope whatever for the future. For him things would never get any better; except as age or illness altered the nature of his tasks, things were not even going to change much. The white bondsman could at least see the end of his servitude somewhere ahead.

Yet this probably did most of the white laborers little good. Many blacks would willingly have traded with them, no doubt, but for most derelicts or convicts out of Hogarth's London, there was no such word as "hope," no notion of a future that might be better. The built-in advantages of being white in the land of opportunity were of little use to such folk. Opportunity was something they could hardly imagine, let alone actually pursue. The average planter was neither a sadist nor a fool; it was natural for him to work white bondsmen harder than he worked blacks, on the cruel but economically sensible theory that the white laborer would only be there a few years and might as well be worked to the limit before he departed, while the black man represented a permanent investment whose resources should be husbanded more carefully. For this and other reasons, all too many white indentures emerged from their labor experience with neither the incentive, the spirit, the skills, nor the energy to swim well in the middle-class mainstream.

If not all white indentured servants represented the lowest dregs of English society, nor labored till they broke at the thankless tasks of plantation agriculture, the fact remained that the flow of white migrants to the New World, once the great Puritan exodus of the 1630s had ended, included a pump at the Old World end of the line that needed priming more frequently than is generally realized, and in ways that need more attention than they usually get. Voluntary new-comers never arrived in sufficient numbers during the colonial period to fill a fraction of the demand. Small settlements might endure and survive in the far-off wilderness, but the architects of the colonial enterprises wanted to make a profit. For this, empty land was only half of it. Profit would not come until settlers, buyers, tenants, producers, and consumers — in short, people — were established there in sufficient quantity to make the whole thing go.

This was elementary, of course. But is was far easier to see the need for warm bodies than it was to get enough of them over here. On both sides of the English Channel there were enterprising men who proved capable of doing this — a motley and not overly attractive assortment of merchants, ship captains, recruiting agents, propagandists, thugs, and various related dealers who collectively acted as middlemen in the complicated business of getting folk to the New World. There were men of similar ilk, similarly engaged, in the older and bigger business of bringing blacks from Africa to the New World. The trade in white bodies required a bit more finesse and subtlety but was not strikingly different.

The point is that not very many of the poor folk wanted to go — not nearly enough of them, at any rate, to satisfy even the minimum demand. America would someday become a great magnet, attracting poor Europeans by the million and exerting its attraction in every corner of the Old World. This process, which was central to one of the greatest migrations in all human history, also required its complex machinery of ships, agents, recruiters, and brokers. But the latter group had one big advantage over their seventeenth- and eighteenth-century forebears in the immigrant trade — the real reputation that America as a great land of opportunity came to have after 1800. The country became its own best selling point; even the most exaggerated hopes of Mediterranean or Eastern European emigrants in the late nineteenth century, even the embellishments and exaggerations contained in the brochures of the transatlantic steamship companies, were built upon a solid substratum of truth: the land *was* good; opportunity *did* exist; this was known.

No such reputation surrounded colonial America, at least not for the poorest of migrants. By the eighteenth century the opportunities available to farmers and artisans — those already in the middle class or close enough to it to peak in the window — were acquiring a deserved reputation in England and parts of Western Europe. But for the very poor it was different. Many of them lacked the incentives and the skills necessary for middle-class status, and many were so submerged in the ignorance and squalor that went with their condition that America was not even a name to them, certainly nothing more than that.

This the assortment of middlemen set out to rectify. At their worst, they were outright crimps cruising the slums and grogshops in search of defenseless folk and employing a combination of muscle, gin, and fast talk to get their senseless or befuddled victims off the streets and aboard ship. Children were sometimes lured by offers of sweets. If this beginning of a voyage across the ocean was the fate of a small minority, a much larger number were conned into signing indentures by fabulous and altogether deceitful promises and descriptions of what awaited them in the New World. Many others, including those with a few possessions and a little money to apply toward the expense of the trip, found themselves ultimately stripped of all this by a series of unknown extra charges and fees that kept being levied, so that they arrived on the farther shore as penniless as their poorer brethren.

Thus migration for many began under unfortunate auspices. Some came under duress and larger numbers were grossly deceived; still more were fleeced. Add to this, for all save that minority who could afford to go as fare-paying passengers, and not for all of these, a long ocean voyage under conditions of discomfort, peril, sickness, and high mortality only a notch or two better than those endured by Africans on the middle passage. Cap it off with a reception in the New World in which indentured servants were herded together, hastily spruced up, and sold off like so many cattle; while the redemptioner and fare-paying arrivals, if they lacked full command of the language or their senses, were apt to find themselves separated from what remained of their cash by official-looking "helpers" at dockside. The totality of this experience left a whole range of physical and psychic scars. It is hardly surprising that some never healed.

Homogeneity was altered in a different way by the increasing infusion of non-English elements into the colonial bloodstream. This did not become noticeable until late in the seventeenth century and assumed its largest proportions in the eighteenth, when the seaboard colonies entered upon their great period of sustained growth. Of greatest significance was the large-scale influx of men and women of African descent. Next in importance were those from the Rhine Valley and the north of Ireland. By the Revolution, the German element in colonial America may have numbered up to 8 per cent of the total population, and the Scotch-Irish — descendants of Scots who had migrated to northern Ireland during the early seventeenth century — may have numbered 10 per cent.

The Germans were mainly redemptioners, though some also came as indentures and others as full-fare freemen. They filled up and expanded the back country in eastern Pennsylvania and the Susquehanna Valley, then pushed on southwestward to form many new settlements in western Maryland, the Valley of Virginia, and interior Carolina. They added strong dashes of Lutheranism and various brands of Pietism to the colonial religious mixture; they tended to be politically passive, socially self-sufficient in their well-knit communities, and economically invaluable as skilled and devoted husbandmen who made their farming regions the most productive and well kept of any in America.

The Scotch-Irish added something special to the colonial brew. They tended to be hard cases politically — unyielding Presbyterians, schooled and scarred by generations of turmoil in Ireland, caught in the middle between oppressed Irish Catholics and the Anglican establishment, hated from both sides, returning the hatred at compound interest. (Where Ireland was concerned, the English, whose overall record as colonists does not compare unfavorably with that of other Western nations, were mired from first to last in a deeper bog than any that dotted the landscape of the Emerald Isle. Even their better-intentioned efforts never turned out right, and such efforts were usually overshadowed or canceled out by all of the heavy-handedness, myopia, prejudice, arrogance, and fumbling ineptitude of which the British at their worst were capable. Ireland represented perhaps the only truly unsuccessful Tudor policy; their successors for the next four centuries built upon these initial mistakes in the same vein, and not a generation passed but what more chickens came home to roost.)

What the Scotch-Irish brought to America, along with their devout Presbyterian animosity toward Papists and Anglicans alike, was a political activism of the querulous and boat-rocking variety. These folk were tough, stubborn, touchy, combative, and full of energy. Like the Germans, many of them went to the back country, where they farmed less skillfully and lived less quietly than their Rhenish neighbors. Their political impact was considerable, and it reverberated in both directions: as the most truculent and activist of frontier settlers, they battled the Indians with the same fierce joy and no-quarter antagonism that marked all their other struggles, and thus provided colonial America with a tough frontier cordon for which settlers in the more established areas had reason to be grateful; yet at the same time the Scotch-Irish became the angriest and most belligerent critics of the seaboard areas, demanding that more sums be spent for defense against Indians and loudly protesting the underrepresentation of frontier counties in provincial assemblies. Not even the original Puritans had added as much ginger to the flavor of American politics.

In addition to the Germans and Scotch-Irish, there were smaller but still sizable migrations from Scotland and

Ireland proper, and from the Netherlands, the latter folk adding to the persistent Dutch stock in the Hudson Valley. Even smaller dashes of Swedes, Finns, Welsh, Swiss, and French added something to the ethnic variety. Though few in number, a sprinkling of French Huguenots rose to wealth and prominence in more than one colony. At a conservative estimate, more than nine in ten colonists were English or of English descent as late as 1690; by the end of the Seven Years' War, the English preponderance was no more than three in five.

Collectively and cumulatively, the waves of migrants had an intangible but perhaps decisive effect upon the developing character of this colonial people. It was a biased rather than a representative sample of British and European populations, as the high incidence of indentures and redemptioners suggests. "The rich stay in Europe," De Crèvecoeur observed, "it is only the middling and the poor that emigrate." Every possible human ingredient was being thrown into this transatlantic stew, but a few elements were outstanding. A great winnowing process was under way. In the most obvious sense, the grinding hardships of ocean crossing and wilderness clearing and frontier existence proved a cruelly effective way of eliminating many of the weak; toughness of body and of spirit was being bred into most of the survivors.

The great Puritan migration of the early seventeenth century left indelible marks, and many of the sober freeholding newcomers of later years — for these men of modest property kept coming, along with the indentures and the very poor — were of like quality. The Reverend Stoughton had said it: "God sifted a whole nation that He might bring choice grain over into this wilderness." If not all of this grain was choice in Stoughton's high-minded sense, nearly all of it was choice in the sense of growing qualities and staying power; the harvests would someday be unforgettable. The best brief description of the leading human qualities was supplied by the eighteenth-century British agriculturist Arthur Young, who had done some thinking about this. "Men who migrate," he wrote, "are from the nature of the circumstances the most active, hardy, daring, bold and resolute spirits, and probably the most mischievous also."

Different though they were, these newcomers had a few broad things in common. In one way or another their lives had been disrupted or threatened by a tangle of economic dislocation and hardship, religious strife, political persecution, war and attendant social turmoil — all of which, in England and in much of the Continent, were taking place as part of the tremendously complicated process whereby the Western world careened into the early stages of the capitalist and nationalist era. Nearly everyone, especially in the middle and lower echelons of European society, was affected by this, felt the pressures, received the buffets that accompany change.

Nearly all were affected, yet only a few came, and in the absence of ways of measuring the difference, one is led to conclude that certain traits set the emigrants apart. Arthur Young had gone to the heart of it; this much more, perhaps, can be ventured. The push, from Europe, was probably more important than the pull. These people were not so much going *to* something as *from* something, and what they were leaving had a grim pattern to it — conflict, upheaval, uncertainty, turmoil, loss or the threat of loss. Things looked bad; these folk wanted out. Even the perils of a transatlantic voyage to an unknown land — about which most of these prospective colonists had few illusions — were preferable to what they had experienced or seemed about to experience in the Old World. Others, equally oppressed, chose to stay at home. Apparently, then, the boldest spirits, the most impatient and restless, the most alienated, the most desperate and quarrelsome, were among those who decided to pull up stakes.

What had got to them, essentially, was the status quo: things as they were. (The fact that the status quo itself was changing in unfathomable ways only made matters worse.) These people were disposed to question and resent authority rather than accept it, to take action rather than remain passive, to fight or run — or both — rather than surrender.

At its peak, this translated itself into a soaring, almost boundless vision of what might be done in a new land, where authority would be an ocean away and things would not be as they were, where a model society with fewer blemishes than the one they were leaving could be built. From such bold and at times utopian visions, the aspirations ranged down-ward through various hopes for new opportunities all the way to a mere blind, urgent desire to escape. But from one end of this broad spectrum to the other, forceful qualities of mind and spirit were at work: venturesome, aggressive, abrasive qualities. These people did not all want the same things, beyond the elemental notions of escape and a fresh start. If, for a determined handful, this meant social engineering and creating communities, for untold larger numbers it meant simply a vague but compelling desire to go where they could be left alone. "Get off my back" is a piece of twentieth-century slang, distinctively American, which well summarized the prime motivation and prevailing mood among immigrants to Britain's mainland colonies. A people so motivated and of such temperament would leave their mark.

I · I · I

Francis Parkman

FRANCE IN THE FAR WEST

FRENCH EXPLORERS. — LE SUEUR ON THE ST. PETER. — CANA-
DIANS ON THE MISSOURI . — JUCHEREAU DE SAINT-DENIS —
BÉNARD DE LA HARPE ON RED RIVER. — ADVENTURES OF
DE TISNÉ. — BOURGMONT VISITS THE COMANCHES. — THE
BROTHERS MALLET IN COLORADO AND NEW MEXICO —
FABRY DE LA BRUYERE.

THE OCCUPATION BY France of the lower Mississippi gave a
strong impulse to the exploration of the West by supplying a
base for discovery, stimulating enterprise by the longing to
find gold mines, open trade with New Mexico, and get a fast
hold on the countries beyond the Mississippi in anticipation
of Spain; and to these motives was soon added the hope of
finding an overland way to the Pacific. It was the Canadians,
with their indomitable spirit of adventure, who led the way
in the path of discovery.

As a bold and hardy pioneer of the wilderness, the Frenchman in America has rarely found his match. His civic virtues
withered under the despotism of Versailles, and his mind
and conscience were kept in leading-strings by an absolute

Church; but the forest and the prairie offered him an unbridled liberty, which, lawless as it was, gave scope to his energies till these savage wastes became the field of his most noteworthy achievements.

Canada was divided between two opposing influences. On the one side were the monarchy and the hierarchy, with their principles of order, subordination, and obedience; substantially at one in purpose, since both wished to keep the colony within manageable bounds, domesticate it, and tame it to soberness, regularity, and obedience. On the other side was the spirit of liberty, or license, which was in the very air of this wilderness continent, reinforced in the chiefs of the colony by a spirit of adventure inherited from the Middle Ages, and by a spirit of trade born of present opportunities; for every official in Canada hoped to make a profit, if not a fortune, out of beaver-skins. Kindred impulses, in ruder forms, possessed the humbler colonists, drove them into the forest, and made them hardy woodsmen and skillful bushfighters, though turbulent and lawless members of civilized society.

Time, the decline of the fur-trade, and the influence of the Canadian Church gradually diminished this erratic spirit, and at the same time impaired the qualities that were associated with it. The Canadian became a more stable colonist and a steadier farmer; but for forest journeyings and forest warfare he was scarcely his former self. At the middle of the eighteenth century we find complaints that the race of *voyageurs* is growing scarce. The taming process was most apparent in the central and lower parts of the colony, such as the Côte de Beaupré and the opposite shore of the St. Lawrence, where the hands of the government and of the Church were strong, while at the head of the colony, — that is, about Montreal and its neighborhood, — which touched the primeval wilderness, an uncontrollable spirit of adventure still held its own. Here, at the beginning of the century, this spirit was as strong as it had ever been, and achieved a series of explorations and discoveries which revealed the plains of the Far West long before an Anglo-Saxon foot had pressed their soil.

The expedition of one Le Sueur to what is now the State of Minnesota may be taken as the starting point of these enterprises. Le Sueur had visited the country of the Sioux as early as 1683. He returned thither in 1689 with the famous *voyageur* Nicolas Perrot.[1] Four years later, Count Frontenac sent him to the Sioux country again. The declared purpose of the mission was to keep those fierce tribes at peace with their neighbors; but the governor's enemies declared that a contraband trade in beaver was the true object, and that Frontenac's secretary was to have half the profits.[2] Le Sueur returned after two years, bringing to Montreal a Sioux chief and his squaw, — the first of the tribe ever seen there. He then went to France, and represented to the court that he had built a fort at Lake Pepin, on the upper Mississippi; that he was the only white man who knew the languages of that region; and that if the French did not speedily seize upon it, the English, who were already trading upon the Ohio, would be sure to do so. Thereupon he asked for the command of the upper Mississippi, with all its tributary waters, together with a monopoly of its fur-trade for ten years, and permission to work its mines, promising that if his petition were granted, he would secure the country to France without expense to the King. The commission was given him. He bought an outfit and sailed for Canada, but was captured by the English on the way. After the peace he returned to France and begged for a renewal of his commission. Leave was given him to work the copper and lead mines, but not to trade in beaver-skins. He now formed a company to aid him in his enterprise, on which a cry rose in Canada that under pretence of working mines he meant to trade in beaver, — which is very likely, since to bring lead and copper in bark canoes to Montreal from the Mississippi and Lake Superior would cost far more than the metal was worth. In consequence of this clamor his commission was revoked.

Perhaps it was to compensate him for the outlays into which he had been drawn that the colonial minister presently authorized him to embark for Louisiana and pursue his enterprise with that infant colony, instead of Canada, as his base of operations. Thither, therefore, he went; and in April, 1700, set out for the Sioux country with twenty-five men, in a small vessel of the kind called a "felucca," still used in the Mediterranean. Among the party was an adventurous youth named Penecaut, a ship-carpenter by trade, who had come to Louisiana with Iberville two years before, and who has left us an account of his voyage with Le Sueur.[3]

The party slowly made their way, with sail and oar, against the muddy current of the Mississippi, till they reached the Arkansas, where they found an English trader from Carolina. On the tenth of June, spent with rowing, and half starved, they stopped to rest at a point fifteen leagues above the mouth of the Ohio. They had staved off famine with the buds and leaves of trees; but now, by good luck, one of them killed a bear, and, soon after, the Jesuit Limoges arrived from the neighboring mission of the Illinois, in a canoe well stored with provisions. Thus refreshed, they passed the mouth of the Missouri on the thirteenth of July, and soon after were met by three Canadians, who brought them a letter from the Jesuit Marest, warning them that the river was infested by war-parties. In fact, they presently saw seven canoes of Sioux warriors, bound against the Illinois, and not long after, five Canadians appeared, one of whom had been badly wounded in a recent encounter with a band of Outagamies, Sacs, and Winnebagoes bound against the Sioux. To take one another's scalps had been for ages the absorbing business and favorite recreation of all these Western tribes. At or near the expansion of the Mississippi called Lake Pepin, the voagers found a fort called Fort Perrot, after its builder;[4] and on an island near the upper end of the lake, another similar structure, built by Le Sueur himself on his last visit to the place. These forts were mere stockades, occupied from time to time by the roving fur-traders as their occasions required.

Towards the end of September, Le Sueur and his followers reached the mouth of the St. Peter, which they ascended to Blue Earth River. Pushing a league up this stream, they found a spot well suited to their purpose, and here they built a fort, of which there was great need, for they were soon after joined by seven Canadian traders, plundered and stripped to the skin by the neighboring Sioux. Le Sueur named the new post Fort l'Huillier. It was a fence of pickets, enclosing cabins for the men. The neighboring plains were black with buffalo, of which the party killed four hundred, and cut them into quarters, which they placed to freeze on scaffolds within the enclosure. Here they spent the winter, subsisting on the frozen meat, without bread, vegetables, or salt, and, according to Penecaut, thriving marvelously, though the surrounding wilderness was buried five feet deep in snow.

Band after band of Sioux appeared, with their wolfish dogs and their sturdy and all-enduring squaws burdened with the heavy hide coverings of their teepees, or buffalo-skin tents. They professed friendship and begged for arms. Those of one band had blackened their faces in mourning for a dead chief, and calling on Le Sueur to share their sorrow, they wept over him, and wiped their tears on his hair. Another party of warriors arrived with yet deeper cause of grief, being the remnant of a village half exterminated by their enemies. They, too, wept profusely over the French commander, and then sang a dismal song, with heads muffled in their buffalo-robes.[5] Le Sueur took the needful precautions against his dangerous visitors, but got from them a large supply of beaver-skins in exchange for his goods.

When spring opened, he set out in search of mines, and found, not far above the fort, those beds of blue and green earth to which the stream owes its name. Of this his men dug out a large quantity, and selecting what seemed the best, stored it in their vessel as a precious commodity. With this and good store of beaver-skins, Le Sueur now began his return voyage for Louisiana, leaving a Canadian named D'Éraque and twelve men to keep the fort till he should come back to reclaim it, promising to send him a canoe-load of ammunition from the Illinois. But the canoe was wrecked, and D'Éraque, discouraged, abandoned Fort l'Huillier, and followed his commander down the Mississippi.[6]

Le Sueur, with no authority from government, had opened relations of trade with the wild Sioux of the Plains, whose westward range stretched to the Black Hills, and perhaps to the Rocky Mountains. He reached the settlements of Louisiana in safety, and sailed for France with four thousand pounds of his worthless blue earth.[7] Repairing at once to Versailles, he begged for help to continue his enterprise. His petition seems to have been granted. After long delay, he sailed again for Louisiana, fell ill on the voyage, and died soon after landing.[8]

Before 1700, the year when Le Sueur visited the St. Peter,

little or nothing was known of the country west of the Mississippi, except from the report of Indians. The romances of La Hontan and Mathieu Sâgean were justly set down as impostures by all but the most credulous. In this same year we find Le Moyne d'Iberville projecting journeys to the upper Missouri, in hopes of finding a river flowing to the Western Sea. In 1703, twenty Canadians tried to find their way from the Illinois to New Mexico, in hope of opening trade with the Spaniards and discovering mines.[9] In 1704 we find it reported that more than a hundred Canadians are scattered in small parties along the Mississippi and the Missouri;[10] and in 1705 one Laurain appeared at the Illinois, declaring that he had been high up the Missouri and had visited many tribes on its borders.[11] A few months later, two Canadians told Bienville a similar story. In 1708 Nicolas de la Salle proposed an expedition of a hundred men to explore the same mysterious river; and in 1717 one Hubert laid before the Council of Marine a scheme for following the Missouri to its source, since, he says, "not only may we find the mines worked by the Spaniards, but also discover the great river that is said to rise in the mountains where the Missouri has its source, and is believed to flow to the Western Sea." And he advises that a hundred and fifty men be sent up the river in wooden canoes, since bark canoes would be dangerous, by reason of the multitude of snags.[12]

In 1714 Juchereau de Saint-Denis was sent by La Mothe-Cadillac to explore western Louisiana, and pushed up Red River to a point sixty-eight leagues, as he reckons, above Natchitoches. In the next year, journeying across country towards the Spanish settlements, with a view to trade, he was seized near the Rio Grande and carried to the city of Mexico. The Spaniards, jealous of French designs, now sent priests and soldiers to occupy several points in Texas. Juchereau, however, was well treated, and permitted to marry a Spanish girl with whom he had fallen in love on the way; but when, in the autumn of 1716, he ventured another journey to the Mexican borders, still hoping to be allowed to trade, he and his goods were seized by order of the Mexican viceroy, and, lest worse should befall him, he fled empty-handed, under cover of night.[13]

In March, 1719, Bénard de la Harpe left the feeble little French post at Natchitoches with six soldiers and a sergeant.[14] His errand was to explore the country, open trade if possible with the Spaniards, and establish another post high up Red River. He and his party soon came upon that vast entanglement of driftwood, or rather of uprooted forests, afterwards known as the Red River raft, which choked the stream and forced them to make their way through the inundated jungle that bordered it. As they pushed or dragged their canoes through the swamp, they saw with disgust and alarm a good number of snakes, coiled about twigs and boughs on the right and left, or sometimes over their heads. These were probably the deadly water-moccason, which in warm weather is accustomed to crawl out of its favorite element and bask itself in the sun, precisely as described by La Harpe. Their nerves were further discomposed by the splashing and plunging of alligators lately wakened from their wintry torpor. Still, they pushed painfully on, till they reached navigable water again, and at the end of the month were, as they thought, a hundred and eight leagues above Natchitoches. In four days more they reached the Nassonites.

These savages belonged to a group of stationary tribes, only one of which, the Caddoes, survives to our day as a separate community. Their enemies, the Chickasaws, Osages, Arkansas, and even the distant Illinois, waged such deadly war against them that, according to La Harpe, the unfortunate Nassonites were in the way of extinction, their numbers having fallen, within ten years, from twenty-five hundred souls to four hundred.[15]

La Harpe stopped among them to refresh his men, and build a house of cypress-wood as a beginning of the post he was ordered to establish; then, having heard that a war with Spain had ruined his hopes of trade with New Mexico, he resolved to pursue his explorations.

With him went ten men, white, red, and black, with twenty-two horses bought from the Indians, for his journeyings were henceforth to be by land. The party moved in a northerly and westerly course, by hills, forests, and prairies, passed two branches of the Wichita, and on the third of September came to a river which La Harpe calls the southwest branch of the Arkansas, but which, if his observation of latitude is correct, must have been the main stream, not far from the site of Fort Mann. Here he was met by seven Indian chiefs, mounted on excellent horses saddled and bridled after the Spanish manner. They led him to where, along the plateau of the low, treeless hills that bordered the valley, he saw a string of Indian villages, extending for a league and belonging to nine several bands, the names of which can no longer be recognized, and most of which are no doubt extinct. He says that they numbered in all six thousand souls; and their dwellings were high, dome-shaped structures, built of clay mixed with reeds and straw, resting, doubtless, on a frame of bent poles.[16] With them were also some of the roving Indians of the plains, with their conical teepees of dressed buffalo-skin.

The arrival of the strangers was a great and amazing event for these savages, few of whom had ever seen a white man. On the day after their arrival the whole multitude gathered to receive them and offer them the calumet, with a profusion of songs and speeches. Then warrior after warrior recounted his exploits and boasted of the scalps he had taken. From eight in the morning till two hours after midnight the din of drums, songs, harangues, and dances continued without relenting, with a prospect of twelve hours more; and La Harpe, in desperation, withdrew to rest himself on a buffalo-robe, begging another Frenchman to take his place. His hosts left him in peace for a while; then the chiefs came to find him, painted his face blue, as a tribute of respect, put a cap of eagle-feathers on his head, and laid numerous gifts at his feet. When at last the ceremony ended, some of the performers were so hoarse from incessant singing that they could hardly speak.[17]

La Harpe was told by his hosts that the Spanish settlements could be reached by ascending their river; but to do this was at present impossible He began his backward journey, fell desperately ill of a fever, and nearly died before reaching Natchitoches.

Having recovered, he made an attempt, two years later, to explore the Arkansas in canoes, from its mouth, but accomplished little besides killing a good number of buffalo, bears, deer, and wild turkeys. He was confirmed, however, in the belief that the Comanches and the Spaniards of New Mexico might be reached by this route.

In the year of La Harpe's first exploration, one Du Tisné went up the Missouri to a point six leagues above Grand River, where stood the village of the Missouris. He wished to go farther, but they would not let him. He then returned to the Illinois, whence he set out on horseback with a few followers across what is now the State of Missouri, till he reached the village of the Osages, which stood on a hill high up the river Osage. At first he was well received; but when they found him disposed to push on to a town of their enemies, the Pawnees, forty leagues distant, they angrily refused to let him go. His firmness and hardihood prevailed, and at last they gave him leave. A ride of a few days over rich prairies brought him to the Pawnees, who, coming as he did from the hated Osages, took him for an enemy and threatened to kill him. Twice they raised the tomahawk over his head; but when the intrepid traveller dared them to strike, they began to treat him as a friend. When, however, he told them that he meant to go fifteen days' journey farther, to the Padoucas, or Comanches, their deadly enemies, they fiercely forbade him; and after planting a French flag in their village, he returned as he had come, guiding his way by compass, and reaching the Illinois in November, after extreme hardships.[18]

Early in 1721 two hundred mounted Spaniards, followed by a large body of Comanche warriors, came from New Mexico to attack the French at the Illinois, but were met and routed on the Missouri by tribes of that region.[19] In the next year, Bienville was told that they meant to return, punish those who had defeated them, and establish a post on the river Kansas; whereupon he ordered Boisbriant, commandant at the Illinois, to anticipate them by sending troops to build a French fort at or near the same place. But the West India Company had already sent one Bourgmont on a similar errand, the object being to trade with the Spaniards in time of peace, and stop their incursions in time of war.[20] It was hoped also that, in the interest of trade, peace might be made between the Comanches and the tribes of the Missouri.[21]

Bourgmont was a man of some education, and well acquainted with these tribes, among whom he had traded for years. In pursuance of his orders he built a fort, which he named Fort Orléans, and which stood on the Missouri not far above the mouth of Grand River. Having thus accomplished one part of his mission, he addressed himself to the other, and prepared to march for the Comanche villages.

Leaving a sufficient garrison at the fort, he sent his ensign, Saint-Ange, with a party of soldiers and Canadians, in wooden canoes, to the villages of the Kansas higher up the stream, and on the third of July set out by land to join him, with a hundred and nine Missouri Indians and sixty-eight Osages in his train. A ride of five days brought him again to the banks of the Missouri, opposite a Kansas town. Saint-Ange had not yet arrived, the angry and turbid current, joined to fevers among his men, having retarded his progress. Meanwhile Bourgmont drew from the Kansas a promise that their warriors should go with him to the Comanches. Saint-Ange at last appeared, and at daybreak of the twenty-fourth the tents were struck and the pack-horses loaded. At six o'clock the party drew up in battle array on a hill above the Indian town, and then, with drum beating and flag flying, began their march. "A fine prairie country," writes Bourgmont, "with hills and dales and clumps of trees to right and left." Sometimes the landscape quivered under the sultry sun, and sometimes thunder bellowed over their heads, and rain fell in floods on the steaming plains.

Renaudière, engineer of the party, one day stood by the side of the path and watched the whole procession as it passed him. The white men were about twenty in all. He counted about three hundred Indian warriors, with as many squaws, some five hundred children, and a prodigious number of dogs, the largest and strongest of which dragged heavy loads. The squaws also served as beasts of burden; and, says the journal, "they will carry as much as a dog will drag." Horses were less abundant among these tribes than they afterwards became, so that their work fell largely upon the women.

On the sixth day the party was within three leagues of the river Kansas, at a considerable distance above its mouth. Bourgmont had suffered from dysentery on the march, and an access of the malady made it impossible for him to go farther. It is easy to conceive the regret with which he saw himself compelled to return to Fort Orléans. The party retraced their steps, carrying their helpless commander on a litter. First, however, he sent one Gaillard on a perilous errand. Taking with him two Comanche slaves bought for the purpose from the Kansas, Gaillard was ordered to go to the Comanche villages with the message that Bourgmont had been on his way to make them a friendly visit, and, though stopped by illness, hoped soon to try again, with better success.

Early in September, Bourgmont, who had arrived safely at Fort Orléans, received news that the mission of Gaillard had completely succeeded; on which, though not wholly recovered from his illness, he set out again on his errand of peace, accompanied by his young son, besides Renaudière, a surgeon, and nine soldiers. On reaching the great village of the Kansas he found there five Comanche chiefs and warriors, whom Gaillard had induced to come thither with him. Seven chiefs of the Otoes presently appeared, in accordance with an invitation of Bourgmont; then six chiefs of the Iowas and the head chief of the Missouris. With these and the Kansas chiefs a solemn council was held around a fire before Bourgmont's tent; speeches were made, the pipe of peace was smoked, and presents were distributed.

On the eighth of October the march began, the five Comanches and the chiefs of several other tribes, including the Omahas, joining the cavalcade. Gaillard and another Frenchman named Quesnel were sent in advance to announce their approach to the Comanches, while Bourgmont and his followers moved up the north side of the river Kansas till the eleventh, when they forded it at a point twenty leagues from its mouth, and took a westward and southwestward course, sometimes threading the grassy valleys of little streams, sometimes crossing the dry upland prairie, covered with the short, tufted dull-green herbage since known as "buffalo grass." Wild turkeys clamored along every watercourse; deer were seen on all sides, buffalo were without

number, sometimes in grazing droves, and some times dot-
ting the endless plain as far as the eye could reach. Ruffian
wolves, white and gray, eyed the travellers askance, keeping
a safe distance by day, and howling about the camp all
night. Of the antelope and the elk the journal makes no mention. Bourgmont chased a buffalo on horseback and shot
him with a pistol, — which is probably the first recorded example of that way of hunting.

The stretches of high, rolling, treeless prairie grew more
vast as the travellers advanced. On the seventeenth, they
found an abandoned Comanche camp. On the next day as
they stopped to dine, and had just unsaddled their horses,
they saw a distant smoke towards the west, on which they set
the dry grass on fire as an answering signal. Half an hour
later a body of wild horsemen came towards them at full
speed, and among them were their two couriers, Gaillard
and Quesnel, waving a French flag. The strangers were eighty Comanche warriors, with the grand chief of the tribe at
their head. They dashed up to Bourgmont's bivouac and
leaped from their horses, when a general shaking of hands
ensued, after which white men and red seated themselves on
the ground and smoked the pipe of peace. Then all rode together to the Comanche camp, three leagues distant.[22]

Bourgmont pitched his tents at a pistol-shot from the Comanche lodges, whence a crowd of warriors presently came
to visit him. They spread buffalo-robes on the ground,
placed upon them the French commander, his officers, and
his young son; then lifted each, with its honored load, and
carried them all, with yells of joy and gratulation, to the
lodge of the Great Chief, where there was a feast of ceremony lasting till nightfall.

On the next day Bourgmont displayed to his hosts the
marvellous store of gifts he had brought for them, — guns,
swords, hatchets, kettles, gunpowder, bullets, red cloth,
blue cloth, hand-mirrors, knives, shirts, awls, scissors, nee-
dles, hawks' bells, vermilion, beads, and other enviable
commodities, of the like of which they had never dreamed.
Two hundred savages gathered before the French tents,
where Bourgmont, with the gifts spread on the ground before him, stood with a French flag in his hand, surrounded

by his officers and the Indian chiefs of his party, and harangued the admiring auditors.

He told them that he had come to bring them a message from the King, his master, who was the Great Chief of all the nations of the earth, and whose will it was that the Comanches should live in peace with his other children, — the Missouris, Osages, Kansas, Otoes, Omahas, and Pawnees, — with whom they had long been at war; that the chiefs of these tribes were now present, ready to renounce their old enmities; that the Comanches should henceforth regard them as friends, share with them the blessing of alliance and trade with the French, and give to these last free passage through their country to trade with the Spaniards of New Mexico. Bourgmont then gave the French flag to the Great Chief, to be kept forever as a pledge of that day's compact. The chief took the flag, and promised in behalf of his people to keep peace inviolate with the Indian children of the King. Then, with unspeakable delight, he and his tribesmen took and divided the gifts.

The next two days were spent in feasts and rejoicings. "Is it true that you are men?" asked the Great Chief. "I have heard wonders of the French, but I never could have believed what I see this day." Then, taking up a handful of earth, "The Spaniards are like this; but you are like the sun." And he offered Bourgmont, in case of need, the aid of his two thousand Comanche warriors. The pleasing manners of his visitors, and their unparalleled generosity, had completely won his heart.

As the object of the expedition was accomplished, or seemed to be so, the party set out on their return. A ride of ten days brought them again to the Missouri; they descended in canoes to Fort Orléans, and sang Te Deum in honor of the peace.[23]

No farther discovery in this direction was made for the next fifteen years. Though the French had explored the Missouri as far as the site of Fort Clark and the Mandan villages, they were possessed by the idea — due, perhaps, to Indian reports concerning the great tributary river, the Yellowstone — that in its upper course the main stream bent so far southward as to form a waterway to New Mexico, with which it was the constant desire of the authorities of Louisiana to open trade. A way thither was at last made known by two brothers named Mallet, who with six companions went up the Platte to its South Fork, which they called River of the Padoucas, — a name given it on some maps down to the middle of this century. They followed the South Fork for some distance, and then, turning southward and southwestward, crossed the plains of Colorado. Here the dried dung of the buffalo was their only fuel; and it has continued to feed the camp-fire of the traveller in this treeless region within the memory of many now living. They crossed the upper Arkansas, and apparently the Cimarron, passed Taos, and on the twenty-second of July reached Santa Fe, where they spent the winter. On the first of May, 1740, they began their return journey, three of them crossing the plains to the Pawnee villages, and the rest descending the Arkansas to the Mississippi.[24]

The bold exploit of the brothers Mallet attracted great attention at New Orleans, and Bienville resolved to renew it, find if possible a nearer and better way to Santa Fé, determine the nature and extent of these mysterious western regions, and satisfy a lingering doubt whether they were not contiguous to China and Tartary.[25] A naval officer, Fabry de la Bruyère, was sent on this errand, with the brothers Mallet and a few soldiers and Canadians. He ascended the Canadian Fork of the Arkansas, named by him the St. André, became entangled in the shallows and quicksands of that difficult river, fell into disputes with his men, and after protracted efforts, returned unsuccessful.[26]

While French enterprise was unveiling the remote Southwest, two indomitable Canadians were pushing still more noteworthy explorations into more northern regions of the continent.

ENDNOTES

1. *Journal historique de l'Établissement des Français à la Louisiane*, 43.

2. *Champigny au Ministre*, 4 Novembre, 1693.

3. *Relation de Penecaut.* In my possession is a contemporary manuscript of this narrative, for which I am indebted the kindness of General J. Meredith Reade.

4. Penecaut, *Journal. Procès-verbal de la Prise de Possession du Pays des Nadouessioux, etc., par Nicolas Perrot,* 1689. Fort Perrot seems to have been built in 1685, and to have stood near the outlet of the lake, probably on the west side. Perrot afterwards built another fort, called Fort St. Antoine, a little above, on the east bank. The position of these forts has been the subject of much discussion, and cannot be ascertained with precision. It appears by the *Prise de Possession,* cited above, that there was also, in 1689, a temporary French post near the mouth of the Wisconsin.

5. This weeping over strangers was a custom with the Sioux of that time mentioned by many early writers. La Mothe-Cadillac marvels that a people so brave and warlike should have such a fountain of tears always at command.

6. In 1702 the geographer De l'Isle made a remarkable MS. map entitled *Carte de la Rivière du Mississippi, dressée sur les Mémoires de M. Le Sueur.*

7. According to the geologist Featherstonhaugh, who examined the locality, this earth owes its color to a bluish-green silicate of iron.

8. Besides the long and circumstantial *Relation du Penecaut,* an account of the earlier part of La Sueur's voyage up the Mississippi is contained in the *Mémoire du Chevalier de Beaurain,* which, with other papers relating to this explorer, including portions of his Journal, will be found in Margry, vi. See also *Journal historique de l'Établissement des Français à la Louisiane,* 38-71.

9. *Iberville à —,* 15 *Février,* 1703 (Margry, vi 180).

10. *Bienville au Ministre,* 6 *Septembre,* 1704.

11. Beaurain *Journal historique.*

12. Hubert, *Mémoire envoyé au Conseil de la Marine.*

13. Penecaut, *Relation,* chaps. xvii., xviii. Le Page de Pratz, *Histoire de la Louisiane,* i. 13-22. Various documents in Margry, vi. 193-202.

14. For an interesting contemporary map of the French establishment at Natchitoches, see Thomassy *Géologie pratique de la Louisiane.*

15. Bénard de la Harpe, in Margry, vi. 264.

16. Beaurain says that each of these bands spoke a language of its own. They had horses in abundance, descended from Spanish stock. Among them appear to have been the Ouacos, or Huecos, and the Wichitas, — two tribes better known as the Pawnee Picts. See Marcy, *Exploration of Red River.*

17. Compare the account of La Harpe with that of the Chevalier de Beaurain; both are in Margry, vi. There is an abstract in *Journal historique.*

18. *Relation de Bénard de la Harpe. Autre Relation du même. Du Tisné à Bienville.* Margry, vi. 309, 310, 313.

19. *Bienville au Conseil de Régence, 20 Juillet,* 1721.

20. *Instructions au Sieur de Bourgmont,* 17 *Janvier,* 1722, Margry, vi. 389.

21. The French had at this time gained a knowledge of the tribes of the Missouri as far up as the Arickaras, who were not, it seems, many days' journey below the Yellowstone, and who told them of "prodigiously high mountains," — evidently the Rocky Mountains. *Mémoire de la Renaudière,* 1723.

22. This meeting took place a little north of the Arkansas apparently where that river makes a northward bend, near the twenty-second degree of west longitude. The Comanche villages were several days' journey to the southwest. This tribe is always mentioned in the early French narratives as the Padoucas, — a name by which the Comanches are occasionally known to this day. See Whipple and Turner, *Reports upon Indian Tribes, in Explorations and Surveys for the Pacific Railroad* (Senate Doc., 1853, 1854).

23. *Relation du Voyage du Sieur de Bourgmont, Juin-Novembre,* 1724, in Margry, vi. 398. Le Page du Pratz, iii. 141.

24. *Journal du Voyage des Frères Mallet, présenté à M.M. de Bienville et Salmon.* This narrative is meagre and confused, but serves to establish the main points. *Copie du Certificat donné à Santa Fé aux sept [huit] Français par le Général Hurtado, 24 Juillet,* 1739. *Père Rébald au Père de Beaubois, sans date. Bienville et Salmon au Ministre, 30 Avril,* 1741, in Margry, vi. 455-468.

25. *Instructions données par Jean-Baptiste de Bienville à Fabry de la Bruyère, 1 Juin,* 1741. Bienville was behind his time in geographical knowledge. As early as 1724 Bénard de la Harpe knew that in ascending the Missouri or the Arkansas one was moving towards the "Western Sea," — that is, the Pacific, — and might, perhaps, find some river flowing into it. See *Routes qu'on peut tenir pour se rendre à la Mer de l'Ouest,* in *Journal historique,* 387.

26. *Extrait des Lettres de Sieur Fabry.*

I · V

Henry Steele Commager

AMERICANS BRING FORTH
A NEW NATION

It took centuries for the peoples of Britain, France, Spain, and Denmark to establish national monarchies and governments, develop a sense of community, and acquire an awareness of common nationalism. It took even longer for those of Italy, Germany, Austria, and Russia. But Americans brought forth a new nation in a single generation. How did it happen that as early as 1775 the ardent Patrick Henry could declaim, however rhetorically, that "the distinctions between Virginians, Pennsylvanians, New Yorkers and New Englanders are no more," and that the newcomer Thomas Paine could write, more accurately, that "our citizenship in the United States is our national character . . . Our great title is Americans."?[1] How did it happen that the miscellaneous British and European peoples who had transplanted themselves to the New World and spread out over an area larger than that of any two Western nations, acquired a sense of nationalism on the battlefield and in diplomacy, organized it into political and administrative institutions, and provided it with so many of the essential cultural ingredients —

myths and legends, heroes and villains, symbols and mottoes, the consciousness of a meaningful past, and the assurance of a glorious future — all in two or three decades?[2]

Not only was American nationalism achieved with a swiftness unprecedented in history, but what was achieved was a new kind of nationalism. It was not imposed by a conqueror or by a monarch. It was not dependent on an Established Church at whose altars all worshipped alike, or upon the power of a ruling class. It did not draw its inspiration from a national past or its strength from a traditional enemy. It came from the people; it was an act of will.

There were, needless to say, antecedents and anticipations. The most important of these were rooted not in history but in circumstances: the separation from Europe, and the "climate" of the new land. The settlement of America was indeed the unsettlement of Europe;[3] for perhaps the majority of newcomers it was a repudiation, conscious or unconscious, of the Old World. It was not just a migration; it was, more often than not, a flight. No one saw this more clearly than the "American Farmer," Hector St. John de Crèvecoeur, whose *Letters* are the first perceptive study of the American character:

> In this great American asylum, the poor of Europe have by some means met together; . . . to what purpose should they ask each other what countrymen they are? Alas, two-thirds of them had no country . . . Urged by a variety of motives, here they came. Everything has tended to regenerate them: new laws, a new mode of living, a new social system; here they are become men . . . by the power of transplantation, like all other plants, they have taken root and flourished
>
> What attachment can a poor European have for a country where he had nothing? The knowledge of the language, the love of a few kindred as poor as himself, were the only cords that tied him; his country is now that which gives him land, bread, protection, and consequence. *Ubi panis, ibi patria*, is the motto of all emigrants.[4]

That among the more sophisticated and literate Americans there was pride in the British connection and loyalty to the British Crown cannot be gainsaid;[5] that this pride inspired farmers and fishermen and indentured servants, the Germans who had been driven out of the Palatinate and the Scots who had fled after the Forty-five, seems improbable. Such loyalties as these had were to their adopted country: *Ubi panis, ibi patria.*

If there was one common denominator more powerful than any other that united farmers and workingmen, merchants, lawyers and clergy, the English, the Germans, the Scots-Irish, and the Huguenots, it was quite simply the recognition that America was not Europe, but something new in history. The sense of uniqueness came before the reality.[6] America was not Europe! Here men and women, if white, were free to live where they would and as they would and to marry whom they would; free to worship in their own churches — or not to worship; to work at their own trades, to go to their own schools and colleges; free to have souls and minds of their own and, what is more, to bare their souls and speak their minds. Even the most cosmopolitan among them could rejoice that here they could escape the luxury which enervated society in the Old World and the corruption that debased it. For the repudiation of the Old World was not just political, or religious, economic or social; it was — or sought to be — moral. Thus, on the eve of the war Franklin could deplore "the extream Corruption prevalent among all Orders of Men in this old rotten State" with its "desperate Circumstances, Injustice, and Rapacity."[7] Thus, Jefferson blessed "the Almighty Being who in gathering together the waters under the heavens in one place, divided the land of your [Old World] hemisphere from the dry land of ours."[8] The poet-editor, Philip Freneau, had recourse to almost the same metaphor:

> Blest in their distance from that bloody scene,
> Why spread the sail to pass the Guelphs between?

And the puritanical Dr. Rush advised that Americans cultivate an indifference to Europe; what concern, he asked, do we have with "the quarrels or the vices of the old world, with duels, elopements, the kept mistresses, the murders, the suicides, the thefts, the forgeries, the boxing matches, the wagers for eating, drinking . . . "?[9]

The America into which men and women of the Old World escaped was new in a more positive sense than in being merely not-Europe. It was new in its spaciousness — land enough, Jefferson was to say, for our descendants to "the thousandth and thousandth generation." By comparison with Europe, that spaciousness was so astonishing that it took on not just a quantitative but a qualitative character. Together with freedom from the limitations of class and from the demands of the military, it accounted for that mobility which was social as well as geographical: It provided not only an economic safety valve but a psychological one. This, too, Crèvecoeur perceived that "There is room for everybody in America," and added that

> An European, when he first arrives, seems limited in his intenions as well as in his views; two hundred miles formerly appeared a very great distance, it is now but a trifle. He no sooner breathes our air than he forms schemes and embarks in designs he never would have thought of in his own country. There the plenitude of society confines many useful ideas, and often extinguishes the most laudable schemes which here ripen into maturity. Thus Europeans become Americans.[10]

Like the land, the Indians belonged to what the philosophes called the "Climate" of the New World, and it is difficult to exaggerate their contribution in war and in peace to the growth of the sense of American community.[11] There they were, from the first landfall of the English, all the way from Massachusetts Bay to Georgia, and in the new territory that was added from the Appalachians to the Mississippi and beyond. They were there to give us the Pocahantas story and the story of the wonderful Squanto of the Pawtuxet tribe who taught the Pilgrims "how to set their corne and where to take fishe";[12] they were there as guides into the wilderness and as instructors in the trapping of beaver and the fashioning of canoes. They were there to be converted to Christianity and to "civilization" — an enterprise that enlisted the talents of

John Eliot with his Indian Bible in the 1660s and of the most enlightened of amateur ethnologists, Thomas Jefferson, through much of his life.[13] They provided the colonials with what they otherwise lacked for effective unity — a national enemy, and one who, after the mid-seventeenth century, carried with him a providential guarantee of victory for the white invaders. They presented the paradox, dear to the Enlightenment, of a savage Satanic in his cruelty but at the same time Noble; the savage who inflicted fiendish tortures on his victims, and who — through the high-minded Chief Logan — pronounced one of the most eloquent declamations in the history of oratory; we have Jefferson's word for that![14] Everywhere they taught the lesson of co-operation, whether by the model of the Iroquois Confederacy and the formidable alliance that Chief Pontiac welded together, or by the inescapable logic of necessity: The Confederacy of New England in the mid-seventeenth and the Albany Plan of - Union in the mid-eighteenth centuries were called into being by threats of Indian warfare. More than anything except Nature herself they fired the imagination of poets and storytellers, historians and ethnologists, and provided the stuff for myth and legend. From John Smith's *General Historie of Virginia* and Thomas Morton's *New English Canaan* to the *Travels* of John Bartram and Jefferson's *Notes on Virginia*; from Robert Rogers's *Ponteach* — which has some claim to be the first drama written in America — and the innumerable captivity narratives, to the Indian poems of the gifted Philip Freneau; from John Lawson's *New Voyage to Carolina* to the *Journals* of the Lewis and Clark expedition, they provided a voluminous and a romantic library of American literature. They wrote their names indelibly on the land: half the states east of the Mississippi bear Indian names, and rivers and lakes from the Kennebec to the Suwannee, the Susquehanna to the Ohio, and so too most of those we call the "Finger" and "Great" Lakes.[15] More than any other element except Nature herself, they furnished the materials for romanticism in literature, history, and mythology. From Powhatan to Geronimo they were part of the American experience, and after they ceased to be a danger they became part of the American imagination; generations of children built tents in their back yards and played at being Indians, and their parents satisfied their yearning for excitement by reading narratives of Indian captivity or of frontier wars. When that, too, passed, the Indian lingered on as a problem both of politics and of conscience.

All of these pressures for unity were circumstantial; something inherent in the flight from Europe, the settlement of America, the immensity of the continent, and the westward sweep of population with its inevitable conflict with the Indians over the control of their hunting grounds. They set the stage for nationalism; they did not call it into being.

It was institutional pressures that nourished and eventually created an American nationalism. Of these perhaps the most important at the outset was religion.[16] We are in the presence here of a paradox: Where in the Old World religious differences divided society and were thought pernicious, in the New they made for unity. By mid-eighteenth century not only did a score of religions flourish in the American colonies, but a substantial majority even of those who attended any church,* worshipped outside the Congregational and Anglican Establishments. Presbyterians, Baptists, Dutch Reformed, Quakers, Catholics, Lutherans, and other German sectaries outnumbered those who enjoyed official support — a situation inconceivable in the Old World† Imagine Huguenots outnumbering Catholics in France, or Lutherans outnumbering Catholics in Bavaria!

Even the regional pattern was a variegated one. The Congregational Church was established in most of New England, but the Baptists dominated Rhode Island, and there were large numbers of Presbyterians, Baptist, and Anglicans in the other New England colonies. The Quakers had founded Pennsylvania, but they were by now greatly outnumbered by Presbyterians and by German sectaries. Even in South Carolina, where the Anglican Church had power, wealth, and distinction, it could not hold its own numerically with Piedmont and up-country "dissenters"; though the Constitution

---

* Even in devout New England there was apparently only one church member to every eight persons.

† Except, of course, in Ireland where the religion of the majority was ruthlessly suppressed.

of 1778 reaffirmed the Anglican Establishment, that of 1790 swept it away — and it went without a struggle.[17] Increasingly throughout the eighteenth century churches ignored colonial and state boundary lines and built up loose intercolonial networks as religion was the chief preoccupation of Americans in these years,[18] the religious connections often proved stronger than the political divisions.

In this development the Great Awakening, which swept the colonies in the second and third quarters of the century, played an explosive role.[19] It was not only a vehicle for the expression of new religious enthusiasm, but for social and political as well. It was — to invoke Edmund Burke's phrase — a kind of dissent from dissent; it arose spontaneously as a reaction to the formalism even in dissenting churches (the New England revival led by Jonathan Edwards in Northampton is an exception here); it was led by newcomers — self-appointed revivalists, most of them drawn from miscellaneous backgrounds, and often without ardent denominational loyalities, like Gilbert Tennent, Devereux Jarrett, and George Whitefield himself. It swept the colonies like a prairie fire, overleaping both political and denominational barriers; it turned away from the religion of the pulpit and the Seminary to the religion of inspiration and the open fields. It rallied dissenters of all denominations against all Establishments, and inevitably attacked political establishments as well as religious; it was democratic in its origins, its inspiration, and its appeal. It made Philadelphia a religious before it became a political capital and created new colleges that drew students from all of the Colonies and sent them out to carry the Gospel to distant frontiers — College of New Jersey, which became Princeton, the College of Rhode Island, which became Brown, the Hampden-Sydney College in Virginia, which opened the year of the Declaration — and it reinvigorated older colleges like Yale. In George Whitefield, who was surely its most eloquent spokesman, and whom many thought the greatest orator of his age, it gave colonial America the only "national" figure to rank with Benjamin Franklin.[20]

Meantime, Americans were learning to work together in other areas than religion. Of these the military and the political were the most enduring and the most importunate. It was the New England Colonies which had banded together to capture the frowning fortress of Louisbourg in 1745 — only to see it handed back to the French. All the colonies were involved (though in varying degrees) in the French and Indian War, the first major enterprise that can be called truly "continental," and it was that war which transformed George Washington from a Virginia surveyor and planter into a continental figure, thus giving Americans not only their first native military hero but also their most durable.[21]

The Revolution itself was perhaps the most powerful instrument in creating a sense of common destiny and of nationalism — the revolution with its fears and hopes, its defeats and victories, its anguish and glory; with heroes and villains, symbols and legends. Americans from every state fought side by side all through the years that tried men's souls. Old World wars did not customarily inspire or strengthen a national spirit; they were fought, for the most part, by professional soldiers or by mercenaries — over one-half the Danish Army, for example, were mercenaries, and the language of the Army was German; they were fought at the will of the King, not by decision of the people; and they were fought in distant lands for purposes exotic and obscure. But the Revolutionary War was not something imposed upon the American people; it was, if not quite spontaneous, largely voluntary, and the American imagination is not wholly misguided in dwelling with affection on the Minute Men who gathered at Concord Bridge, the Green Mountain Boys who fought at Bennington, the Mountain Men who repulsed Major Ferguson at King's Mountain, or the Swamp Foxes who followed General Marion. The War, too, affected every part of the country (though unevenly) and every segment of a literate and knowledgeable society. It was an experience that might have fragmented the nation, but that provided, rather, the sinews for unity; the flight or expulsion of some eighty thousand loyalists contributed here. It was almost inevitable that after Yorktown, the most passionate spokesmen for a stronger union were those who had served "their country" during the war, in the Army or the council: Washington himself, Hamilton, Pickering, Knox, McHenry, Franklin, Jefferson,

Madison, Tom Paine, and Robert Morris among them.[22]

The War gave Americans a common cause, one that could be both rationalized and sentimentalized. The rationalization could be read in those state papers that were to constitute an American Testament; the sentiment in the legends that clustered about Washington and Valley Forge, Marion and Mad Anthony Wayne, Nathan Hale who had but one life to give for his country, and John Paul Jones who had just begun to fight; in the symbols of the flag and the bald eagle and in the seals and the mottoes — three of them, no less — and in patriotic poems, jocular like Yankee Doodle or elevated like Timothy Dwight's

> Columbia, Columbia, to glory arise,
> The Queen of the world, and the child of the skies

or, at the end of the era, Joseph Hopkinson's exultant national anthem

> Hail, Columbia, happy land!
> Hail, ye heroes! heaven-born band!

What country before 1776 had equipped itself with all this patriotic paraphernalia in one generation?[23]

The war provided an enemy, too, one more formidable than the Indian, and more worthy, for the distinction of defeating Britain on the battlefield, and in the pages of history, was more exalted by far than that of overcoming even the fiercest of Indian tribes. Surprisingly, it vindicated American nationalism abroad even before it had been vindicated at home. Franklin and Adams, Jefferson and Jay, spoke for the United States as a nation, and it was as representatives of a nation that they were accepted and won allies.[24] Tom Paine put this well, as he put everything else well:

> That which includes and renders easy all interior concerns is the UNION OF THE STATES. On this our great national character depends. It is this which must give us importance abroad and security at home. It is through this only that we are, or can be, nationally known in the world; it is the flag of the United States

which renders our ships and commerce safe on the seas . . . All our treaties . . . are formed under the sovereignty of the United States, and Europe knows us by no other name or title.[25]

Political experience was intertwined with military. That had been true for the making of Dutch nationalism in the seventeenth century; it might have been true of the Irish and the Scottish revolts, had they been successful. Elsewhere, in eighteenth-century wars, political like military direction came from the Crown, not the people. Franklin and his associates had projected something very like a colonial government as early as 1754 with the remarkable Albany Plan of Union. A decade later came the Stamp Act Congress which brought together delegates from nine colonies; among the delegates were many who were to play stellar parts in the Revolution, even some who were to be Founding Fathers:[26] James Otis of Massachusetts, Robert Livingston and Philip Livingston from New York, John Dickinson from Pennsylvania, Caesar Rodney — whose all-night ride was to swing the vote for Independence — from Delaware, and Christopher Gadsden and John Rutledge from South Carolina. A few more years and Committees of Correspondence[27] wove their network from colony to colony. By the time of the First Continental Congress most of the colonial leaders knew one another, and something like an American party had come into existence. Formal union did not come until the ratification of the Articles of Confederation in 1781, just six months before Yorktown; had there not been an effective union before this, there might never have been a Yorktown.[28]

As an organized Church attracts inchoate religious sentiments and institutionalizes them into good works, and as a political party absorbs miscellaneous political sentiments and directs them to governmental purposes, so the first formal union, for all its inadequacies and infirmities, provided a focal point for latent and overt Continental sentiments. As the residuary legatee of the British Government on a continental scale, the Association and the Confederation almost inevitably concentrated and institutionalized all the potential forces of nationalism.[29] Somewhat surprisingly, Americans found themselves with a government that had, or assumed, authority to conduct a war and to make peace, own and dispose of a national domain as large as the original thirteen states, exercise jurisdiction in a score of interstate disputes, and attract to its services some of the ablest minds in the nation. They found themselves thinking "continentally" — there was a Continental Congress and a Continental Army whose soldiers were called quite simply Continentals: currency was called Continental, and there was even a Continental Fast and a Continental Thanksgiving. There was a national capital more like those of the Old World than Washington was to be for half a century, for Philadelphia was not only the political but the religious and cultural center of the nation and, for a time, its financial center as well as its most populous city.[30] And, what with the war and the Congress and the Convention, Americans found themselves with leaders who were indubitably national, and with a ready-made set of Founding Fathers, headed up by the God-like Washington.[31]

It was a revolutionary and a spectacular achievement, this creation of a nation overnight. Many of the ingredients of nationalism long thought to be essential were lacking from the beginning: no King, no Court, no aristocracy, no Capitol, no body of laws, no professional Army, no Established Church, no history, no tradition, no usable past, and as for that most essential element — territory — here was so much of it that it constituted a danger rather than an immediate asset. But if these ingredients were lacking, so thought many of the shrewdest Old World observers, the essentials were lacking, and hopes for creating a durable union were illusory. "As to the future grandeur of America, and its being a rising empire under one head," wrote Dean Josiah Tucker of Gloucester — he had opposed the war all along and thought it as absurd as the Crusades — "it is one of the idlest and most visionary notions that was ever conceived."[32] So, too, said the great financier Turgot, an ardent friend of America: "in the general union of the States I do not see a coalition, a melting of all the parts together, making but one body, one and homogeneous; it is only an aggregate of parts, always

too separate and preserving always a tendency to division...
It is only a copy of the Dutch republic."[33] And even that ardent patriot Patrick Henry lamented that a republican government on a continental scale was "a work too great for human wisdom."[34]*

But it turned out that Americans could manage very well with such ingredients as they had, and could create the others on order. From the most heterogeneous elements, they welded together a people. Crèvecoeur himself was able to conjure up the image of a "melting pot." They set up independent state and national governments. Thanks to the farsighted provisions of the Northwest Ordinance, extensive road building, a river system which made it easy to link up the seaboard and the interior, and, within a few years, steamboats and canals, they made their extensive territory an asset rather than a debit. They got along without an Established Church, and their morals did not suffer. They got along without a military too, and thanks to geographical isolation and to the preoccupation of Old World powers with the French Revolution and Napoleon, they were secure until the crisis of 1812, and thereafter for a generation. Jefferson could say in his First Inaugural Address that "this is the strongest government on earth . . . the only one where every man, at the call of the law, would fly to the standard of the law and would meet invasions of the public order as his own personal concern." The War of 1812 was to prove that rhetoric romantic folly, but it proved, too, that distance and size were indeed a protection. Needless to say, they got along without a monarchy: as Tom Paine put it, in America the Law is King.[35] They even got along for some time without a

---

* Note Alexis de Tocqueville's prediction half a century later: "Whatever faith I may have in the perfectibility of man, until human nature is altered, and man wholly transformed, I shall refuse to believe in the duration of a government which is called upon to hold together forty different peoples, disseminated over a territory equal to one-half of Europe in extent, to avoid all rivalry, ambition and struggles between them, and to direct their independent activity to the accomplishment of the same designs." (*Democracy in America*, Vol. I.)

real capital, and if the peevish Tom Moore could write of the residents of Washington that

> ... nought but woods and Jefferson they see,
> Where streets should run, and sages ought to be[36]

Americans themselves were quite content with the woods, and Mr. Jefferson, too. They needed History and Traditions, and manufactured these more expeditiously than any people had ever done before, so that past and present telescoped, and yesterday became antiquity; thus Jefferson's reference in 1787 to the Articles of Confederation of 1781 as, "the good, old and venerable fabric."[37]

To an extent unimaginable in the Old World, American nationalism was a creation of the people themselves: it was self-conscious and self-generating. Elsewhere nationalism was cultivated and sustained by Kings and Barons, Marshals and Admirals, Prelates and clergy, Judges and Magistrates, Landlords, Proprietors, Magnates, Junkers and Seigneurs, all of whom looked to the Crown and the Church for their support. They professed loyalty to the nation as embodied in monarch and Church, and in symbols and traditions. They served its government, its church, and its armed forces. Increasingly, in the eighteenth and nineteenth centuries, they were joined by the merchants, traders, and bankers who helped formulate a special economic philosophy designed to prosper nationalism and their own interests.

What the new United States lacked in such contributions, it made up in a popular participation, which involved most of its free population. Here it was the farmers and frontiersmen, the fishermen and woodsmen, the shop keepers and apprentices, the small-town lawyers (there were no barristers), the village clergy (there were no bishops), the country schoolteachers (there were no dons) who provided the warp and the woof for the fabric of nationalism. Only the large slaveholders represented the kind of widespread and continuous special interest that sustained the State or the Monarch in Europe, and these, as it turned out, contributed as much to the disintegration of the nation as to its nourishment. It was women as well as men who made the nation, for from the beginning they played a more active role in society and the economy, and even in the Church, than had been their lot in the Old World. And children, who were not only more numerous than elsewhere — for most of them survived infancy — but enjoyed greater freedom and more expansive education than did their European cousins, were prepared from childhood to take their place as citizens in a republic. It was indentured servants who, after they earned independence, blended imperceptibly into society and were accepted as equals; it was newcomers from abroad who found room (though not always welcome) in all the colonies, and who — as with the Germans and the Scots-Irish — all but created their own commonwealths within existing commonwealths. All worked the land together; they intermingled in churches and town meetings and militia training; they fought side by side against Indians and British; they moved down the valleys and across the mountains, setting up new communities and States. They erected churches and imported preachers who did not suffer for their non-conformity; they built schoolhouses where their children learned a common language and a common history out of Mr. Noah Webster's Blue-Backed Spellers and Readers. They conducted their public and private affairs under a common law and an equity which they could, themselves, change by statute, and they were guided by the same Bible where they read — in different tongues — the same moral precepts. All of this, as it turned out, provided a foundation for national unity quite as firm as that provided by Monarchy, History, and the Church in the Old World.

Nation making in the United States was not only new and democratic, it was enlightened. If Americans did not write upon paper that was blank, neither were they condemned to be content with marginal annotations to the black-letter books of the past. Antiquity was picturesque and edifying, but originality and invention had more substantial advantages. In the Old World nations were encrusted with centuries of tradition, bound by a thousand commitments, imprisoned by a thousand precedents, hobbled by a thousand compromises, bemused by a thousand memories. The new-made nation was as yet innocent of traditions, commitments, or memories, although these were speedily provided. It was rooted not in the exhausted soil of some remote past, but in the virgin land of a new continent; it found inspiration not in dubious mythology masquerading as history (that, too, was to come) but in the public will openly proclaimed. Its institutions were fashioned not by the vicissitudes of history, but by the laws of Reason and the dictates of Common Sense. Because the United States was really new, it was free from most of those inherited ambitions and animosities which had for so long made a shambles of many of the nations of Europe. How striking that with the exception of Aaron Burr the new nation did not produce a single adventurer* of the type so familiar in the Old World — an upstart Struensee, an incendiary Wilkes, an imperious Napoleon, a quixotic Miranda.[38] Where it was unable, or unwilling, to free itself from the past — as with the iniquity of slavery — it paid a high price for its failure, a failure all the more tragic in that Jefferson and his co-workers had opened the path to emancipation and freedom. And because the nation was deliberately new-made, in the full light of day, it escaped most of the mysticism and romanticism that suffused those new nations which were quickened into life by the revolutionary spirit blowing out of France. There was romanticism, to be sure, especially in the South, which in its class structure and its yearning for the past, gravitated more and more toward the Old World; the romanticism of New England tended to be transcendental rather than traditional. It required centuries of history to confer sanctity on the State, and America had no such history, so the American State escaped anything remotely resembling sanctity. Centuries of history hedged monarchy about with divinity, but there was nothing divine about the office of the President, and although Washington was doubtless immortal — Parson Weems made that clear — he was wholly unable to transmit any of his majesty or his immortality to his successors, as Bourbon did to Bourbon, Hapsburg to Hapsburg, and even by some strange alchemy, Tudor to Stuart and Stuart to Hanoverian.

* John Paul Jones, perhaps, but it can scarcely be said that the new nation produced him. He arrived in America in 1773 and left it, pretty much for good, in 1783.

ENDNOTES

1. Henry's "Give me liberty or give me death" speech can be found in W. W. Henry, *Patrick Henry: Life, Correspondence, and Speeches*, I (N.Y., 1891), 266; Paine's statement is in *The Crisis Papers*, No. 13.

2. The achievement of nation making has not been accorded the attention it · merits. See Hans Kohn, *American Nationalism* (N.Y., 1957) and his *The Idea of Nationalism* (N.Y., 1944), Ch. vii; C. J. H. Hayes, *Essays on Nationalism* (N.Y., 1937); Boyd C. Shafer, *Nationalism: Myth and Reality* (N.Y., 1955); William P. Murphy, *The Triumph of Nationalism* (Chicago, 1967); and H. S. Commager, "The Origins and Nature of American Nationalism," in *Jefferson, Nationalism, and the Enlightenment* (N.Y., 1975), Ch. 7.

3. Lewis Mumford, *Sticks and Stones* (N.Y., 1924), and see also the opening pages of his *Golden Day* (N.Y., 1926).

4. *Letters from an American Farmer*, Letter III.

5. Merle Curti, *Roots of American Loyalty* (N.Y., 1946), and Max Savelle, "Nationalism and Other Loyalties in the American Revolution," LXVII *American Historical Review* (July 1962), 901 ff.

6. It is not surprising that Tom Paine and Crèvecoeur, both of whom came to America when mature, saw this more clearly than did most Americans except perhaps Jefferson himself. See S. William Sachse, *The Colonial American in Britain* (Madison, Wis., 1956) which unfortunately stops with the outbreak of the Revolution. See too some passages in H. S. Commager, *The Defeat of America* (N.Y., 1975), Ch. 1. See also, for illuminating insights, Hans Huth, *Nature and the American* (Berkeley, Calif., 1957); Daniel J. Boorstin, *The Americans: the Colonial Experience* (N.Y., 1958); Perry Miller, *Nature's Nation* (Cambridge, 1967); Howard Mumford Jones, *O Strange New World* (N.Y., 1964); John Bakeless, *Eyes of Discovery* (N.Y., 1950); Roderick Nash, *Wilderness and the American Mind* (New Haven, 1967); Charles Sanford, *The Quest for Paradise* (Urbana, Ill., 1961); and Leon Baritz, "The Idea of the West," LXVI *American Historical Review* 618 (1961).

7. Letter to Galloway, 25 February 1775, in VII *Writings*, ed., Smyth, 82.

8. Jefferson to the Earl of Buchan, 10 July 1803, *Memorial Edition*, 400.

9. Quoted in Goodman, *Rush* (Philadelphia, 1934), 285.

10. *Letters from an American Farmer*, Letter III.

11. The literature on the impact of the Indian on the American imagination and history is immense. See William Fenton, ed., *American Indian and White Relations to 1830* (chiefly bibliographi-

cal), (Chapel Hill, 1957); Roy Pearce, *The Savages of America: A Study of the Indian and the Idea of Civilization* (Baltimore, 1953); and, for contemporary material, *The Travels of William Bartram* (various editions) and Jefferson's *Notes on the State of Virginia* (various editions).

12. William Bradford, *Of Plymouth Plantations*, S. E. Morison, ed., (N.Y., 1952), 61.

13. Bernard Sheehan, *Seeds of Extinction: Jeffersonian Philanthropy and the American Indian* (Chapel Hill, 1973).

14. Logan's speech is reproduced in Jefferson's *Notes on the State of Virginia*, (Query VI), and can be found in Ford's edition of the *Writings*, III, or in the recent editions of the Notes by Thomas P. Abernethy (N.Y., 1964), or by William Peden (Chapel Hill, 1955), 62-63, 226-58, 274-75.

15. George R. Stewart, *Names on the Land: a Historical Account of Place-naming in the United States* (N.Y., 1945).

16. On religion and the Great Awakening, see Anson Phelps Stokes, *Church and State in the United States*, Vol. I (N.Y., 1950); Wesley Gewehr, *The Great Awakening in Virginia* (Durham, N.C., 1930); Cedric B. Cowing, *The Great Awakening and the American Revolution* (Chicago, 1971); William W. Sweet, *Religion in Colonial America* (N.Y., 1942); Alan Heimert and Perry Miller, eds., *The Great Awakening* (Indianapolis, 1967); Edwin S. Gaustad, *The Great Awakening in New England* (N.Y., 1957); Herbert L. Osgood, *The American Colonies in the Eighteenth Century* (N.Y., 1924), Vol. III, Pt. III, Ch. l.

17. Stokes, *Church and State*, analyzes some of these figures in Vol. I, 228 ff.

18. Carl Bridenbaugh, *The Spirit of Seventy-Six* (N.Y., 1975), Ch. III, and 118.

19. See references in Note 16 above.

20. On Whitefield, see L. Tyerman, *The Life of the Rev. George Whitefield*: 2 vols., (L., 1876-77); and Stuart Clark Henry, *George Whitefield: Wayfaring Witness* (N.Y., 1957).

21. James Thomas Flexner, *Washington: The Indispensible Man* (Boston, 1974); and the Introduction to Richard H. Kohn, *Eagle and Sword* (N.Y., 1975)

22. Kohn, *Eagle.*, 9 ff.

23. H.S. Commager, *The Search for a Useable Past* (N.Y., 1967).

24. See Irving Brant, *James Madison: The Virginia Revolutionary* (Indianapolis: 1941), Ch. xviii.

25. *Crisis*, No. XIII.

26. Richard Frothingham, *Rise of the Republic of the United States* (Boston, 1872).

27. See E. D. Collins, "Committees of Correspondence in the American Revolution," *Am. Hist. Assoc. Annual Report* 1901, Vol. I; J. Leake, *The Virginia Committee System* (Baltimore, 1882); Frothingham, op. cit.

28. Stanley Elkins and Eric McKitrick, "The Founding Fathers: Young Men of the Revolution," 76 *Pol. Sci. Qtly.* 181 ff.

29. All the major histories of the Revolution cover this: John Fiske, *Critical Period;* A. C. McLaughlin, *Confederation and Constitution;* E. C. Burnett, *The Continental Congress;* John C. Miller, *Origins of the American Revolution;* C. H. Van Tyne, *Causes of the War of Independence;* Merrill Jensen, *The New Nation;* and so forth.

30. Carl and Jessica Bridenbaugh, *Rebels and Gentlemen: Philadelphia in the Age of Franklin* (N.Y., 1942).

31. On Washington idolatry, see Gilbert Chinard, *Washington as the French Knew Him* (Princeton, 1940); W. S. Baker, ed., *Character Portraits of Washington* (Philadelphia, 1867); Bryan, "George Washington: Symbolic Guardian of the Republic," *Wm. and Mary Qtly.*, 3d series, VII (January, 1950); and the portrait in W. M. Thackeray's *The Virginians.* Jefferson did not always approve of Washington's policies, but his final judgment of Washington was just and sagacious: "On the whole, his character was, in its mass, perfect, in nothing bad, in few points indifferent; and it may be truly said that never did nature and fortune combine more perfectly to make a man great, and to place him in the same constellation with whatever worthies have merited . . . an everlasting remembrance." Letter to Dr. Walter Jebb, 2 Jan. 1814, *Writings*, ed., H. A. Washington, VI (Washington, 1855).

32. J. Tucker, *Cui Bono.* (Gloucester, Mass., 1781), 117.

33. The Turgot letter to Dr. Price is printed in C. G. Adams' edition, IV *Works of John Adams*, 273ff.

34. Commager, *Jefferson, Nationalism, and the Enlightment*, 176.

35. *Common Sense* (Foner edition, N.Y., 1945), I, 29.

36. *Poetical Works of Thomas Moore* (Boston, 1856), I, 95-96.

37. Thomas Jefferson to John Adams, 13 November, 1787, XII Boyd, 351.

38. Goethe, "Amerika, du hast es besser." Hans Kohn has translated this poem — one difficult to render into English — in his book on *American Nationalism*, 250:
> America, thou are more fortunate than our old continent. Thou hast no ruined castles, no venerable stones. No useless memories, no vain feuds, harry thee in thy soul when thou wishest to live in the present. Make something happy out of today. And when thy children start to write, may a kind Providence preserve them from tales of chivalrous knights, robber barons, and ghosts.

V

Bernard A. DeVoto

A MORE PERFECT UNION

Pierre clement laussat came to New Orleans by command of the First Consul to administer the restored French Empire in North America, the re-arisen New France. There were delays and he smouldered with helpless anger in a still Spanish town. The Spanish gentry and officials began by hating him but soon ignored and despised him. The French inhabitants were of many factions. Some, especially merchants who profited from the smuggling that was universal under the lax administration they were used to, adhered to the Spanish interest. Some looked forward to a Terror to renew the liberty that seemed so antique a notion in the improved world of the Consulate. Some appeared to have been debauched by American ideas. But, impotently waiting for the Province of Louisiana to be transferred to France, he busied himself making plans for its security and development — plans to substitute Napoleon's firm control of maritime commerce for the fatuous Spanish makeshifts under which the Americans had prospered, to nourish French sympathies in the American West, to attach the Indian tribes of the American Southwest to French interest. He forwarded his results, for its information and guidance, to a colonial office where they were tossed into the wastebin of yesterday's debris. When in a moment of curiosity Talleyrand asked what he and his staff might be engaged in, the colonial minister replied, "*Il peut être mort.*"

Almost as soon as Laussat arrived he had to deny a monstrous rumor which the Louisianans and the Americans who were resident among them came increasingly to believe. But it was, he shockingly found out, true. On November 30 1803 he received for the French Republic the enormous domain of Louisiana, transferred by His Catholic Majesty in accordance with a secret treaty made three years before, and this was the first of the duties he had been sent to America to perform. But he was a mere commissioner for the exchange of deeds and he administered Louisiana for just twenty days. On December 20 he added his signature to those of an American governor "with charming private qualities" but "great awkwardness" and a general "full of queer whims and often drunk." The American flag stuck halfway up the pole, then reached the top, and a small crowd of Americans cheered it uncouthly. It signified that a real-estate transaction of incalculable value had been completed, that the French Empire would never return to North America, and that one of the most momentous events in history had occurred.

Upper Louisiana remained. The dream had been that Laussat would direct it toward the prosperity latent in it for the health and strength of the restored Empire. (Who could help dreaming too that some day armies would march from it to raise the tricolor above the Citadel at Quebec where no French banner had flown for forty-four years?) Ended. St. Louis was, on the average, more than two months away and winter had set in. Laussat asked for the name of the American army officer at Kaskaskia whom the awkward governor and the queer general had appointed to receive the transfer of Upper Louisiana.

Thus Amos Stoddard, a Yankee who had been a lawyer but was now a captain in the Corps of the United States Artillerists, became Agent and Commissioner of the French Republic. He accompanied a detachment of that corps which, marching from Kaskaskia, reached Cahokia, across the Mississippi from St. Louis, on February 25, 1804. A cold wave came down from the north, the river filled with ice, and it seemed unwise to cross till March 9. They marched to Government House, where the whole population of the town (increased in the last few years by a startling number of Americans) had assembled. Commissioner Stoddard signed the documents for France, everyone made speeches of rejoicing and congratulation, and the flag of Spain was lowered. That of France was raised while the popguns of the old fort, whose foundation had been laid when the British threatened St. Louis during the Revolution, fired a salute. The lieutenant who commanded the American detachment marched it to the fort, whose garrison was paraded under arms, and the stars and stripes replaced the tricolor that had attested French sovereignty for a few minutes. The Missouri River, all the lands it drained, and all the Indians who lived in them were American. So was the route to the Pacific Ocean.[1]

The documents had also been signed by a captain of the First Infantry, the personal representative of the President of the United States. He had been on detached duty as Jefferson's private secretary for two years but he was now in camp a few miles up the river on the Illinois side. He was Meriwether Lewis and with George Rogers Clark's younger brother William he was commanding a United States Army organization which the President had ordered, thirteen months before, to ascend the Missouri and discover the water route to the Pacific.

A dictatorship must be kept in motion. The dictator is a ruler who must maintain the momentum of events in order to control them or he will fall. This necessity of absolutisms accounts both for Napoleon's attempt to restore the French Empire in North America and for his abandonment of the attempt.

England was the everlasting enemy. In 1798 General Bonaparte led to Egypt an army whose eventual purpose was to shatter the British Empire by reclaiming India for France. Horatio Nelson cut its lifeline by destroying the French fleet in the harbor of Abukir, and sea power had frustrated the

imperial design. Later, leaving the army to rot or be saved
by diplomacy or by victories in Europe, whose map was now
to become the map of France, Napoleon sailed for home
with two new plans matured in his mind. He would build up
the French navy, an enterprise which would require many
years, and he would transfer the imperial contest to the Western Hemisphere.

A month after reaching France he was First Consul. The
energy that no other ruler of men has ever had in equal measure reached the incandescence it was to maintain until, in
Victor Hugo's phrase, God grew bored with him. During the
next year while he attacked the victorious Austrians in Italy,
crumpling them at Marengo, and launched Moreau against
them in Germany to the triumph of Hohenlinden, his mind
played with France and with the world as if they were made of
building blocks that could be arranged in new structural designs at his desire. He began the internal reorganization of
France that was to be his lasting gift to society. Where vor-
texes of force whirled without direction on the margins of Europe, he touched several so that they would now converge.
And as the man of whom Europe had this same summer
learned the terror which was to last till Waterloo he approached Charles IV and his queen, Maria Luisa of Parma
who was the actual ruler of Spain. In return for creating in
Tuscany a Bourbon kingdom for the Duke of Parma, their
son-in-law, he demanded possession of Louisiana. The shat-
tering of the British Empire was to occur in North America.

This was the deal ratified by the secret treaty of San Ildefonso in October 1800. Charles IV removed the last stay to
the dissolution that had begun in South America and
smoothed the way of the liberators and adventurers who within twenty years brought down the whole structure that had
been built on the discovery of the Indies. France recovered
the vastness which it had given away to keep it from Great Britain and to end a war, and which it had never ceased planning and conspiring to recover. Napoleon repossessed it
first of all as an attack on the everlasting enemy. Yet it was
also a move in the war he was fighting to bring Europe to an
armistice, which in turn was a move toward the unification of
Europe. His ruthlessness to Spain was a little the less cynical

in that he thought of Spain, seven years too early, as already his. There was, moreover, at least a twofold purpose in regard to the United States, to the Presidency of which Jefferson had just succeeded after an election that had almost torn it apart. The United States, which had fought a bitter and victorious if undeclared naval war with France under John Adams, must be appeased or it would be driven into alliance with Great Britain, and Napoleon put the diplomatic machinery to work at the very moment when he demanded Louisiana from the Spanish king. And possession of Louisiana was the most powerful force he could direct against the republican and democratic principles which as the post-Thermidor heir of the French Revolution he considered a danger to well-governed societies.

Singularly little ever got written down about the new French Empire in North America. Of the men who have tried to conquer the world, no other had a mind commensurable with Napoleon's, which was infinitely subtle and in much concealed from scrutiny. It played with continents as with dice, with nations as with the markers of the game, and seems to have produced intricate and detailed plans as instantaneously as a reflex. Clearly, his design for the colonial empire in North America which would challenge and eventually overturn the British Empire was as specific as that by which he blueprinted the political and juridical reorganization of France. But what can be said about it is in great part inference — inference from his dispatches and official correspondence and military orders, from the memoirs and conversations at St. Helena, from the memoirs of his ministers, and even less aptly from a handful of state papers.[2]

It may be said that the conception was his own, for it went far beyond what either Talleyrand or the colonials and their conspiracies had urged, and that it derived from a geopolitical concept. He was a conqueror: he saw the shape and contour of empires as issuing from grand strategy. New France had been organized on the axis of the St. Lawrence, whose mouth is one of the strategical keys of North America. The axis of its successor was to be the Mississippi, whose mouth is the master key. It was to have military power not only to maintain itself secure but to defend the Sugar Islands, whose restoration after more than a decade of conquest and revolution was to be completed. Its agricultural wealth was to feed them, and its wealth in furs and raw material was to sustain the French Empire — not only directly under Napoleon's conception of maritime commerce but by competition with whatever of the British Empire could not be conquered.

Strategic security demanded, as well for the Sugar Islands as for the continental empire, control of the Gulf of Mexico and of the highway to it from the south, the Caribbean. Control of the first meant in addition to the mouth of the Mississippi the peninsula of Florida, which another master of geopolitics, President Jefferson, had long been trying to get from Spain for the nation to whose land continuum it belonged. Napoleon had tried to have Florida included in the cession of San Ildefonso but Charles refused. The return to power of Manuel de Godoy, "Prince of the Peace," who was neither afraid of him nor his inferior in guile, kept it out of his hands in the diplomatic game which they played incessantly for the ensuing two and a half years.

Control of the Caribbean required a second stronghold to dominate the island screen. Martinique and Guadeloupe, often fought over but still French, held the Windward Islands at the southern end of the great arc but the central pier of this outpost barrier, instantly seen to be dominant when one looks at a map and even more visibly so in the era of sailing ships, was San Domingo. It was ruled by a Negro genius, Toussaint L'Ouverture, who ostensibly had saved it for Revolutionary France but actually had converted it into a personal and most Napoleonic dictatorship. Horrors and cruelties all but inconceivable, yet inconsiderable compared to those that now lay ahead, had supported the military and diplomatic skill with which Toussaint had manipulated French, Creoles, Spanish, English, Americans, and native blacks till the whole island of Haiti was French in appearance but his in fact. To the American view he had heroic stature in that he had made a Revolution and a Constitution, somewhat less so in that he had freed the slaves, and most of all in that his wars had worked to our safety and had much enriched our merchants. This was the man of whom Wendell Phillips in an orgasmic burst of rhetoric said that the muse of history, dipping her pen in sunlight, would write his name in the clear blue of heaven above those of Brutus, Hampden, and Washington. Napoleon (after perhaps rejecting an idea that he could be used to command a Negro army which would conquer North America) said that by means of him the scepter of the New World might pass into the hands of the blacks. To initiate the first phase of his western empire, he moved to destroy Toussaint and reclaim San Domingo. He prepared the largest amphibious operation the world had yet seen . . . and was to say at St. Helena that it was the greatest act of folly of his life.

Concurrently he prepared an expeditionary force of ten thousand to occupy Louisiana, with the army in San Domingo to make it perhaps twice as large when they had won their victory. The ten thousand (whose start was delayed by the chronic lack of shipping that always hampered Napoleon's maritime plans) were twice as great a force as the sum of the American army and the British garrisons in Canada. No trouble was expected from the Spanish troops in Louisiana; indeed sailing orders were held up till the peaceful cession was assured, and there was talk of hiring them till the army of the Republic could arrive. The purpose of this strength was not only to hold Louisiana for the ten or fifteen years needed to make of the French and tributary fleets a force that could challenge the British navy. It was to insure tractable behavior by the riotously expansive Americans. As for its eventual enlargement from the army in San Domingo, no one knows — but after all New Orleans was the beginning of the road to Quebec.

San Domingo must come first. The army sent there did indeed break Toussaint's armies and capture Toussaint, incidentally destroying what was left of the island's economy. But it was promptly broken in turn by guerrilla warfare, insurrections, and a terrible epidemic of yellow fever. There was nothing to do but to pour into this whirlpool of massacre and pestilence the army that was mustering in Holland for Louisiana and such others as could be raised. The act of folly was completed swiftly. The first army reached the island in January 1802; it was decimated and its commander was dead by November. When, a year later, the commander of its suc-

cessor, besieged by another Negro general and hemmed in
by a British fleet, chose to surrender to the whites, France
had lost upward of 50,000 men and Napoleon had sold his
western empire to the republicans.

Events must be kept in motion. In March 1802 he had procured the European armistice known as the Treaty of
Amiens. The everlasting antagonists regrouped their forces
and diplomatic chessmen for a showdown. News of the
death of his first commander in San Domingo reached Napoleon in January 1803 and confronted him with the ineluctable fact of failure. In the global war he was a Robert E. Lee
who, having in Egypt and the West Indies lost the attacks on
the Round Tops and Culp's Hill, had left no possible action
but to break the center at Cemetery Ridge. He abandoned
the overseas efforts altogether: the road to empire must run
through Germany and across the English Channel. "I renounce Louisiana." But not to Great Britain, the mistress of
the seas, whose fleet would seize it as soon as the war he must
now make broke out. "To emancipate nations from the commercial tyranny of England, it is necessary to balance her influence by a maritime power that may one day become her
rival; that power is the United States."[3]

Godoy had succeeded in delaying the transfer of Louisiana, even after Napoleon had peremptorily demanded it.
Meanwhile, the Spanish intendant at New Orleans had seen
in the impending transfer a chance to rectify what he considered a mistake in statecraft and a weak surrender to the
Americans. Without consulting the governor of Louisiana or
the Spanish minister at Washington, he reverted to the policy of the early 1790's and closed the Mississippi to American
commerce, which by now had multiplied many times. News
that Spain had bound herself to "retrocede" Louisiana had already produced acute tension in the United States. The nation was fully aware that the return of France to the North
American continent would, as Jefferson said, "change the
face of the world." No American could doubt that the expedition to San Domingo was the beginning of imperial aggression in the Western Hemisphere. And while the one to Louisiana was concentrating at the seaports the American minister at Paris learned what its destination was to be.[4]

The intendant's closure of the Mississippi brought both tensions to crisis. As a first move to resolve it Jefferson sent a minister plenipotentiary to assist the minister's effort, now more than a year old, to buy New Orleans or, failing that, some other site at the mouth of the Mississippi and thus secure an outlet to the Gulf. Talleyrand had ignored the minister, played with him, scorned him, misled him, lied to him. But now, "I renounce Louisiana . . . Obstinacy in trying to preserve it would be madness." On April 11 1803 the minister, Robert R. Livingston, fatalistically beginning one more routine discussion with Talleyrand on the purchase of New Orleans, was greeted with a decisive question. What, Talleyrand asked him, what would the United States pay for all Louisiana?[5]

Little need be said about the American background of the Louisiana Purchase. This narrative has shown that among the forces which produced the United States, a recurring one had been imperial war. As has been said here and must be emphatically repeated, the United States was itself an empire before it was a nation, though it was first a people who had made a society. Historians have been fond of drawing a distinction: the Peace of Amiens brought the wars of the French Revolution to an end and led on to the Napoleonic wars. It is a distinction for convenience only, for both groups of wars issued, as the American Revolution did, from the collapse of the world order completed by the Seven Years' War, and both were on the way to the stabilization that followed when the final defeat of the unification of Europe at Waterloo permitted the nineteenth century to begin. For a distinction between the groups of wars, for the bridge between them, the Peace of Amiens is perhaps less convenient than the Treaty of San Ildefonso which preceded it. That treaty did most surely, in French and British no less than in American eyes, "change the face of the world." And it brought the greatest military power, under the man who would presently be Emperor and intended to conquer the world, to the western boundary of the Republic that was just twelve years old.

On September 17 1796 George Washington had said, "The

period is not far off . . . when belligerent nations, under the impossibility of making acquisitions upon us, will not lightly hazard the giving us provocation." He went on to ask the question which down to this day has lowered like a thunderhead whenever the nation has come in peril, "Why, by interweaving our destiny with that of any part of Europe, entangle our peace and prosperity in the toils of European ambition, rivalship, interest, humor, or caprice?" Always when that cloud has gathered it has been dispelled by the same inexorability that faced Jefferson when Louisiana again became French. It was now that he wrote, and to Robert Livingston as minister, "There is on the globe one single spot, the possessor of which is our natural and habitual enemy." And he went on to say, "The day that France takes possession of New Orleans fixes the sentence which is to restrain her forever within her low water mark. It seals the Union of two nations who in conjunction can maintain exclusive possession of the ocean. From that moment we must marry ourselves to the British fleet and nation."[6]

This realism of the sometime Francophile preceded by thirteen months the British minister's report to his chief that "the most desirable state of things seems to be that France should become mistress of Louisiana, because her influence in the United States would be by that event lost forever, and she could only be dispossessed by a concert between Great Britain and America in a common Cause, which would produce an indissoluble bond of union and amity between the two countries."[7]

Jefferson expected to resolve the problem by peaceful means, as he had been able to do when it was a Spanish problem eight years before.[8] But as President now he no more disregarded the possibility that war with France might become necessary, than as Secretary of State then he had disregarded the possibility that war with Spain might become necessary.[9] Among alternatives, at the extremity he was prepared to abide the presence of France in Louisiana till the force which he knew nothing could withstand should take care of it, "till we shall have planted such a population on the Mississippi as will be able to do their own business, without the necessity of marching men from the shores of the Atlantic."

To do their own business: to take New Orleans, open the river, control the French. At almost the exact date of that quotation, the frustrate prefect Laussat was writing from New Orleans, "The Anglo-American [United States] flag eclipses by its number here those of France and Spain. In front of the city and along the quays there are at this moment fifty-five Anglo-American ships to ten French . . . The Anglo-Americans are the most dreaded rivals in the world in point of commerce . . . If New Orleans has been peopled and has acquired importance and capital, it is due neither to Spain nor to the Louisianans properly so-called. It is due to three hundred thousand planters who in twenty years have swarmed over the eastern plains of the Mississippi and have cultivated them and have no outlet than this river and no other port than New Orleans."[10] Either Laussat or Jefferson had only to glance from the Spanish Province of Louisiana to the American Territory of Mississippi just across the river from it. Such a glance, like a single line of type that told the number of emigrants who had crossed the mountains in the last year, was evidence enough that the force would ultimately be irresistible.

But French possession of New Orleans, which meant that the river would continue to be closed, was the extremity. Though Jefferson knew that the extremity would be temporary and calculated that it would prove tolerable, he had no intention of accepting it. He would neither wait for the population that could do its own business nor become the prisoner of events. He intended to be master of events. His sending the plenipotentiary, James Monroe, to support Livingston's efforts to buy the Floridas and New Orleans was a measure of domestic policy. It was to restrain the Westerners from taking matters into their own hands and precipitating a war which he calculated was avoidable, and the eastern Federalists from inciting them to. (It worked out precisely as he had foreseen.) But his letter to Monroe following the appointment was written in full knowledge that the French army in San Domingo had been annihilated and that the crisis between France and Great Britain was sharpening. (And it was written just five days before his secret message to Congress asking funds for an exploring expedition to traverse Louisi-

ana.) He told Monroe that on his success depended "the future destinies of this republic. If we cannot by a purchase of
the country insure to ourselves a course of perpetual peace
and friendship with all nations, then as war cannot be distant, it behooves us immediately to be preparing for that
course, without, however, hastening it, and it may be necessary (on your failure on the continent) to cross the channel."[11] To cross the channel and, as a measure of prepara-
tion for a certain and early war, to propose marriage to the
British fleet and nation.

It was the French possession of Louisiana that would
change the face of the world, but it was the Spanish closure
of the Mississippi that precipitated the domestic crisis. Jefferson had been President less than two years, following the
first of our political revolutions. The Western interest that
had forced Washington to require of Spain the reopening of
the river in 1795 had by now increased many times over. So
Eastern Federalism was curiously focused on supporting
Western Republicanism, and New England separatism was
even more curiously focused on intensifying Western separatism. Jefferson said quite truly that "the fever into which the
western mind is thrown by the affair at N. Orleans stimulated
by the mercantile, and generally the Federal, interest threat-
ens to overbear our peace."[12] The maritime war which had
ended in the last months of Adams's administration might,
as a result of that fever, be followed by the war for the mouth
of the Mississippi that Washington had averted. Jefferson believed that it could be averted now: he sent Monroe to
France to quiet the fever of the Western mind. The rest he
confided to the unfolding of events: he saw that in the world
turmoil lay the chance of achieving all the results the war
could, of achieving them without a war. No statesman ever
interpreted events more accurately than Jefferson did at this
crisis, or bent them to his ends with more fastidious calculation of the forces they contained. It was Jefferson, not Napoleon, who charted the channel through the whirlpool.

And if the envoys he directed to buy a village secured instead a domain which more than doubled the area of the
United States, the surprise, though stunning, was only that
this had come about in one step, so easily, and so soon. "I

believed the event not very distant but acknowlege it came on sooner than I had expected," he wrote to Dr. Priestley. That was afterward but it was not hindsight. He had told Livingston that the British alliance would "make the first cannon which shall be fired in Europe the signal for tearing up any settlement [France] may have made and for holding the two continents of America in sequestration for the common purposes of the United British and American nations." And he had notified the governor of Mississippi Territory on the vital frontier that if France forced us to war, "we should certainly seize and hold [New Orleans and the Floridas] *and much more.*"[3] The inescapable fact was that either the alliance with Great Britain or war with France, or anything else that made New Orleans American, must immediately or very soon carry with it the rest of Louisiana. In London Rufus King, the American minister, had freely discussed the military acquisition of all Louisiana, and the correspondence between Livingston and King discusses the same possibility.[4] When nations light a war the peace settlement will involve more than a free port. There had never been a time when war for the mouth of the Mississippi had not meant war for the western half of the Mississippi Valley.

That was in the event of war. The contingency had been allowed for in circumstances other than war. Madison, the Secretary of State, wrote to the envoys after the great deed was done, "It was not presumed that more could be sought by the United States with a chance of success, or perhaps without being suspected of a greedy ambition, than the island of New Orleans and the Floridas . . . It might be added that the ample views of the subject carried with him by Mr. Munroe, and the confidence felt that your judicious management would make the most of favorable occurrences, lessened the necessity of multiplying provisions for every turn which your negotiations might possibly take."[5] That is the language of diplomats: at least the possibility had been envisaged. Likewise, proposals to guarantee the western bank of the river to France, to withdraw either the entrepôt or the boundary to Natchez, to accept this or that condition, were items of diplomatic maneuver, pawns authorized to be offered in position play. So far as the administration accepted the very remote possibility that it might be forced to sacrifice any such pawn, it was for a few years only, to hold the position till the advancing West should reach the Mississippi in force.

For neither Jefferson nor Madison nor anyone else who watched the emigration supposed that the frontier would stop at the Mississippi, which the pioneer fringe had in fact already crossed throughout its entire length south of St. Louis. Every chancellery in Europe was on repeated notification from its ministers that, as Carondelet wrote in 1794, the Americans "advancing with an incredible rapidity toward the north and the Mississippi will unquestionably force Spain to recognize the Missouri as their boundary within a short time, and perhaps they will pass over that river. . . If such men succeed in occupying the shores of the Mississippi or of the Missouri, or to obtain their navigation, there is, beyond doubt, nothing that can prevent them from crossing those rivers and penetrating into our provinces on the other side." That nothing could prevent them was clear to the Spanish governor of Louisiana in 1794. It was no less clear to the President of the United States in 1803. He had, in fact, written to the governor of Virginia in 1801, "However our present interests may restrain us within our own limits, it is impossible not to look forward to distant times, when our rapid multiplication will expand itself beyond those limits & cover the whole northern, if not the southern continent, with a people speaking the same language, governed in similar forms & by similar laws."[16]

King in London had discussed an American Louisiana as a buffer to protect Canada. Livingston had proposed to France, even before the Intendant closed the river, the cession of all Louisiana or, alternatively, all of it north of the Arkansas River. To this proposal he repeatedly came back.[17] And Livingston may be taken as representative: a Republican, an Easterner, in no way a visionary, a member of the committee that had been appointed to draft the Declaration of Independence, a member of Congress, a veteran and very skillful diplomat. He had shared the entire national experience of the United States . . . and he took its expansion across Louisiana as a thing given, only the factor of time being in question. As for that champion of reserved powers, Jefferson, in January 1803 he took up with Gallatin the question of acquiring territory and was sure "that there is no constitutional difficulty."[18] This was two months before Monroe sailed for France, six months before Jefferson had to face the acquisition of the territory in view and hastily sketched an amendment that would sanction it, only to decide that the constitutional question had better not be raised at all. And in that same January he asked Congress for an appropriation "for the purpose of extending the external commerce of the United States" by exploring Louisiana.

Part of the price paid for Louisiana was the assumption by the United States of claims against France by American citizens for damage suffered from depredations in the various naval wars. These later produced the litigation that invariably follows such settlements, and they were not finally extinguished until 1925. In 1939 the Geological Survey, summing up Louisiana, reported that the United States had paid in cash settlement of them the sum of $3,747,268.96. Beyond this "assumption" the price of Louisiana was 60,000,000 francs, $11,250,000. In addition the Survey counts $8,221,320.50 in interest, less discounts of $5021.75. The total is $23,213,567.73.

No one knew what the bonds had bought, for France did not know what had first been transferred to Spain or what had later been repossessed from it. The documents were both ambiguous and contradictory; some specifications they contained had been made futile by events, some meaningless by the progress of discovery. When the minister of finance mentioned this confusion to Napoleon he was told "that if the obscurity did not already exist, it would perhaps be good policy to put it there,"[19] and there is sense as well as cynicism in the conqueror's remark. The ambiguities were on the territorial margins, were of the boundaries. Thus though few could believe that France had any claim to land west of the Mississippi drainage, there were some who read the tortuous legalities otherwise. Livingston himself considered that Louisiana reached the Pacific and Dr. Samuel Latham Mitchill, scientist, friend of Jefferson, Congressman from New York, and the author of legislation concerning Louisiana, supposed that it reached the Pacific north of California and somewhere, south of whatever part of the Northwest coast might be British. Dr. Mitchill, in fact, so reported to the House of Representatives.[20] Again there was a matted tangle of uncertainties about the boundaries of what is now the State of Louisiana. The resolution of disputes about them, honest or factitious, required local uprising, militia occupation, annexation by fiat, the War of 1812, the purchase of Florida, and indeed the Mexican War of 1846. The final definition of Louisiana had to be arbitrary. The nation which Livingston and Monroe represented had an area computed at 869,735 square miles. The three instruments of cession dated April 30 1803 but signed four days later transferred to it, the arbitrary summation says, 909,130 square miles.[21]

It included (subject to the disputes mentioned) parts of Mississippi and Alabama as well as the part of Louisiana that is east of the river. The rest was the actual western extent of the region which on April 9 1682 the Sieur de la Salle had added to the domain of Louis XIV. It was the western half of the Mississippi drainage basin to the as yet undetermined Continental Divide, except as treaties or the acceptance of conventions had trimmed it . . . Later there would thus be trimmed from it an area instantly and poignantly at issue as soon as the transfer to the United States was made. This is the portion of Missouri River drainage north of 49°, a strip in Alberta and Saskatchewan that amounts to 9715 square miles . . . Excluded at the south was whatever land was legally Spanish before 1783 — and again this was not determined till the purchase of Florida, when the boundary was established as the Red River to the 100th meridian, north to the Arkansas River, and west along the Arkansas.

Louisiana: Minnesota west of the Mississippi. Louisiana west of the Mississippi and the city of New Orleans east of it. Arkansas, Iowa, Nebraska, North and South Dakota. Oklahoma except "the Public Land Strip," that is Oklahoma east of the 100th meridian. Kansas except for the corner west of the 100th meridian and south of the Arkansas River. Colorado north of the Arkansas and east of the Continental Divide

Wyoming and Montana east of the Divide.

When the determinations were made none of the maps they were based on were accurate. In the end, the land itself had to be surveyed to accord with the accepted determinations. An exactly equivalent empiricism governed the American acceptance of the Purchase: all legal, indeed all abstract, questions about it were meaningless and Jefferson was right not to raise the constitutional issue. In the presence of the tremendous fact the laws were silent: the land itself reduced all other meanings to nonentity. And among the meanings thus nonplused was a threefold irony: that Napoleon sold Louisiana before the "retrocession" from Spain was executed, and so it was not his to sell; that he sold it without consulting the Senate of the French Republic and the Legislative Assembly, so that the sale was unconstitutional and therefore invalid; and that the Treaty of San Ildefonso, which alone could give France title to Louisiana, contained an article of absolute reversion to Spain in case there should be any attempt to cede or alienate it, and so whatever warranty or claim he was acting to transfer perished with his act.

The Louisiana Purchase was a resultant. It was the resultant of four systems of imperial energies forced to conform to the unmalleable reality of geographical fact. Because that is what it was, April 30 1803 is one of history's radical dates. "The annexation of Louisiana," Henry Adams wrote, "was an event so portentous as to defy measurement."

In the sector of partial measurements, two remarks of Napoleon's, both quoted by Barbé-Marbois, the minister of finance who conducted the negotiations, are germane. "This accession of territory consolidates the power of the United States forever, and I have given England a maritime rival who sooner or later will humble her pride."[22] The unifier of Europe and the remaker of the world, who had also ended forever the dream of a North American France, was here looking down a long arc of time with great clarity . . . And yet.

(And yet it is always summer afternoon, they say, on the bank of the Styx to which the Elysian Fields come down. Statesmen there watch without concern the flowing of the asphodel-bordered river of time, tranquil because all doubts are ended and nothing is to be done. So sometimes they fall to talking about *if*s that have no force. George Canning and John Quincy Adams may thus discuss the Monroe Doctrine in terms of the alliance with Great Britain which Jefferson was willing to envisage, which Napoleon perhaps averted by the cession, and which would have given the nineteenth century, in its third year, an experiment in international discipline based on allied sea power.)

With the threat of France on the Mississippi dissipated, the United States and Great Britain did revert to the antagonism implicit in their respective situations, as the world upheaval went on to define them further. That was the first step in what Napoleon foresaw, and he supplied the pressures that intensified the antagonism to war nine years later. As he foresaw, the maritime rival humbled British power, turned back invasions down the Champlain corridor and up his (and La Salle's) Mississippi route, and as a nation came to understand permanently the natural channels for the application of military force on this continent.

The power added to the United States by the Louisiana Purchase is indeed beyond measurement, and its torque has been exerted on the nations increasingly since 1803. Napoleon's second remark shows that he missed something in it: he missed the core-meaning of what he had done. "Perhaps," he said to Marbois, "perhaps I will also be told in reproach that in two or three centuries the Americans may be found too powerful for Europe, but my forethought cannot encompass such distant fears. Besides, in the future rivalries inside the Union are to be expected. These confederations that are called perpetual last only till one of the confederating parties finds that its interest can be served by breaking them."[23] He was wrong on his oath: Louisiana made the confederation perpetual.

Louisiana welded the implicit significance of the American political experiment to the implicit logic of continental geography. Thereafter they were not to be distinguished from each other. From them came the strength which not only held the confederation secure against exterior force but could not be overcome when the rivalries of its members that Napoleon took for granted produced a revolution intended to break it. When that time came, the land itself forbade.

As Abraham Lincoln understood it must.

Fifty-nine years after the Louisiana Purchase, December 1 1862, President Lincoln sent his second annual message to Congress. He had a dolorous year to look back on when he reported the state of the nation. The invasion of Maryland, it was true, had been stopped at Antietam but the full victory which might have destroyed the Army of Northern Virginia had slipped from McClellan's grasp. There had followed the heartbreaking delays of a general who felt confident that he would be invincible tomorrow and certain that the enemy was invincible today. So McClellan had had to be replaced for the second time. There was the failure that produced the earlier removal to look back on: the glorious promise of the Peninsular Campaign, the timid management of the Seven Days, the magnificent parrying by first Johnston and then Lee, the humiliating withdrawal. There were other humiliations of this year to be remembered: repeated defeats in the Valley, Second Bull Run, smaller actions that seemed everywhere to go against the Union. In the West there had been significant victories in 1862 but they were far away and easily forgotten in the city where every foul bird came abroad and every dirty reptile rose up — where defenders of the Union seemed the most likely to destroy it — where the Secretary of the Treasury preferred the impotence of the government to the continuance in office of the Secretary of State — where part of the Cabinet was hostile to the President and in Congress much of his own party had rebelled against him.

Surely here was a powerful tendency of confederating parties to destroy a confederation. Yet as far back as September 22 Lincoln had read his draft of the Emancipation Proclamation to the Cabinet, telling them they might criticize the phrasing but not the act, which was determined upon, not open to question. Now, on December 1, his message explained to Congress that the Proclamation must be supported, as a war aim, by amendments to the Constitution abolishing slavery. The war, he said . . . "our strife pertains to ourselves, to the passing generations of men — and it can without convulsion be hushed forever with the passing of one generation of men." This was a dark saying to a nation almost at its darkest hour, and in order to make its meaning clear the President had to preface it with another explanation.

He quoted from his inaugural address the moving passage that begins, "Physically speaking we cannot separate. We cannot remove our respective sections from each other nor build an impassable wall between them. A husband and wife may be divorced and go out of the presence and beyond reach of each other, but the different parts of our country cannot do this." On to the end. When he first addressed that solemn warning to the South there had been no fighting. But now there had been much fighting and God only could sum up how much waste, destruction, agony, and death — and still the inexorable truth of that warning held. So he went on:

> There is no line straight or crooked, suitable for a national boundary upon which to divide. Trace through from east to west, upon the line between the free and slave country, and we shall find that a little more than one-third of its length are rivers easy to be crossed and populated or soon to be populated thickly on both sides; while nearly all its remaining length are merely surveyors' lines, over which people may walk back and forth without any consciousness of their presence. No part of this line can be made any more difficult to pass by writing it down on paper as a national boundary. . . . A glance at the map shows that territorially speaking [the vast interior region] is the great body of the Republic. The other parts are but marginal borders to it. . . . And yet this region has no seacoast — touches no ocean anywhere. As part of one nation its people now find, and may forever find, their way to Europe by New York, to South America and Africa by New Orleans, and to Asia by San Francisco. . . And this is true *wherever* a dividing or boundary line may be fixed. Place it between the now

free and slave country, or place it south of Kentucky or north of [the] Ohio, and still the truth remains that none south of it can trade to any port or place north of it, and none north of it can trade to any port or place south of it, except on terms dictated by a government foreign to them. These outlets, east, west, and south, are indispensable to the well-being of the people inhabiting and to inhabit this vast interior region. *Which* of the three may be the best is no proper question. All are better than either and all of right belong to that people and to their successors forever. True to themselves, they will not ask *where* a line of separation shall be, but will vow rather that there shall be no such line. Nor are the marginal regions less interested in these communications to and through them to the great outside world. They too, and each of them, must have access to this Egypt of the West without paying toll at the crossing of any national boundary.

Our national strife springs not from our permanent part; not from the land we inhabit; not from the national homestead. There is no possible severing of this but would multiply and not mitigate evils among us. In all its adaptations and aptitudes it demands union and abhors separation. In fact it would ere long force reunion, however much of blood and treasure the separation might have cost. Our strife pertains to ourselves, to the passing generations of men. . . .

Here is the inherence of the physical conditions that have shaped American life, expressed by the man who at the Gettysburg cemetery and in his second inaugural address would express the deepest faith and the highest aspiration of American life. It states what Napoleon's prophecy left out of account, when for sixty million francs he relinquished to the young Republic the West that completes the physical unity.

And there is a striking thing about Thomas Jefferson. He sometimes said that the continental area was too big for the

United States to govern. He could tranquilly contemplate the possibility of other republics in the Far West peopled by Americans but independent. "We think we see their happiness in their union [with us] & we wish it. Events may prove it otherwise; and if they see their interest in separation, why should we take side with our Atlantic rather than our Missipi descendants? It is the elder and the younger son differing."[24] Again, "I confess I look to this duplication of area for the extending a government so free and economical as ours as a great achievement to the mass of happiness which is to ensue. Whether we remain in one confederacy or form into Atlantic and Mississippi confederacies, I believe not very important to the happiness of either part . . . and did I now foresee a separation at some future day, yet I should feel the duty & the desire to promote the western interests as zealously as the eastern." So he could believe and say. Nevertheless it is possible without any distortion whatever to make a chronological sequence of his actions in regard to the American land, from the reports and ordinances he wrote for the government of the Northwest Territory as a member of the Congress of the Confederation, through his ministry to France, his term of Secretary of State, and on to the Louisiana Purchase — and, looking at this sequence, to decide that though he may sometimes have *thought* that the nation could not permanently fill its continental system, he *acted* as if, manifestly, it could have no other destiny.

Or more simply, this: after 1803 the phrase "the United States" in Jefferson's writing, usually plural up to now, begins increasingly to take a singular verb.

History cannot suppose that because the intangibles which alter men's consciousness deposit no documents in the archives they therefore do not affect societies. What constituted the New World a new world, how the new world made Americans out of European stocks, what interactions of men and land established the configuration of American society — these are intangibles which historical thinking has only gingerly considered. Fragmented facts, all commonplaces, await a synthesis. Some are the daily absorption of the humbler sciences immediately at hand and indeed taught to all schoolboys. Others are truisms used by all artists. There is no schoolboy who has not read about "Indian old fields" or does not know that Squanto told his white friends to plant the maize in hills. There is no artist who does not know that the American scythe blade and the American axe handle developed a curve instead of the inherited straight line in response to conditions which the tools must meet. There is no one who does not know that the firstcomers must live in, by, and in spite of an abundance of timber of which not even an ancestral memory was left in Europe, and no one who does not know that the syntax of the American tongue differs in structure from the syntaxes of Europe. . . . The poet MacLeish: "She's a tough land under the corn mister: She has changed the bone in the cheek of many races." The poet Benét: "And they ate the white corn-kernels, parched in the sun, And they knew it not but they'd not be English again. . . And over them was another sort of day, And in their veins was another, a different ghost."

Rivers, mountain ranges, the orientation of glacial lakes, soils, climates, prevailing winds. And, in the late phases of the westering, an acceleration which is the only way time decisively affects the equations. (Time in relation to space; those who thought the space too great to be mastered were miscalculating neither area nor politics but only the rate of acceleration.) These compose an articulation, a pattern, an organic shape. It is not a perfect symmetry nor a perfect unity, but it is incomparably closer to being both than the physical matrix in which any other modern nation developed. The American teleology is geographical.

The Appalachian Highland curves two arms round the state of Maine. Those heavily timbered uplands, incapable of being farmed, were a barrier not worth crossing and therefore an implicit boundary. They remain essentially a wilderness, detoured not crossed, today. The rivers that flow north from them to the St. Lawrence (like those that flow south to it) are short. That is, the valley of the St. Lawrence is narrow. That is further, throughout almost the whole length of the valley agriculture had from the beginning not only a rigid limitation but a visible one. It had another limitation in the northern winter, from which agronomical adaptations could not free it till after the economic pattern had been fixed.

The society of the St. Lawrence Valley, then, must conform to the fisheries, to which the river led eastward — and which the English colonies could reach more easily from Massachusetts than from Maine, where they were nearest to Canada. And it must conform to the fur trade to which the river led west, all the way west, and its tributaries led north, all the way north. By the time settlement reached the first widening of the agricultural horizon, the Ontario peninsula, the society of Canada had conformed to the wealth in furs. There never would be agriculture in the north. The Laurentian Highland made it impossible; the bulldozer of the icecap had pushed the topsoil of Canada into the upper American Middle West. The bulk of Canadian agricultural wealth, apart from the Ontario peninsula, is concentrated west and northwest of Lake Winnipeg. It was hardly developed at all before the middle of the nineteenth century; much of its development has occurred in the twentieth century. By the time its West was settled, Canada had a social organism easily able to assimilate disruptive pressures that could easily have destroyed it a century before.

But the society south of Canada had always been of land, not furs: on an agricultural foundation. Its expansion was at a slower rate and got its power from mass.

After inclosing Maine in parentheses, the Appalachian Highland strikes southwest. The agricultural strip widens toward the south, but movement to occupy it was also movement west. This combined movement is repeated by the wide valleys within the uplands, which are agricultural and trend southwestward.

Mountain ranges impede communication, transportation, and settlement. They therefore concentrate populations, whose institutions integrate before they expand. The Appalachian system produced that effect, thus further slowing the momentum of the agricultural society. Yet the Appalachians are not a difficult barrier. There is one entirely unencumbered way through it, by the Hudson and Mohawk Rivers; a railroad that uses it truthfully calls itself "the water-level route." But a social and military obstacle stretched straight across it, the Iroquois. Similarly, at the southern end of the Appalachians, where again there is no serious top-ographical barrier to movement, were the Civilized Tribes, who were most civilized in fighting quality. Between these two extremities, straight west of populous colonies lay a num-ber of comparatively easy passages across the mountains. All of them cluster with names from which our legendry has been spun — and all of them are practically continuous with water routes from the littoral. For the rivers that come down from the mountains could hardly have been better designed for access to the interior. Delaware, Susquehanna, Poto-mac, James, Roanoke, Santee, Savannah — all led to intelli-gible corridors. From the Susquehanna by way of the Juniata and through moderate passes to the Allegheny, or from the Cheat to the Monongahela — either was a simple and coher-ent route to a prime focus, the Forks of the Ohio. From the Potomac to the Kanawha the route through the mountains was less simple but equally coherent. Just as coherent, long-er and more difficult, but by more profitable stages were the routes that converged on Moccasin Gap and Cumberland Gap and emerged on the Tennessee or the Cumberland Riv-er. These truly *crossed* the mountains, yet the mountains were not wide and the streams that cut through them did so by valleys too narrow to be populated. Moreover, all this country could be more easily traversed by horse and even-tually vehicular traffic than the Canadian land, very large areas of which prohibited them altogether.

The Appalachian system, then, though a decelerant, im-plied neither economic nor political discontinuity. The cismontane river system impelled the American society west-ward or northward to it and westward or southwestward across it. Once across the mountains, the society came into the Mississippi Valley, a geographical unity of tremendous centripetal force. The routes were spun round the Ohio River as if by design. The Great Lakes lay to the north, a wat-er route but also an implicit boundary. The ease of commu-nication between the Lakes and the Ohio has been re-peatedly emphasized in this narrative, and so has the ease of communication between the western Lakes and the Mississip-pi. On a map the rivers look like the veining of a leaf.

Miami, Wabash, Illinois, Wisconsin — Kanawha, Kentucky, Cumberland, Tennessee — Ohio, middle Mississippi — and the continental arch through which the Missouri empties into the Mississippi.

To cross the Appalachian system was to come into the American heartland, where nothing could be separated from anything else for very long. Where all cultures and all stocks and all casts of thought and all habits of emotion mingled. Where as Lincoln said the dividing lines were either rivers that could be ferried in a moment or the numbered abstractions of surveyors that could not even be perceived. And where to go west a mile today was to go twain before sundown tomorrow.

This continuity and integration of the land, it must be repeated, was a centripetal force, a unifying, nation-making force. It increased as it progressed, so that the centrifugal thrusts, the separatist actions previous to 1803, could not prevail against it and those of the next decade were still more futile.

In this force, the element reciprocal with physical design, though hard to define and all but impossible to isolate, can never be left out of account. A people that has widened an axehead and changed the angle of its bevel, or that has begun to shock wheat with one bundle for capstone and covering, has already developed a different physiology of thought and feeling. The variations in temperature no less than the abundance of unowned land, new crops and different growing seasons no less than a leveling scarcity of labor, differentiations in the usages of woods, the handicrafts of a wilderness-lapped livelihood, town government and township surveys, a forest pharmacopoeia, the skills of clearing and trail, a clergy made rebellious and an electorate of freehold ownership, the reduction of bog iron or the presentiment of a wider suffrage — all these are metabolic processes in the growth of a new consciousness. Lincoln said that there was no possible severing of the national *homestead*; he also said that its *adaptations and aptitudes* abhorred separation. They were dynamically connected, functions of each other. For the whole he had no word except the mystical one, Union, and no concepts except democracy.

Gathering centripetal energy as it traveled, then, the nation that was coterminously an empire burst through its western limit in 1803. Many accessions of power followed, notably an increase in this same centripetal and nation-making force. Centrifugal, disruptive forces that would oppose it would increase now too, at first gradually, pellmell later on with the slave-labor hegemony, but their true nature could not, in 1803, be understood. Much was withholden but it was dramatically clear that if not in this year then in some other not long distant, the nation would have crossed the Mississippi regardless.

But how far and for how long?

The land remained a continuum. No boundary between nations was ever drawn more justly than the canoe route from Lake Superior to Lake of the Woods. It corresponded exactly to the existing economic systems. Their equipoise sufficed temporarily to make the line of 49° westward from there an acceptable convention to both nations, when it was proved to pass north of the source of the Mississippi. Here, however, there was latent the first possible discontinuity or aberration. It requires a paragraph.

The Red River valley is Hudson Bay drainage and therefore was not geographically a part of Louisiana. (Jefferson, the American commissioners, the British commissioners, almost everyone who thought about those distant regions supposed that 49° had been made the boundary of Louisiana by the Treaty of Utrecht in 1713. Actually it had not been: the treaty provided that the boundary was to be determined by "commissaries," who never determined it.) West of the Red River the great plains begin — and, except climatically, these are as continuous north and south as they are east and west. The southwestern quarter of Manitoba, the southern half of Saskatchewan, perhaps half of Alberta are of the same nature as the Dakotas and Montana and no barrier cut across this enormous area. There was indeed an invisible one, of water flow, climate and especially convertible wealth. Long before the Louisiana Purchase the Canadian economy had determined it: the fur business. Its connection with the Pacific remained an imperial issue — one that had become immediate and urgent even before the Purchase — but the Canadian momentum was furs. Its movement was therefore west and north, not south. By the time the two societies could compete for the Great Plains area both had been integrated past any inner possibility of defying what had been established long before. In the late 1860's and early 1870's the vision that all Western Canada might be American, that the United States might stretch from Lake Winnipeg to Alaska, did indeed excite many Canadian and American minds. Much emotion and some blood was spilled but neither the Red River Rebellion nor any of the lesser plots, dreams, or nightmares ever had a chance. The issue had been settled long before. The acceleration of time had affected the equation and the equipoise held.

The Rio Grande was an implicit boundary between Texas and Mexico. West of the Rio Grande the boundary between the United States and Mexico is even more implicit, the composite of topography, soil, water flow, and climate even more inflexible. The line could have been drawn a few miles north or a few miles south of where it was drawn — but, as the entire history of Spain in the Southwest attested, not many miles.

Northern and southern limits defined a unit that was continentally continuous with the earlier United States. The possible discontinuities, the latent aberrations or refutations of the continental experience, were in the interior West — across the path to the Pacific that the American people had been following since they began to be American, when the Pacific lapped the western foothills of the Cumberland Mountains and could be reached from tidewater in two weeks.

On the map the river system of the eastern half of the Mississippi Valley appears to have been sketched by an artist drawing, freehand, a series of related curves. West of the Mississippi the river system appears to have been blueprinted by a purposive systematic architectural engineer. That latter appearance is profoundly deceptive. The Red River (of Louisiana) was but imperfectly navigable and was navigable at all only in its lower reaches. The statement is no less true of the Arkansas River. Only the Missouri was a water route — and it was infinitely laborious and infinitely circuitous. Contrary to the traditional experience of the westering Americans, most travel, the principal movement, must be by land. And now the land changed. And the climates.

The Americans would leave the forest behind, then the prairies, then the tall grass, and come into the plains. On a steady gradient the land sloped upward to the unknown Rocky Mountains. The end of the tall grass meant the beginning of aridity and the approach of deserts. The deserts were a much more formidable barrier than the Appalachians. Routes across them must be sounded for like the channels in the shallow lakes of Saskatchewan. The valleys of three rivers threaded the maze of deserts, the Arkansas, the Platte, and the Missouri. Then came the Rockies. They could be crossed in only a few places; only two passes were feasible for wheeled vehicles in the travel season and, so it turned out, only one was actually usable during the critical years of Far Western expansion. The Rockies were a succession of ranges, a zone of mountains, in some places more than two hundred miles wide, everywhere precipitous. Beyond them were additional deserts and then another mountain wall, the Sierra and Cascades, much narrower than the Rockies but even harder to cross.

Deserts and mountains composed just such a barrier as political systems had broken on in Europe. Though the land remained a continuum an ellipsis interrupted its coherence. In the event, the westward thrust reached this barrier with the dynamics of expansion stepped up to the greatest power it ever had, the rush of the 1840's. It hurdled the barrier. The Pacific coast was brought within the American system of energies before the interior West was. Precisely here the acceleration of time had become decisive. Industrial development was the final centripetal force in American expansion: it enabled the single system, the single social and political combination, to absorb the ellipsis and fill out the continuum. There was never a chance that Oregon and California would fall away, as there had once been a strong chance that Kentucky might. The clipper ships, steamships, telegraph lines, railroads, and the subsidiary accelerants of communication and trade developed too fast.

None of this could be foreseen in 1803. In particular no

American knew anything about any of the deserts or any of the mountain ranges. But an energy in addition to the uninterrupted westward thrust had been in operation for ten years. A detached portion of the American system existed at and near the known mouth of a river called the Columbia, which was unknown above its mouth. It was as if a whirling sphere had detached an asteroid that traveled in a concentric orbit, and yet the attractive force was in the direction of the asteroid — pulling the sphere toward it. Jefferson truly called the land between "terra incognita." But if a water passage across Louisiana to the Columbia River could be found, then the detached portion of the American system could be brought in circuit . . . or drawn within it. And a feeling of incompleteness, hardly to be diagnosed on the margin of Jefferson's emotion but one of the "adaptations and aptitudes" which the land had wrought as it created the continental consciousness, would be eased.[25]

The determination to send an exploring expedition overland to the Columbia must have been fully matured in Jefferson's mind when he entered on his Presidency in March 1801, for there was no other reason to make Meriwether Lewis his private secretary.[26] Lewis, a family friend, had sought his help when trying to get a place on the abortive expedition of André Michaux and he knew that, as Lewis said, the exploration of Louisiana "had formed a darling project of mine for the last ten years."[27] In March Louisiana remained Spanish (Jefferson did not learn till May that it was becoming French) and he had been dealing with it as a Spanish problem since the beginning of Washington's first term. To what sovereignty the land west of Louisiana belonged, the land drained by the Columbia, was wholly conjectural if not beyond conjecture. Neither the Spanish nor the conjectural sovereignty mattered in the least: he would send out the expedition, wrapping it in the usages of diplomacy. No one who knew the earlier history and no President, least of all our first geopolitician, could doubt that once a water route across Spanish Louisiana had been found the continental issue would be joined. The imperialism is peculiarly, even uniquely, our own kind but the dispatch of the Lewis and Clark expedition was an act of imperial policy. Even while he moved to buy New Orleans the President of the United States was moving to possess Louisiana.

The narrative must turn back forty-seven years, to 1756, and to the Virginia piedmont in from the actual frontier but on the edge of the wilderness. Three years earlier, in 1753, George Washington had been sent to order the French out of the Ohio Valley. The year after that, at the Great Meadows, he had opened the global war in which the mastery of the West was the central issue. And in June 1755, just a year ago, pushing past the Great Meadows and on toward Fort Duquesne at the Forks of the Ohio, General Braddock had suffered a defeat that came close to settling that great issue for France.

That was a year ago. On June 10, 1756, in Fredericksville Parish, Louisa County, Virginia, a learned clergyman sits down to write to an uncle of his in England. He reminds the uncle that in an earlier letter he has told how his parish and plantation can be located on the map of Virginia which two of his neighbors, Joshua Fry and Peter Jefferson, published in 1751. Now he has another map to describe, a "map of the middle British colonies in America" drawn by Lewis Evans and published last year. The map, the war, and Braddock's defeat have increased his already intense concern about the Western wilderness. He is thinking continentally on the basis of the information at hand.

His thesis is simple, central, and very old. Whichever nation finds itself "master of [the] Ohio and the [Great] Lakes at the end of [the present war] must in the course of a few years . . . become sole and absolute lord of North America." And it follows that within a few years either the Hudson River or the Potomac will therefore become "the grand emporium of all East Indian commodities."

This idea, the reverend gentleman explains, though it may startle one who lives in England, is not chimerical. It rests on the swiftness and carrying capacity of canoes, and on the affluents of the Mississippi River that lead into the Western wilderness. He specifies. . . . It is not clear whether he himself has read the Baron Lahontan but he reproduces Lahontan's geography, which is taken over in the book that

113

he says he has read, Daniel Coxe's *Carolana.* Also he has read a book that appears to confirm Coxe, "a History of the travels of an Indian towards those regions." His having read it shows that he was indeed interested and alert, for this is Moncacht-Apé — and in the amusing plagiarism by Dumont (or the Abbé Le Mascrier) in *Mémoires sur la Louisiane* published in Paris in 1753, three years before. (The plagiarism preceded the publication of the original invention, Le Page du Pratz's *Histoire de la Louisiane,* 1758.) But Moncacht-Apé is only gratifying support; his reasoning is based on Lahontan's fiction and Coxe's wonderful nonsense. He erroneously makes Coxe say that he has sailed seven hundred miles up the Missouri but otherwise quotes him faithfully.

The headwaters of the Missouri, Coxe had learned from the Indians, are in a mountain (range) on the western side of which a river flows down to "a large lake called Thayago, which pours its water through a large navigable river into a boundless sea." That sea is the Pacific, and both accounts have described the masted European ships to be seen there. And Coxe's facts and descriptions "are said to have been found by late discoveries, as far as discoveries have been made."

(Coxe had actually said that the Missouri was navigable to the source, "which proceeds from a *ridge of hills* [italics added here] somewhat north of New Mexico, passable by horse, foot or wagon in less than half a day" — and thence the river to the big lake, to the big river, to the South Sea.)

This route, the clergyman says, is certain to make the English plantations, by way of the Hudson or the Potomac, "the general mart of the European World, at least for the rich and costly products of the East, and a mart at which chapmen might be furnished with all those commodities on much easier terms than the tedious and hazardous and expensive navigation to those countries can at present afford." The quest for the northeast Passage can be abandoned at last. (For this will *be* the Northwest Passage.) There will be no more interminable voyages to the East Indies, no more seamen dying "like rotten sheep" of scurvy. "What an exhaustless fund of wealth would be opened, superior to Potosi and all the other

South American mines! What an extent of region! What a —! But no more!'"

No more, certainly, for Sir Humphrey Gilbert, and indeed Columbus, had said it all before.

Not the rector's enthusiasm is the important point, nor even the "aggrandizing and enriching this spot of the globe," but instead "a grand scheme formed here about three years ago." Mark this:

"Some persons were to be sent in search of that river Missouri, if that be the right name for it, in order to discover whether it had any such communication [as Coxe says] with the Pacific Ocean: they were to follow that river if they found it and make exact reports of the country they passed through, the distance they traveled, what sort of navigation those rivers and lakes afforded &c., &c." The outbreak of the war prevented this expedition but it had been organized. (It is still so live a project that this letter is to be kept secret and the writer has directed its bearer to throw it overboard if his ship is attacked by a French privateer.) The head of the expedition was to be "a worthy friend and neighbor of mine," who had already made many discoveries to the westward.

That would be Dr. Thomas Walker. A medical man who was also a piedmont planter, a surveyor, a speculator in lands, he was the first explorer known certainly to have entered Kentucky from Virginia and the discoverer of Cumberland Gap. In 1748 he accompanied a group of land viewers to the Holston River and East Tennessee, but his great exploit began in December 1749 and lasted till the following July. It preceded Christopher Gist's first Kentucky journey by more than a year and took Walker to the Holston again and on to Clinch and Powell's Rivers, through Cumberland Gap, to the headwaters of the Kentucky River and back across New River and the Valley of Virginia. Made on behalf of a land company, this was a notable, influential, and immediately famous journey. And Walker was a notable man and an influential wilderness thinker. He had had a hand in making the map which the clergyman mentions in his letter. . . . He had married the widow of a Meriwether and his oldest daughter married Nicholas Lewis, the uncle and legal guardian of Meriwether Lewis.[28]

The man who wrote that letter in June 1756 was the Reverend James Maury. To increase his income he conducted a small school for the sons of neighboring planters. One of his neighbors and friends was Peter Jefferson, a wealthy planter, the lieutenant of his county, a surveyor and to some degree an explorer of the wilderness. In 1746 Peter Jefferson helped to mark "the Fairfax line," seventy-six miles straight across the Blue Ridge to determine the extent of the great Fairfax grant. In 1749 with his friend and neighbor Joshua Fry he was employed to run the Virginia-North Carolina boundary some ninety miles farther west than the celebrated William Byrd of Westover had run it on the first survey, and this took him deeper into the wilderness. And in 1751 Jefferson and Fry were commissioned to make the map of Virginia to which Maury alludes in his letter and which was by a good deal the most accurate yet drawn.

In August 1757 Peter Jefferson died, attended to the end by Dr. Walker, and the next year his son Thomas, fourteen years old, went to board with the Reverend James Maury and attend his school. As one of the executors of his father's will, Dr. Walker must have had a voice in sending him there[29] . . . Jefferson's intellectual heritage from the frontier cannot be itemized but it is so well recognized as enormous that nothing need be said about it here. Enough that as early as his tenth year he could have been familiar with proposals to ascend the Missouri as a way of reaching the Pacific — and as a way of possessing Louisiana and so winning the conflict of empires. Jefferson himself expressed his gratitude to the Reverend James Maury for sound instruction in the classical languages. Perhaps the United States should thank him for first planting in Jefferson's mind an idea that matured as the expedition of Lewis and Clark.

ENDNOTES

1. Robertson, I, 361-76; II, 29-59. Also E. P. Renaut, "La Question de la Louisiane," *Revue de L'Histoire des Colonies Françaises* (Paris, 1918), and citations from *Archives du Ministre de la Marine, Série A*, III and IV, and *Archives des Affaires Etrangères*, XXXVII and XLII; André Laforgue, "Pierre Clement Laussat," *Louisiana Historical Quarterly*, XX (1937). Also Lyon, *op. cit.*, Chap. V. My quotation

from Decrés is taken from Renaut, p. 140.

2. *Correspondence de Napoleon Ier*, VIII and IX (Paris, 1861). *Oeuvres de Napoléon à Sainte Hélène*. F. Barbé-Marbois, *Histoire de la Louisiane* (Paris, 1829). A. Thiers, *Histoire du Consulat*, IV and V (Paris, 1874). Adams, I and II. Renaut, *op. cit.* Lyon, *op. cit.* Laforgue, *op. cit.* Baron Marc de Villiers, *Les Dernières Années de la Louisiane Française* (Paris, 1904). Fletcher Pratt, *The Empire and the Glory* (N.Y., 1949). Ralph Korngold, *Citizen Toussaint* (Boston, 1944).

3. Barbé-Marbois, p. 282. The preceding quotation, p. 298.

4. Livingston to Madison, April 24 1802 (*American State Papers: Foreign Relations*, II, 515-16; cited henceforth as ASP).

5. Livingston to Madison, April 11 1803 (ASP, II, 552); see also his summary, II, 557. Barbé-Marbois, p. 301.

6. Ford, IX, 364, 365.

7. Thornton to Hawkesbury, May 30 1803 (Robertson, II, 21).

8. See Chap. IX. "Whenever they [the Westerners who use the Mississippi for commerce] shall say, 'We cannot, we will not be longer shut up,' the United States will be reduced to the following dilemma: 1. To force them to acquiescence. 2. To separate from them, rather than take part in a war against Spain. 3. Or to preserve them in our Union by joining them in the war. . . . The third is the alternative we must adopt." (Ford, VI, 125-26.) As for the British possibility, he had written the year before, "Weigh the evil of this new accumulation of debt Against the loss of market and eternal danger and expence of such a neighbor. But no need to take a part as yet. We may choose our own time for that. Delay gives us many chances to avoid it. . . ." (*Ibid.*, 91.)

9. Adams, II, 55: "President Jefferson had chiefly reckoned on this possibility [that Napoleon would not provoke the United States to a hostile alliance] as his hope of getting Louisiana; and slight as the chance seemed, he was right." Coming at the end of a hundred pages designed to show that in the questions which the Louisiana Purchase involved Jefferson's policy was naïve, unrealistic, blindly foolish, and intellectually dishonest, this is one of the most ironical sentences ever written by a historian. Note that so careful a writer as Adams would not have made it "Louisiana" instead of "New Orleans" inadvertently.

10. Jefferson quotation, to John Bacon, April 30 1803 (Ford, IX, 464). Laussat to Decres April 18 1803 (Robertson, II, 33-36).

11. To Monroe, January 13 1803 (Ford, IX, 419).

12. To Monroe, January 10 1803, three days before the above (Ford, IX, 416).

13. This letter to Claiborne is not printed in Ford. It is cited in

Vol. II of Randall's *Life of Thomas Jefferson*, p. 62, and quoted in W. P. Cresson, *James Monroe*, p. 187. The letter to Livingston is the one cited in note 6 above and the sentence is on p. 365. The letter to Priestley is January 29 1804 (Ford, X, 69-72).

14. See for example Livingston to King, March 10 1802 (ASP, II, 515), and King to Madison April 2 1803 (p. 551). Cf. Thornton above.

15. Madison to Livingston and Monroe, July 29, 1803 (ASP, II, 566).

16. To Monroe, November 24, 1801 (Ford, IX, 317).

17. ASP, II: 530, 531, 533, 535, 551, 552, 554, 557, 566, etc.

18. Ford, X, 3.

·19. Barbé-Marbois, p. 312.

20. *The Medical Repository*, Second Hexade, I (1804), 406.

21. Edward M. Douglas, *Boundaries, Areas, Geographic Centers and Altitudes of the United States and Several States. Geological Survey Bulletin*, No, 817 (Washington, 1939).

22. Barbé-Marbois, p. 355.

23. *Ibid.*, p. 300.

24. Ford, X, 6. But note, four sentences later, "When we shall be full on this bank we may [that is, with the method just described we will be free to] lay off a range of States on the Western bank from the head to the mouth, & so, range after range, advancing compactly as we multiply." The second quotation in my text is from the previously cited letter to Priestley (*ibid.*, 71).

25. As my text turns to a study of the Lewis and Clark expedition, the reader must be notified that impressive authority dissents in part from my reading of its imperial purposes. In deference to that authority I have phrased portions of this chapter and the next one more tentatively than, in my judgment, the visible facts would warrant. Evidence is supplied in the text. The fullest and best statement of the opposed view is Ralph B. Guinness, "The Purpose of the Lewis and Clark Expedition," MVHR, XX (June 1933).

26. This is the conclusion of John Bakeless and in my judgment it cannot be questioned. See his *Lewis and Clark*, pp. 3-5 and *passim*. For Lewis's desire to join Michaux, Jefferson's letter, printed as "Memoir of Meriwether Lewis," Coues, I, xix.

27. *Journals*, I, 285.

28. J. Stoddard Johnston, ed., *First Explorations of Kentucky* (Louisville, 1898); Thomas P. Abernethy, *op. cit.*; Robert L. Kincaid, *The Wilderness Road* (Indianapolis, 1947).

29. Maury's letter is printed in Ann Maury, *Memoirs of a Huguenot Family* (N.Y., 1872). The date is there given erroneously as January. The correct date was supplied from the manuscript by Mr. Henry Reck, who at my request made a search of the Maury papers

in the Alderman Library, University of Virginia. He was unable to find the earlier letter to which Maury alludes in this one. I am much indebted to him and to Mr. Francis L. Berkeley, Jr., of the Alderman Library. The significance of Maury's letter was first pointed out to me by Mr. John Dos Passos, who had encountered it in manuscript without realizing that it had been published. For Peter Jefferson: Dumas Malone, *Jefferson the Virginian*, Chap. II; Marie Kimball, *Jefferson: the Road to Glory*, Chap. II. For the Evans map, Lawrence H. Gipson, *Lewis Evans*.

V · I

Oscar Handlin

THE AMERICAN–A NEW MAN

INDEPENDENCE MARKED THE political separation of the United States from Europe. But another kind of separation had already been effected by the time that the new state took form. The Americans had become a distinct people. The widening gulf that prevented the colonists and the English ministers from understanding one another was the result of a fundamental divergence of experience. The men on the western shore of the Atlantic had ceased to be the same as those on its older, eastern, shore. In the hearts and minds of those who fought it, therefore, the Revolution was already consummated before the first shot was fired. Even had political developments taken some other turn that permitted the colonies to remain within the empire, the Americans would still have been a nation apart.

The signs of distinctiveness appeared in the middle of the eighteenth century. Earlier, writers who referred to the Americans had in mind the Indian native of the soil. Now the term came consistently to apply to the provincials, as if they were no longer Englishmen living abroad but a separate species. The British officers and men who served in the New World in the wars against France habitually differentiated themselves from the colonists. The Americans did the same. The encounters of travelers — whether the provincials were abroad or the Europeans in the colonies — elicited the same sense of distinctiveness. On the eve of the Revolution, it was clear that a new nationality held together the people of the New World.

Neither then nor later could Americans explain the bonds that held them together as the products of inheritance. The Frenchman or German or Englishman was what he was by virtue of his patrimony; his ancestors had passed down to him a territory, a language, customs and religion which cemented individuals into a unity. Not so the American. His language, laws and customs were mostly English; but that heritage did not establish an identity with the people of the mother country. That was already evident on the eve of the Revolution and the events of the years after 1774 strengthened the convictions that this nation was not simply the derivative offshoot of any other. Heatedly Americans insisted that their English inheritance was only one, if the largest, of several. They were a mixture of many varieties of Europeans who by the alchemy of the New World were fused into a new kind of man.

What then was this new man — the American? Several questions lay hidden in the inquiry. Why did Americans think they were different from other people? Were they actually different? And what made them identify themselves as one nation — rather than as several, as their separate provincial experiences might have forecast. The answers were embedded in the institutions the colonies had developed, in their character as people, and in their aspirations for the future.

Shortly before his death in 1753, William Douglass, a Boston physician, commented on the problem in his *Summary View* of the history and present condition of the British colonies in North America. Douglas had observed that a difference in their experience had set the Americans apart from other Englishmen. Life in the wilderness, the effects of constant mobility, and the necessity of adjusting to strange conditions had nurtured among them novel customs and manners and had created new social forms. He initiated thus a long line of speculation that attributed the nationality of the Americans to their distinctive institutions.

Certainly these factors were important. By the middle of the eighteenth century a variety of circumstances made the culture of the colonies American, in the sense that it was both intercolonial and different from that of England. The provinces were all contiguous, so that men and goods moved freely among them. Ties of trade drew them together; stagecoaches, inns, and a regular post facilitated communications, as did the numerous vessels that plied the coastal sea. Newspapers passed from town to town and made the dispersed population familiar with a common fund of information and ideas. Despite local variations, all the governments were unmarked by significant feudal elements, and notable similarities in the style of life knit the several colonies together.

In addition, a common enemy pressed the Americans toward unity. At first it was the French, who for a century were a continuing danger to the frontier. After 1763, when that peril abated, the threat came from the mother country; and the necessity of joining forces in the struggle developed a consciousness of common interest. As the crisis unfolded and as men thought of their differences with England, they became increasingly aware of the similarities among themselves. In 1765 at the Stamp Act Congress, Christopher Gadsden had already proclaimed that *there ought to be no New England man, no New Yorker, known on the Continent; but all Americans.* And ten years later, Patrick Henry had boldly affirmed, *I am not a Virginian but an American.*

The War for Independence was itself a unifying experience and after the peace the recollection of shared sufferings held the victors together. The new governments had many features in common and their emphasis upon free institutions added strength to the sentiment of nationalism. History had thus created a network of common institutions that endowed Americans with nationality.

But here was a paradox! One could speak of American

institutions; but for a long time there was no America, except insofar as the term vaguely applied to the whole hemisphere. That designation could be attached to no political entity in existence before 1774. Each colony was separate and related not to its neighbors but to the Crown. Boston's governmental, cultural and business contacts were at least as close with London as with Charleston, South Carolina. Efforts to devise schemes for intercolonial co-operation among the governments were futile; and when the provinces met together it was in congresses, as if they were separate states.

Furthermore, not all the English possessions were American in the sense that they joined the rebellion and became states in the Union. Nova Scotia, Quebec and the West Indian islands remained apart, yet they shared some experiences and institutions with those that became independent. South Carolina, in climate, history and economy, was closer to Barbados than to Massachusetts.

Indeed, diversities were as striking as uniformities in the cluster of mainland colonies that formed the nation. Differences in antecedents, history, habits, religious affiliations, and style of life set the New Englander off from the Virginian, the New Yorker from the Pennsylvanian. Nor did those people learn to discount the differences simply by common exposure to the wilderness. In many respects the diversities remained significant; and, in any case, the towns distant from the frontier were as American as the back-country.

Remoteness from the Old World was no criterion at all of the degree of national identification. The Americans were by no means those who were un-European; indeed ties across the Atlantic had never been closer than in the quarter-century before Independence. No colonist seemed more representative of his countrymen than Benjamin Franklin and none was more familiar than he in the cosmopolitan salons of Paris.

And who most eloquently expressed the aspirations of the nation as it approached the test of revolution? The Americans commonly agreed that two works, *Letters from an American Farmer* and *Common Sense*, most carefully described them as a people, most accurately enunciated their ideas and attitudes. Yet Michel de Crèvecoeur, the author of the one, was a Frenchman who had only migrated from Canada after 1763; and Thomas Paine had come off the ship from England little more than a year before he wrote the other. Neither could have been shaped by the influence of distinctive institutions or experience in the brief period after his arrival.

There was no America before 1774. But there were Americans. The people of Maine and Georgia did feel a sense of identification with the nation and did regard their institutions and experience as common unifying forces. The circumstances of their lives in the New World alone were not enough to create a national sentiment; but the people, under those circumstances, developed traits of character that drew them together in pursuit of common goals.

That was Crèvecoeur's conclusion when he attempted to account for the identity of his adopted countrymen. He too had puzzled over the question of who the Americans were. He could see clearly enough that they were a mixture of English, Scotch, Irish, French, Dutch, Germans, and Swedes. From this promiscuous breed that race, now called Americans, had arisen. *He was an American, who, leaving behind him all his ancient prejudices and manners, received new ones, from the new mode of life he embraced, the new government he obeyed, the new rank he held.* But, by what invisible power had this surprising metamorphosis been performed? In part, by that of the laws and of a new social system. But whence proceeded these laws? From the government. Whence the government?

There was the difficulty. The colonies were, after all, English; and although the original genius and the strong desire of the settlers influenced the laws, in the last analysis it was the Crown that ratified and confirmed them. Furthermore, these institutions were neither uniform through the many provinces of British America nor entirely distinctive of them. Crèvecoeur pointed to the significant differences between men who lived in the North and those who lived in the South, between those who earned their livelihood by the sea and those who tilled the soil, between the residents of the frontier and the German Moravians.

It was therefore necessary to look not merely at the laws, but at the mode of living in a new society which shaped the character of the people. To do so Crèvecoeur narrowed the focus of his vision from the continent as a whole to a tiny corner of it — the island of Nantucket. Here a society of five thousand individuals exemplified the traits distinctive of the Americans.

Crèvecoeur reviewed at length the topography of the place, the manners of the inhabitants, the way in which they earned their bread, the upbringing of their children and the form of their government. He then passed to a description of the whale fishery, which had begun as the simple pursuit of offshore strays but which now carried the Nantucketers far from home, northward by the coast of Labrador to Cape Desolation and southward by Brazil to the Falkland Islands and even the South Seas.

In one of these characteristic ventures, a little company forms and sets out in a brig of about 150 tons burden. They have no wages; each draws a certain established share in partnership so that all are equally vigorous and determined. They sail for weeks in readiness for the moment of their great encounter. When they sight the whale, two boats are launched, each with a crew of six, four at the oars, one on his feet in the bow holding a harpoon, and the other at the helm. At a reasonable distance, one boat stands off as a witness, the other approaches.

The harpooner is still; *on him principally depends the success of the enterprise. In his hands he holds the dreadful weapon — made of the best steel, to the shaft of which the end of a cord is firmly tied. The other end is fastened to the bottom of the boat. They row in profound silence, leaving the whole conduct of the contest to the harpooner and to the steersman. At a distance of about fifteen feet, the harpooner bids them stop.*

He balances high his harpoon, trying at this important moment to collect all the energy of which he is capable. He launches it forth — the whale is struck! Sometimes, in the immediate impulse of rage, she will attack the boat and demolish it with one stroke of her tail. At other times she will dive and disappear from sight or swim away and draw the cord with such swiftness that it will set the edge of the boat on fire by the friction. The boat follows her course until, tired at last with convulsing the elements, she dies and floats on the surface.

The handful of men, venturing freely forth to impose their will upon the natural power of sea and whale, are American in character. Why?

The Nantucketers are not alone in the pursuit of the great whale; in the eighteenth century, vessels from England and Scandinavia also expose themselves to the danger. But the motive that leads Nantucketers to the sea marks them off from other seafaring men. Neither failure at home nor despair sends them to that element; it is a simple plan of life, a well-founded hope of earning a livelihood. The sea becomes to them a kind of patrimony; they go to whaling with as much pleasure and tranquil indifference, with as strong an expectation of success, as the landsman undertakes to clear a piece of swamp.

And they go to come back home. Not for them the wild bouts of carousing in port, by which other seamen punctuate their repeated encounters with danger. There are no material irregularities when the fleet returns to Nantucket. All is peace and a general decency prevails. The long abstemiousness to which these men are exposed, the frequent repetitions of danger, the boldness in surmounting them, do not lead, when on shore, to a desire for inebriation and a more eager pursuit of those pleasures of which they have been so long deprived and which they must soon again forego. They come home to their wives and children; and the pleasures of returning to their families absorb every other desire. In their absence, their wives have managed their farms and transacted their business. The men at their return, weary with the fatigue of the sea, full of confidence and love, carefully give their consent to every transaction that has happened during their absence, and all is joy and peace. "Wife, thee hast done well," is the general approbation for application and industry.

The Nantucketers were distinctive not in their willingness to take risks or in the fact that they had homes to which to return, but in the unique juncture of the two qualities. They were stable men who cherished ties to family and friends, who left home not because there was no place, but voluntarily and with the intention of returning. The hazards they accepted were not a desperate alternative to, but an accepted part of, an orderly life.

By the 1770's that situation had become characteristically American. The men who moved along the northern and southern frontiers were not simply isolated drifters, placeless individuals, cut loose from any ties. They were often the sons of respectable families who left decent homes, not driven away but drawn on by impatience with the limits of the present. As a matter of course they subjected themselves to hardship and danger, strengthened as they were by the certainty of a limitless future. Habituated to a landscape without horizons, they had no fear of venturing into the unknown distances.

That situation the Nantucket whalemen shared with the Virginia planter. So the young Washington, well connected by good family, hardly hesitated to take himself off to the wilderness, abandoning comfort for the life of the shelterless forest and exchanging the company of the cultivated local gentry at Mount Vernon for that of rude trappers and Indians. It was a matter of course that such men should put in the balance the security of what they already had as against the hazards of a boundless potential.

At every level of society the speculative temperament asserted itself. The son of the prosperous merchant was more likely to go to sea than to college; he carried his wares in little craft subject to all the hazards of the elements, from port to port, appeasing hostile officials, negotiating with strangers, his mind ever occupied in calculation, his will ever hardened to gain. What fortune he accumulated was never secure, but always passed through his hands back to new enterprises. The farmer and artisan could fall in with no rhythm of production, they could not adjust to a regular round of sowing and reaping, of building and making. They too were occupied in the effort to extend themselves. They borrowed and lent, worked to save and saved to invest, driven on by the hope of great winnings, yet recognizing the possibility of great losings.

None of them liked the necessity. All their dreams revealed occasional glimpses of a distant resting place which offered surcease from their constant striving; there the husbandman divided the fruits of his fields with his family, the patriarchal master graciously guided the·operations of his great plantation, the merchant neatly balanced his books and all was contentment, harmony and peace. Such was the stability and order these people valued. But there was no confusing dreams with the reality of constant striving and ever-present danger. A situation that compelled men who cherished security constantly to seek out and to take risks formed the character of the Americans.

The willingness to accept risks had originated in the very nature of the first settlement and had been perpetuated by a society that allowed few individuals stability enough to relax in the security of exemption from further hazards. All was and remained precarious; whatever was achieved was not enough to sustain itself without further effort. Nothing stood of itself. Ceaseless striving and mobility were necessary to hold on, for only expansion could preserve what had already been created. The venture to the South Seas or to the Ohio wilderness was necessary to keep the Nantucket home or Mount Vernon from crumbling.

The risk and the constant strain of taking it were tolerable because there was a reasonable chance of reward. Space and opportunity — and therefore hope — were abundant. Every man, whatever his past, could have a future. Europeans became Americans because they no sooner arrived than they immediately felt the effects of plenty. Their toils were no less heavy than before but of a very different nature. They had put behind them involuntary idleness, servile dependence, penury and useless labor. An ample subsistence was within reach. They became landowners and for the first time in their lives, counted for something. *They ceased to be ciphers and felt themselves men because they were treated as such.* They were then Americans.

The sense of nationality was essentially the awareness of the common situation they shared. They recognized one another not by the identity of their antecedents, nor by similarities in appearance, habits, manners, or institutions, but by those traits of character that came from the effort to maintain a balance between the longing for stability and the exposure to risks. This was their environment and the environment alone molded the nature of men and established the differences among species.

Therefore it was possible for the foreign-born to come off the boat and be transformed immediately into Americans, as Paine was and as countless later immigrants would be. Indeed some could identify themselves with the nation and already be American before even leaving the Old World, if the circumstances of their own lives projected them into the same precarious situation. That identification brought scores of Europeans to fight in the revolutionary armies; and it would continue to pull others across the Atlantic on into the nineteenth century.

Independence gave political form to American nationality and deepened the characteristic traits associated with it. Pride in the achievement of having humbled the great empire, confidence in the ability to do without the trappings of traditional monarchy, and faith in man's capacity for fresh creation stimulated every imagination. It was only necessary to be daring enough! Any risk was worthwhile; and there were no limits to what the independent citizens of a republic could do.

The travelers set themselves ever more distant goals. One of Jefferson's neighbors in Virginia took to dreaming in 1792 of an overland route to the Pacific. He was only eighteen then, of a good family, bright and attractive, with every prospect before him. But he would not settle down to planting. It was ten years before Meriwether Lewis had his chance to make that long tedious journey westward to the mouth of the Columbia River. President Jefferson, who had dispatched him, no doubt remembered another genius who had also yearned to lay eyes on the Pacific. John Ledyard had sailed with Cook to the South Seas, but refused to serve the British against his countrymen. A romantic escape; wanderings through Europe; a meeting with Jefferson and John Paul Jones in Paris; then Ledyard had his idea. He would walk eastward across Russia and Siberia. He left England in 1786, passed through Norway, Sweden, and Lapland to St.

Petersburg, reached Yakutsk in 1787 and Irkutsk in 1788, then, seized by order of the suspicious empress, was sent back to Poland. Frustrated, he took it into his head to locate the sources of the Niger and never returned to his native Connecticut. For such men the wish to add to knowledge was but a way of describing their restless curiosity.

Everywhere the pace of movement quickened. Settlers in the thousands hastened to the West; merchants sent their ships along hitherto untraveled lands to remote harbors; and every type of fresh enterprise attracted speculative investors. They could hardly wait, any of them, to expose themselves to risk. They were now conscious of their newness as a people; new principles animated them; and they had to assert themselves in new ideas and new achievements.

The awareness of their peculiar situation which shaped their character as a people gave a national meaning to the culture and institutions of the Americans. The looseness of their society and their desire for order, the local sources of political power and the concern with individual rights, the disregard for tradition and the eagerness for new knowledge, the tolerance of difference and the concern with ethical behavior were the accommodations of men who lived precariously in an environment that did not limit their future.

The few who stood apart alienated themselves from the rest. At the Revolution they mostly became Tories and many left the country; after Independence those who stayed were citizens but did not share the spirit of the Republic. In that sense they were not Americans; though born in the New World, they were not part of it. Particular quirks of their personal situations accounted for the difference in their response. Some great merchants whose business connections were fixed and secure, some great landowners who valued stability on their estates, men of all sorts who clung to political or religious tradition or who refused to surrender the social standards of the Old World formed the minority that emigrated or that remained querulously in opposition at home.

Tiny enclaves, like those of the Pennsylvania Amish, which retained a character of their own and resisted national tendencies also stood apart but were no problem. There was space for them, they did not interfere with others, and the distance they maintained was the result of their own desire. But other, larger groups — in the population yet not fully identified as Americans — posed an intellectual and social challenge of the first magnitude.

The Indians, after all, were the original inhabitants of the New World and had longest been subject to its beneficent environment. Yet despite the effort to persuade them to settle down and enter into the new mixture that was brewing, they preferred their tribal identities. Indeed, there was disconcerting evidence that contact with the white man only introduced them to vice and disease. By the end of the eighteenth century the prospect seemed slight that they would amalgamate with other Americans. Clearly they were separate and independent nations.

That was inconvenient. The lands they occupied were within the territorial jurisdiction of the United States and were covetously regarded by settlers and speculators. The polite fiction had it that the tribes, uncivilized as they were, needed the tutelage of the Great Chiefs in the East who best knew how to safeguard the Indian interests. Solemnly signed treaties spelled out the kindly arrangement. However, they left unsolved the question of how to remove the obstacles to the advance of settlement.

President Jefferson supplied the practical answer in his advice to Governor Harrison of the Indiana Territory: It was the duty of the Indians to *withdraw themselves to the culture of a small piece of land.* Soon they would *perceive how useless to them were extensive forests* and would be willing *to pare them off from time to time in exchange for necessities for their farms and families.* That inclination could be promoted by setting up trading houses where *the good and influential among them would run up debts beyond what they could pay* and then would be willing *to lop them off by a cession of lands.* The formula only omitted the whiskey. That was the usual course, before the Revolution and after. Broken promises, bloody wars and deceptive treaties marked the whole history of Indian removal. But these tactics, which might well be expected of European despots, were not appropriate to the representatives of the free people of a republic.

The intellectual question remained. Wistfully, Americans told themselves that the Indians really did not like it where they were. Beyond the Mississippi there was more than enough space where they could better lead the life they preferred. It was in their own self-interest that they should go, until some future time when they would be able to associate, as they should, on equal terms with other Americans. There was no better answer.

The situation of the Negroes was more anomalous still, for they lived not in tribes of their own but thoroughly intermingled with the rest of the population. Earlier in the century, slavery had explained their differences from the whites; lacking freedom or the capacity to make choices, they were cut off from the influences that formed other Americans. But after 1750, and increasingly as the Revolution approached, slavery was condemned as an evil. Those who claimed the natural rights of life, liberty and the pursuit of happiness for themselves could hardly deny them to others. In all the Northern states, slavery disappeared with Independence.

Thereafter, it was expected, the blacks would merge with their neighbors. Few in number, they readily made a place for themselves in the expanding cities. Their peculiarities were explicable in terms of environmental forces; even their color — the result of long exposure to the tropic sun or, as Dr. Benjamin Rush explained, of a disease that had once raged through Africa — ultimately would fade to the whiteness befitting Americans. The polite stanzas of Phillis Wheatley's little book of poems, published in Boston, showed the levels of cultivation to which a former slave could aspire.

In the plantation South, the question had altogether different dimensions. The men of Jefferson's generation were no less ready than their countrymen in the North to admit that slavery was an evil. Abolition was a moral imperative and would shortly have to be effected. The difficulty arose from adjustments to the political and social implications. Gradual emancipation created more problems than it solved; freedom extended to some Negroes made control of the rest less secure, and unscrupulous slaveholders were sometimes tempted to use manumission to rid themselves of those too old to work. Liberty, when it came, would have to come to all.

Yet the consequences of such a radical change were unthinkable. In a republic, citizenship went with freedom; when the Negroes ceased to be slaves they would become potential voters and in some places would surely acquire political power. Was it reasonable to suppose that men who had suffered the cruelest wrongs for generations would then fail to seek revenge? Their own sense of guilt for the crimes of their ancestors gave Southerners the answer even before Toussaint in Santo Domingo confirmed it. Emancipation would lead to violence, bloodshed and the collapse of all order. Everyone would suffer in the aftermath.

Prudential considerations added to the hesitation. Would the freedmen be able to support themselves without capital and land? Those who drove the reluctant bondsman to the fields could not see in him the makings of an enterprising yeoman. Was the Negro really constitutionally equal? Those who did not treat him so found it hard to believe. Would it be safe to mix on terms of equality, two races so different in manners and antecedents? The masters who had always had their will of the slaves feared the loss of advantages power gave them. The doubts were not strong enough to persuade many to argue that slavery ought to be preserved; but they were strong enough to postpone the day of decision.

Better wait. Soon, perhaps, the problem would solve itself. With the author of the widely read legal commentary on Blackstone, St. George Tucker, many a planter indulged in the dream. If only the Negro would go away! There was land enough in the West, or better still, in Mexico. There the freedmen, removed from the scenes of their past indignities, separated from the masters who had once wronged them, could build their own life in their own way. No doubt the future would reveal the means of consummating this happy outcome. The Negro, like the Indian, was assigned a promissory portion of the New World. For the time being, these people were awkward exceptions to the American's conception of his own identity as a new man, liberated from his past and free to live as an individual by the rule of risks of his own choosing.

For the Americans there was always the future to redeem the shortcomings of the present; their experience and ideas encouraged a faith in improvement and infused fresh vitality into the old conception of mission.

The image of the city on the hill had persisted since the days of the first settlers; and the events of the revolutionary period only confirmed the certitude that a great destiny awaited the Republic. The environment shaped the character of men; and there was nowhere a more bounteous setting for achievement than the continent the Americans were in process of occupying. Painstakingly Jefferson, in the *Notes on Virginia*, marshaled the evidence: nature here was on a grander scale; man would be so too. He thereby reaffirmed Franklin's earlier estimate of the future grandeur of the country.

Their own character was also evidence that the Americans were a new race whose labors and posterity would one day cause great changes in the world. In them were incorporated the sum of all past achievements; and the situation which had made them a nation would soon give their experience universal significance. They were, Crèvecoeur proclaimed, *the western pilgrims, carrying along with them that great mass of arts, sciences, vigor and industry which began long since in the east.* They were the heirs of all the ages, the vanguard of human destiny.

The Revolution proved it was all true, not only by its success, but by its implications for the rest of the world. Enthusiasm, in 1794, swept that cautious divine the Reverend Timothy Dwight into poetry. He hailed the Republic, *by heaven design'd, th' example bright, to renovate mankind.* Its sons would soon claim their home on far Pacific shores, and *their rule, religion, manners, arts, convey and spread their freedom to the Asian sea.* And actions spoke louder than words. In 1806, a small group of students in Williams College, in rural Massachusetts, recalled their duty to the millions living in *the moral darkness of Asia.* Their resolution to do something led to the formation of the American Board of Commissioners for Foreign Missions in 1810. Soon farm wives in every countryside would be saving pennies for the redemption and Americanization of the waiting millions.

Behind such efforts was the utter conviction that the American brought to his mission the irresistible weapons of an entirely new political and social system. Unhampered by a feudal past, he had created forms of government grounded on natural law and universally applicable. His situation made him a trader; nature, which did nothing in vain, had so arranged his geography that all nations, *by a free intercourse with this vast and fertile continent would again become brothers* and forget war. And above all, he had space — to advance agriculture to its summit of perfection and to welcome, in limitless numbers, immigrants from every end of the earth who, becoming free, would all become American.

Laboriously Joel Barlow measured the syllables in the endless lines of his epic. As a youth he had fought for Independence, then had tried his hand at diplomacy and had done what he could for the revolution in France. After years away he came back home in 1805 and converted an earlier innocent poem into a gigantic glorification of his country. *The Columbiad* surveyed the whole span of human history, past and prospective. At the end, man — liberated from fraud, folly, and error, holding sovereign sway over earth's total powers which yield their fruit at his mere call — has banished contention and bound all regions in one confederate league of peace. This was the work the first American, Columbus, had initiated when

> his pinions led the trackless way
> and taught mankind such useful deeds to dare,
> To trace new seas and happy nations rear;
> Till by fraternal hands their sails unfurl'd
> Have waved at last in union o'er the world.

This was the work it was the destiny of other Americans to pursue.

V · I · I

Winston Churchill

AMERICAN EPIC

THE YEAR 1815 had marked the end of a period of American development. Up to this time the life of the continent had been moulded largely by forces from Europe, but with the conclusion of the war of 1812 against England America turned in upon herself and with her back to the Atlantic looked towards the West. The years following the Peace of Ghent are full of the din of the Westward advance. In politics the vehement struggles of Federalist and Republican were replaced by what a contemporary journalist called "the era of good feelings." But underneath the calm surface of the first decade lay the bitter rivalry of sectional interests which were soon to assume permanent and organised party forms. As in all post-war periods, the major political issue was that of finance. The ideas of Alexander Hamilton on Protection and banking were reluctantly accepted by the Republican administration under the stress of war conditions. The tariff of 1816 had created a régime of Protection under which New England turned from her shipping interests to manufacture and laid the foundations of her nineteenth-century prosperity. The old suspicions of Jefferson about a Federal banking system were overcome, and in 1816 a charter replacing the one which had expired was issued for the foundation of a new Federal Bank.

The ties with Europe were slowly and inexorably broken. Outstanding disputes between England and America were settled by a series of commissions. The boundaries of Canada were fixed, and both countries agreed to a mutual pact of disarmament upon that storm centre, the Great Lakes. In 1819, after straggling warfare in Spanish Florida, led by the hero of New Orleans, Andrew Jackson, the Spanish Government finally yielded the territory to the United States for five million dollars. Spain had withdrawn from the Northern continent for ever.

But the turmoils of European politics were to threaten America once again for the last time for many years to come. The sovereigns of the Old World were bound together to maintain the principle of monarchy and to co-operate in intervening in any country which showed signs of rebellion against existing institutions. The policy of this Holy Alliance had aroused the antagonism of Britain, who had refused to intervene in the internal affairs of Italy in 1821. The new crisis came in Spain. Bourbon France, burning to achieve respectability in the new Europe, sent an army across the Pyrenees to restore the Spanish monarchy. Russia would have liked to go farther. The Czar of Russia had worldwide interests, including large claims to the western coastline of North America, which he now reaffirmed by Imperial decree. Rumours also spread to Washington that the reactionary Powers of Europe, having supported the restoration of the Bourbons in Spain, might promote similar activities in the New World to restore Bourbon sovereignty there. In Southern America lay the Spanish colonies, which had in their turn thrown off the yoke of their mother country.

The British Government under Canning offered to co-operate with the United States in stopping the extension of this threatening principle of intervention to the New World. Britain announced that she recognised the sovereignty of the Latin republics in South America. Meanwhile President Monroe acted independently and issued his message to Congress proclaiming the principles later known as the Monroe Doctrine. This famous Doctrine, as has been related, was at once a warning against interference on the part of any European Powers in the New World and a statement of the intention of America to play no part in European politics. With this valedictory message America concentrated upon her own affairs. A new generation of politicians was rising. The old veterans of the days of the Constitution had most of them vanished from the scene, though Jefferson and Madison lingered on in graceful retirement in their Virginian homes.

Westward lay the march of American Empire. Within thirty years of the establishment of the Union nine new states had been formed in the Mississippi valley, and two in the borders of New England. As early as 1769 men like Daniel Boone had pushed their way into the Kentucky country, skirmishing with the Indians. But the main movement over the mountains began during the War of Independence. The migration of the eighteenth century took two directions: the advance westward towards the Ohio, with its settlement of Kentucky and Tennessee, and the occupation of the northwest forest regions, the fur-traders' domain, beyond Lake Erie. The colonisation of New England and the eastern coastline of America had been mainly the work of powerful companies, aided by the English Crown or by feudal proprietors with chartered rights. But here in the new lands of the West any man with an axe and a rifle could carve for himself a rude frontier home. By 1790 there were thirty-five thousand settlers in the Tennessee country, and double that number in Kentucky. By 1800 there were a million Americans west of the mountain ranges of the Alleghenies. From these new lands a strong, self-reliant Western breed took its place in American life. Modern American democracy was born and cradled in the valley of the Mississippi. The foresight of the first independent Congress of the United States had proclaimed for all time the principle that when new territories gained a certain population they should be admitted to statehood upon an equality with the existing partners of the Union. It is a proof of the quality and power of the West-

erners that eleven of the eighteen Presidents of the United
States between 1828 and 1901 were either born or passed the
greater part of their lives in the valley of the Mississippi.
Well might Daniel Webster upon an anniversary of the landing of the Pilgrim Fathers declaim the celebrated passage:
"New England farms, houses, villages, and churches spread
over and adorn the immense extent from the Ohio to Lake
Erie and stretch along from the Alleghanies [*sic*] onwards beyond the Miamis and towards the falls of St. Anthony. Two
thousand miles westward from the Rock where their fathers
landed may now be seen the sons of pilgrims cultivating smiling fields, rearing towns and villages, and cherishing, we
trust, the patrimonial blessings of wise institutions, of liberty
and religion . . . Ere long the sons of the pilgrims will be
upon the shores of the Pacific."

America was swelling rapidly in numbers as well as in
area. Between 1790 and 1820 the population increased from
four to nine and a half millions. Thereafter it almost doubled every twenty years. Nothing like such a rate of growth
had before been noted in the world, though it was closely
paralleled in contemporary England. The settlement of
great bodies of men in the West was eased by the removal of
the Indian tribes from the regions east of the Mississippi.
They had been defeated when they fought as allies of Britain
in the war of 1812. Now it became Federal policy to eject
them. The lands thus thrown open were made available in
smaller units and at lower prices than in earlier years to the
incoming colonists — for we might as well use this honour-
able word about them, unpopular though it may be. Colonisation, in the true sense, was the task that engaged the Western pioneers. Farmers from stony New England were tilling
the fertile empty territories to the south of the Great Lakes,
while in the South the Black Belt of Alabama and Mississippi
proved fruitful soil for the recent art of large-scale cotton cultivation.

But this ceaseless expansion to the West also changed the
national centre of gravity, and intense stresses arose of interest as well as of feeling. The Eastern states, North and South
alike, presently found their political power challenged by
these settler communities, and the lure of pioneering cre-

ated the fear of a labour shortage in the Eastern factories. In fact the gap was filled by new immigrants from Europe. As the frontier line rolled westward the new communities rising rapidly to statehood forced their own problems and desires upon the exhilarated but also embarrassed Federal Government. The East feared the approaching political dominance of the democratic West. The West resented the financial and economic bias of the Eastern moneyed classes. The forces of divergence grew strong, and only the elasticity of the Federal system around the core of state rights prevented the usual conflict between a mother country and its sturdy children.

The political history of these years between 1815 and 1830 is confused through the lack of adequate national party organisations to express the bitter sectional conflicts and hatreds in the North, South, and West. By 1830 the situation cleared and the great parties of the future stood opposed. With the growth of Federal legislation and the creation of a national economic framework of tariffs, banks, and land policies the Union felt the stress of state jealousies and rival interests. The expansion to the West tilted the political balance in favour of the new Western states, and strenuously the older forces in the North and South resisted the rising power of democracy within the Federal State. They had to confront not only the desires of the West, but also those of the small planters in the South and of the working men in the industrial North. Many of these people now for the first time began to receive the vote as universal manhood suffrage was more widely adopted. The electorate was expanding and eager to make its voice heard. At the same time the convention system was introduced into American politics. Candidates for the Presidency and for lesser public office in the states gradually ceased to be nominated by restricted party caucuses. Instead they were selected at meetings of delegates representing a variety of local and specialised opinion. This obliged the would-be President and other public officeholders to be more responsive to the divergences of popular will. Politicians of conservative mind like Henry Clay and John C. Calhoun feared the menacing signs of particularism and the consequent threat to the Union. These men formulated what they called the "American System."* But their policy was merely a re-expression of the ideas of Hamilton. They sought to harmonise economic interest within a Federal framework. As Calhoun had said in 1817, "We are greatly and rapidly — I was about to say fearfully — growing. This is our pride and our danger, our weakness and our strength . . . Let us then bind the Republic together with a perfect system of roads and canals. Protection would make the parts adhere more closely . . . It would form a new and most powerful cement."

Public works were set on foot; steamboats appeared upon the Mississippi, and the concentration of trade in the Gulf of Mexico roused alarm in the Atlantic states, who saw themselves being deprived of profitable markets. But they hastened themselves to compete with this increasing activity. In 1817 the state of New York began the construction of the Erie Canal, which was to make New York City the most prosperous of the Eastern seaports. The great Cumberland highroad across the Ohio to Illinois was built with Federal money, and a network of roads was to bind the eager West to the Eastern states. But the history of the American nineteenth century is dominated by the continually threatened cleavage of East and West, and, upon the Atlantic seaboard, of the Northern and Southern states. In the early years of the century the keynote of politics was the rival bidding of Northern and Southern politicians for the votes and support of the Western states.

The issue of slavery was soon to trouble the relations of the North and South. In 1819 a Bill was tabled in Congress to admit Missouri as a state to the Union. This territory lay inside the bounds of the Louisiana Purchase, where the future of slavery had not so far been decided by Federal law. As the people of Missouri proposed to allow slavery in their draft constitution the Northerners looked upon this Bill as an aggressive move to increase the voting power of the South. A wild campaign of mutual recrimination followed. But with the increasing problem of the West facing them both, North and South could not afford to quarrel, and the angry sectional strife stirred up by this Bill ended in a compromise which was to hold until the middle of the century. Missouri was admitted as a slave-holding state, and slavery was prohibited north of latitude 36° 30´ within the existing territories of the Union which did not yet enjoy statehood. As part of the compromise Maine, which had just severed itself from Massachusetts, was admitted as a free state, making the division between slave and free equal, being twelve each. Far-seeing men realised the impending tragedy of this division. John Quincy Adams noted in his diary, "I considered it at once as the knell of the Union. I take it for granted that the present question is a mere preamble — a title-page to a great, tragic volume."

It was this cultured New Englander, son of the second President of the United States, who succeeded Monroe in 1825. The so-called era of good feelings was coming to a close, and the four years of his Presidency were to reveal the growth of lively party politics. All the political and economic interests of the Eastern states were forced on to the defensive by the rapid expansion of the West.

The West grouped itself around the figure of the frontier General Andrew Jackson, who claimed to represent the true Jeffersonian principles of democracy against the corrupt moneyed interests of the East. Adams received the support of those classes who feared majority rule and viewed with alarm the growing power of the farmers and settlers of the frontier. The issue between the two factions was joined in 1828, when Jackson stood as rival candidate against Adams's re-election. In the welter of this election two new parties were born, the Democrats and the National Republicans, later called the Whigs. It was the fiercest campaign since Jefferson had driven the elder Adams from office in 1800. As the results came in it was seen that Adams had won practically nothing outside New England, and that in the person of Andrew Jackson the West had reached controlling power. Here at last was an American President who had no spiritual contacts whatever with the Old World or its projection on the Atlantic shore, who represented at the White House the spirit of the American frontier. To many it seemed that democracy had triumphed indeed.

There were wild scenes at Washington at the inauguration

of the new President, dubbed by his opponent Adams as "the brawler from Tennessee." But to the men of the West Jackson was their General, marching against the political monopoly of the moneyed classes. The complications of high politics caused difficulties for the backwoodsman. His simple mind, suspicious of his opponents, made him open to influence by more partisan and self-seeking politicians. In part he was guided by Martin Van Buren, his Secretary of State. But he relied even more heavily for advice on political cronies of his own choosing, who were known as the "Kitchen Cabinet," because they were not office-holders. Jackson was led to believe that his first duty was to cleanse the stables of the previous régime. His dismissal of a large number of civil servants brought the spoils system, long prevalent in many states, firmly into the Federal machine.

Two great recurring problems in American politics, closely related, demanded the attention of President Andrew Jackson — the supremacy of the Union and the organisation of a national economy. Protection favoured the interests of the North at the expense of the South, and in 1832 the state of South Carolina determined to challenge the right of the Federal Government to impose a tariff system, and, echoing the Virginia and Kentucky resolutions of 1798, expounded in its most extreme form the doctrine of state rights. In the party struggles which followed the votes of the Western states held the balance. Their burning question was the regulation of the sale of public land by the Federal Government. As the historian S. E. Morison puts it, "It was all a game of balance between North, South, and West, each section offering to compromise a secondary interest in order to get votes for a primary interest. The South would permit the West to plunder the public domain, in return for a reduction of the tariff. The North offered the tempting bait of distribution [of the proceeds from land sales for public works in the West] in order to maintain protection. On the outcome of this sectional balance depended the alignment of parties in the future; even of the Civil War itself. Was it to be North and West against South, or South and West against North?"[1]

The debates on these themes in the American Senate contained the finest examples of American oratory. In this battle of giants the most imposing of them all was Daniel Webster, of Massachusetts, the best speaker of his day. He it was who stated the case for the Union and refuted the case of South Carolina in one of the most famous of American speeches. His words enshrined the new feeling of nationwide patriotism that was gathering strength, at least in the North. They show that New England in particular was moving away from the sectional views which had prevailed in 1812. A broader sense of loyalty to the Union was developing. "It is to that Union," Webster declared in the Senate, "we owe our safety at home, and our consideration and dignity abroad. It is to that Union that we are chiefly indebted for whatever makes us most proud of our country. That Union we reached only by the discipline of our virtues in the severe school of adversity. It had its origin in the necessities of disordered finance, prostrate commerce, and ruined credit. Under its benign influences these great interests immediately awoke, as from the dead, and sprang forth with newness of life. Every year of its duration has teemed with fresh proofs of its utility and its blessings; and although our territory has stretched out wider and wider, and our population spread farther and farther, they have not outrun its protection, or its benefits. It has been to us all a copious foundation of national, social and personal happiness.

"I have not allowed myself, Sir" he went on, "to look beyond the Union, to see what might lie hidden in the dark recess behind. I have not coolly weighed the chances of preserving liberty when the bonds that unite us together shall be broken asunder. I have not accustomed myself to hang over the precipice of disunion to see whether, with my short sight, I can fathom the depth of the abyss below; nor could I regard him as a safe counsellor in the affairs of the Government, whose thoughts should be mainly bent on considering, not how the Union may be best preserved, but how tolerable might be the condition of the people when it should be broken up and destroyed. While the Union lasts we have high, exciting, gratifying prospects spread out before us, for us and our children. Beyond that I seek not to penetrate the veil. God grant that in my day at least that curtain may not rise! God grant that on my vision never may be opened what lies behind! When my eyes shall be turned to behold for the last time the sun in heaven, may I not see him shining on the broken and dishonoured fragments of a once glorious Union; on states dissevered, discordant, belligerent; on a land rent with civil feuds, or drenched, it may be, in fraternal blood! Let their last feeble and lingering glance rather behold the gorgeous ensign of the Republic, now known and honoured throughout the earth, still full high advanced, its arms and trophies streaming in their original lustre, not a stripe erased or polluted, not a single star obscured, bearing for its motto no such miserable interrogatory as 'What is all this worth?' nor those other words of delusion and folly, 'Liberty first and Union afterwards,' but everywhere, spread all over in characters of living light, blazing on all its ample folds, as they float over the sea and over the land, and in every wind under the whole heavens, that other sentiment, dear to every true American heart — Liberty *and* Union, now and for ever, one and inseparable!"

On the Indiana frontier a young man was moved by this speech. His name was Abraham Lincoln.

President Jackson himself was impressed, and in his warlike approach to politics was prepared to coerce South Carolina by force. But a tactful compromise was reached. The tariff was lowered but rendered permanent, and the Force Act, authorising the President to use the Army if necessary to collect the customs duties, was declared null and void by South Carolina. Here then for a space the matter was left. But the South Carolina theory of "nullification" showed the danger of the Republic, and with the prophetic instinct of the simple frontiersman Jackson pointed to the future: "The next pretext will be the negro or slavery question."

But the next serious issue was the Federal Bank, whose charter was due to come up for renewal in 1836. The National Republicans, or Whigs, now led by Clay, preferred to force it before the 1832 Presidential election. Jackson had long been expected to attack the moneyed power in politics. The position of the Bank illustrated the economic stresses which racked the American Republic. "It was an economic conflict," wrote Charles Beard, "that happened to take a sectional form: the people of the agricultural West had to pay tribute to Eastern capitalists on the money they had borrowed to buy land, make improvements, and engage in speculation." The contest was joined in the election. The triumphant return of Jackson to power was in fact a vote against the Bank of the United States. It was in vain that Daniel Webster was briefed as counsel for the Bank. Jackson informed the Bank president, "I do not dislike your bank more than all banks, but ever since I read the history of the South Sea Bubble I have been afraid of banks." He refused to consent to the passing of a Bill to renew the charter, and without waiting for the Bank to die a natural death in 1836 he decided at once to deprive it of Government deposits, which were sent to local banks throughout the states. When the charter expired it was not renewed, and for nearly thirty years there was no centralised banking system in the United States. The union of Western and Southern politicians had had their revenge upon the North. The Radicalism of the frontier had won a great political contest. Jackson's occupation of the Presidency had finally broken the "era of good feelings" which had followed the war with Britain, and by his economic policy he had split the old Republican Party of Jefferson. The Radicalism of the West was looked upon with widespread suspicion throughout the Eastern states, and Jackson's official appointments had not been very happy.

The election in 1836 of Jackson's lieutenant, Van Buren, meant the continuation of Jacksonian policy, while the old General himself returned in triumph to his retirement in Tennessee. The first incursions of the West into high politics had revealed the slumbering forces of democracy on the frontier and shown the inexperience of their leaders in such affairs.

The westward tide rolled on, bearing with it new problems of adjustment. The generation of the 1840's saw their culmination. During these years there took place the annexation of Texas, a war with Mexico, the conquest of California, and the settlement of the Oregon boundary with Great Britain. Adventurous Americans in search of land and riches had been since 1820 crossing the Mexican boundary into the Texas country, which belonged to the Republic of Mexico, freed from Spain in 1821. While this community was growing, American sailors on the Pacific coast, captains interested in the China trade, established themselves in the ports of the Mexican Province of California. Pioneers pushed their way overland in search of skins and furs, and by 1826 reached the mission stations of the Province. The Mexicans, alarmed at the appearance of these settlers, vainly sought to stem the flood; for Mexican Governments were highly unstable, and in distant Provinces their writ hardly ran. But there appeared on the scene a new military dictator, Santa Anna, determined to strengthen Mexican authority, and at once a revolt broke out. In November 1835 the Americans in Texas erected an autonomous state and raised the Lone Star flag. The Mexicans under Santa Anna, marched northwards. At the Mission House of the Alamo in March 1836 a small body of Texans, fighting to the last man, was exterminated in one of the epic fights of American history by a superior Mexican force. The whole Province was aroused. Under the leadership of General Sam Houston from Tennessee a force was raised, and in savage fighting the Mexican army of Santa Anna was in its turn destroyed and its commander captured at San Jacinto River. The Texans had stormed the positions with the cry "Remember the Alamo!" The independence of Texas was recognised by Santa Anna. His act was repudiated later by the Mexican Government, but their war effort was exhausted, and the Texans organised themselves into a republic, electing Sam Houston as President.

For the next ten years the question of the admission of Texas as a state of the Union was a burning issue in American politics. As each new state demanded entry into the Union so the feeling for and against slavery ran higher. The great Abolitionist journalist, William Lloyd Garrison, called for a secession of the Northern states if the slave state of Texas was admitted to the Union. The Southerners, realising that Texan votes would give them a majority in the Senate if this vast territory was admitted as a number of separate states, clamoured for annexation. The capitalists of the East were committed, through the formation of land companies, to exploit Texas, and besides the issue of dubious stocks by these bodies vast quantities of paper notes and bonds of the new

Texan Republic were floated in the United States. The speculation in these helped to split the political opposition of the
Northern states to the annexation. Even more important was
the conversion of many Northerners to belief in the "Manifest Destiny" of the United States. This meant that their destiny was to spread across the whole of the North American
continent. The Democratic Party in the election of 1844
called for the occupation of Oregon as well as the annexation of Texas, thus holding out to the North the promise of
Oregon as a counterweight to Southern Texas. The victory of
the Democratic candidate, James K. Polk, was interpreted
as a mandate for admitting Texas, and this was done by joint
resolution of Congress in February 1845.

It remained to persuade Mexico to recognise this state of
affairs, and also to fix the boundaries of Texas. President
Polk was determined to push them as far south as possible,
and war was inevitable. It broke out in May 1846. Meanwhile
a similar train of events was unfolding on the other side of
the continent. All this time American penetration of the
West had continued, often with grim experiences of starva-
tion and winter snows. Nothing could stop the migration
towards the Pacific. The lure of the rich China trade and the
dream of controlling the Western Ocean brought the acquisition of California to the fore, and gave her even more importance in American eyes than Texas. In June 1846 the American settlers in California, instigated from Washington,
raised the Bear Flag as their standard of revolt and declared
their independence on the Texan model. Soon afterwards
American forces arrived and the Stars and Stripes replaced
the Bear.

The American advance was rapidly gathering momentum. The Mexican army of the North was twice beaten by
General Zachary Taylor, a future President. A force under
General Winfield Scott was landed at Vera Cruz and
marched on Mexico City. The capital fell to the Americans
after a month of street fighting in September 1847. On this expedition a number of young officers distinguished themselves. They included Captain Robert E. Lee, Captain
George B. McClellan, Lieutenant Ulysses S. Grant, and Colonel Jefferson Davis.

Mexico sued for peace, and by the treaty which followed she was obliged not only to recognise the annexation of Texas, but also to cede California, Arizona, and New Mexico. Lieutenant Grant confided his impressions to his memoirs: "I do not think there was ever a more wicked war than that waged by the United States on Mexico. I thought so at the time, when I was a youngster, only I had not moral courage enough to resign." But the expansive force of the American peoples was explosive. "Manifest Destiny" was on the march, and it was unfortunate that Mexico stood in the path. The legend of Imperialism and the belief in the right of the United States to exploit both continents, North and South, which sprang from the Mexican War henceforward cast their shadow on co-operation between the South American republics and the United States.

The immediate gains were enormous. While the commissioners were actually debating the treaty with Mexico an American labourer in California discovered the first nugget of gold in that region. The whole economy of a sleepy Mexican province, with its age-old Spanish culture, was suddenly overwhelmed by a mad rush for gold. In 1850 the population of California was about eighty-two thousand souls. In two years the figure had risen to two hundred and seven thousand. A lawless mining society arose upon the Pacific coast. From the cities of the East and from the adjoining states men of all professions and classes of society flocked to California, many being murdered, killed in quarrels, by cold and famine, or drowned in the sea voyage round Cape Horn. The gold of California lured numbers to their death, and a few to riches beyond belief.

> Oh! California,
> That's the land for me
> I'm off to Sacramento
> With my washbowl on my knee.

The anarchy of the gold rush brought an urgent demand for settled government in California, and the old, perplexing, rasping quarrel over the admission of a new state was

• *Winston S. Churchill* •

heard again at Washington. For the moment nothing was done, and the Californians called their own state convention and drew up a temporary constitution.

During all this time, farther to the north, another territory had been coming into being. The "Oregon Trail" had brought many men from the more crowded states of the North-East to find their homes and establish their farms along the undefined Canadian frontier to the Pacific. With the prospect of war in the South for the acquisition of Texas and California, the American Government was not anxious to embark upon a quarrel with Great Britain upon its Northern frontier. There was strong opposition by the Southerners to the acquisition of Oregon, where the Northern pioneers were opposed to slavery. Oregon would be another "free soil state." Negotiations were opened with Britain, and in spite of electioneering slogans of "Fifty-four-forty or fight" the boundary was settled in June 1846 by peaceful diplomacy along the forty-ninth parallel. This solution owed much to the accommodating nature of the Foreign Secretary in Peel's Government, Lord Aberdeen. The controversy now died down, and in 1859 the territory of Oregon reached statehood.

Among the many settlements which lay dotted over the whole of the American continent the strangest perhaps was the Mormon colony at Salt Lake City. In the spring of 1847 members of this revivalist and polygamist sect started from the state of Illinois under their prophet leader, Brigham Young, to find homes free from molestation in the West. By the summer they reached the country round Salt Lake, and two hours after their arrival they had begun establishing their homes and ploughing up the soil. Within three years a flourishing community of eleven thousand souls, combining religious fervour, philoprogenitiveness, and shrewd economic sense, had been established by careful planning in the Salt Lake country, and in 1850 the territory received recognition by the Federal Government under the name of Utah. The colony was established in a key position on the trail which led both to Oregon and California. The sale of food and goods to the travellers and adventurers who moved in both directions along this route brought riches to the Mormon settler, and Salt Lake City, soon tainted, it is true, by the introduction of more lawless and unbelieving elements, became one of the richest cities in America.

With the establishment of this peculiar colony the settlement of the continent was comprehensive. The task before the Federal Government was now to organise the Far Western territory won in the Mexican War and in the compromise with Britain. From this there rose in its final and dread form the issue of bond and free.

ENDNOTES

1. *The Oxford History of the United States* (1927), vol. i, p. 391.

V · I · I · I

Roscoe Carlyle Buley

NEW HOMES IN THE WEST

A savage wilderness, resting in primaeval solitude, or inhabited only by a race whose practice it is when they migrate, to leave no trace behind, is suddenly opened to an eager multitude, who pour in like the waters of the sea, and cover it with civilized life. The forest falls around them, and is consumed or converted into habitations; the ground is opened by the industrious ploughshare, to the sun; the vapors and the malaria dry up; the fruits of other climes are planted; the comfortable log house is raised, the rude wagon is built, and the spot where "yesterday" all was silent, save the beast and the bird, becomes today the home of the woodsman — the center of human affections — the nucleus perhaps of an intelligent, social, virtuous community — the focus, where, it may be, light shall emanate to other parts of the world.

Western Monthly Magazine, November, 1836

It was spring at Pittsburgh,[1] wet and cold, but nevertheless, spring. The muddy waters of the Monongahela joined the clear and more rapid current of the Allegheny, and westward between the wooded hills stretched the broad Ohio, *La Belle Rivière* of the French, for a thousand miles an open and inviting pathway to the West. The thriving young city of about 5,000 people was stirring with the bustle of commerce and industry, for the western traffic was booming, and Pittsburgh was the gateway to the West.

Between Pittsburgh and Wheeling the river, studded with alluvial islands, wound back and forth between shores which alternately presented almost level bottoms and headlands which rose three to four hundred feet. Said the traveler,

> Truly, the waters have here chosen a lovely spot for their meeting, and it was but natural that such a stream as the Ohio should spring from such a union. Looking backward now I could see that river, like a young giant rejoicing in its birth, sweeping suddenly on its course, but turning every moment among its green islands, as if to look back till the last upon the home of its infancy. . . . The windings of the river present, at every turn, some of the most beautiful views in the world; but the regular alternations of "bluff" and "bottom" give such a sameness to the landscape, that unless familiar with the points of the country around, one might be dropped in a dozen different places along the river, and not be aware of a change in his situation. Nature seems to have delighted in repeating again and again the same lovely forms, which she first moulded in this favorite region.

This traveler, who first saw the Ohio at Wheeling in 1833, continued:

> The Ohio is beneath your feet. . . . The clear majestic tide, the fertile islands on its bosom, the bold and towering heights opposite, with the green esplanade of alluvion in front, and the for-

est-crowned headlands above and below, round which the river sweeps away, to bless and gladden the fruitful regions that drink its limpid waters, — these, with the recollections of deeds done upon its banks — the wild incidents and savage encounters of border story, so immediately contrasted with all the luxuries of civilization that now float securely upon that peaceful current, — these make a moral picture whose colours are laid in the heart, never to be effaced: — no man will ever forget his first view of the Ohio.[2]

From the pack-train trails and wilderness roads, by Braddock's Road from Virginia, Forbes's Road from Philadelphia, even by the Genesee Road through New York, came the movers. At Redstone on the Monongahela, Kittanning on the Allegheny, and most of all at Pittsburgh at the forks, they assembled. Some had sent their belongings by the big Conestoga freighters, ridden the stagecoaches and stopped at taverns, but the greater numbers traveled in the light wagons drawn by horses or oxen, hauling their plunder with them, or walked with packs, and in some instances pulled carts or pushed wheelbarrows. At the river towns axmen, carpenters, and boatmakers were ready to supply anything from a light skiff for two up to the elaborate seventy-foot barges with sails and poling platforms, but whether the newcomer got a good job of seasoned wood with well-caulked seams, or a green, heavy, and leaky craft, depended upon his own knowledge and shrewdness. Many secured boats by trading their horses; some built their own. Equipping emigrants was almost a business in itself, and to the stores freighted by wagon over the long haul from Philadelphia and Baltimore, Pittsburgh added the products of her own budding manufacturers — the blacksmiths, cutlers, founders, glassmakers, hatters, saddlers, ropemakers, tanners, chandlers, weavers, and bootmakers.[3]

When the river rose and floating ice no longer threatened, the sundry types of craft were loaded and the tide of humanity headed for the land of promise, the West. Armed with only a copy of Cumings' *Western Pilot* or Cramer's *Navi-*

gator, or depending upon hearsay and his own ability, the emigrant faced the dangers of snags and sawyers, planters, and driftwood islands. Little time had he to notice, and none to record, the beauties of bountifully wooded shores, as yet undenuded by the ax, or the majestic stretches of stream bearing their burden of strange craft,

> As down Ohio's ever ebbing tide,
> Oarless and sailless silently they glide,
> How still the scene, how lifeless, yet how fair,
> Was the lone land that met the strangers there!
> No smiling villages, or curling smoke,
> The busy haunts of busy men bespoke,
>
> Nothing appear'd, but Nature unsubdu'd
> One endless, noiseless, woodland solitude.... [4]

The thrill of new ventures in strange lands no doubt was there, but to the man with family it was largely a part of the prosaic day's work. Rather it was the traveler, the Easterner or Englishman with means and education, who was impressed with the pageantry of the scene, the beauties of nature, the manners of the people. To him the collection of floating contrivances was an interesting sight: pirogues, batteaux, barges, schooners, and keelboats; flatboats, broadhorns, arks, and now and then a steamboat.[5] Equally fascinating were the picturesque, hard-spitting and fluently cussing professional rivermen.

Since the Indian shore of the Ohio no longer presented the danger of hostile arrows and bullets, the heavily boarded and enclosed flatboat, or Kentucky boat, was no longer a necessity, and the cumbersome ark began to prove its worth. These craft, shallow and uncovered, ran up to a hundred feet in length and, except for the long sweep at the stern, were largely at the mercy of the current. But for the family or group which wished to take much plunder, the ark had its advantages. In its spacious hulk were packed boxes, bags, and bundles; tools, wagons, chickens, horses, neat cattle, and hogs; dogs, children, and supplies. A shanty in the middle for the family, or several families, if it was a communal affair, offered shelter. A stone- or dirt-filled enclosure housed a fire for domestic purposes. A pillar of smoke by day and of fire by night marked the progress of the crude craft, from which emanated the squalling of infants, the yapping of dogs, and chatter of voices.

The more cautious traveled only by day; but some going far, or fearing the good land would be gone, traveled by night as well, taking turn at the sweeps and on watch. The miles slowly fell behind as the progress varied, dependent upon current and wind, from a few miles a day to forty or fifty. After a sojourn of from ten days to three weeks on the river, the settler, arrived at the point of debarkation, could sell his raft for use downstream or for the timbers in it, or, if he was locating close by, he might knock it apart himself and use the material for a temporary shelter.

The poet, in retrospect, paid his tribute to the river, neglected in sentiment and description by the emigrant:

> O loveliest river of this Western clime!
> Thou shalt not flow unsung, as in the time
> When in the mirror of thy winding waters
> Gazed on their forms, the groups of Indian daughters.
>
> O'er the wide ocean they have borne thy name,
> Thy sons have told thy legends unto fame,
> The enchanted Frank hath fondly lingered here,
> And called thee, in his joy, "La Belle Riviere;"
> The Briton stranger here hath fought and died,
> And then *he* bore thy name o'er ocean's tide; —
> The daring emigrant hath ploughed thy wave,
> The rudest savage hath his tale to tell,
> What deeds of wonder and of war befel,
> Ere the white robber came and drove him far,
> To hunt his game beneath a setting star.
>
> But not alone to swell the harp of Clio,
> Thou windest in thy beauty — bright Ohio?[6]

Not all came by river, for in summer or early fall the low stage of water made such travel precarious. There were those who would rather undertake the laborious travel by land. The Cumberland Road was opened to the Ohio at Wheeling in 1817. West from Pittsburgh ran the road to Steubenville and on to Zanesville and to Columbus, but horseback mail service between Pittsburgh and Steubenville did not come until 1818, and it was two years later before a stage line was in use. Zane's Road from Wheeling to Limestone, laid out in 1796, was so worn in places that the ruts were almost deep enough to bury a horse in. From the South across Kentucky came the streams of emigrants to swell the tide. "We do not recollect of ever having seen so many families emigrating to the western country as are this fall," said a Maysville editor.[7] "Old America seems to be breaking up and moving westward," wrote Birkbeck in 1817. Easterners on the move said they were going to Ohio, but when one got to Ohio the people there were going on to Indiana, Missouri, or Alabama. "The American has always something better in his eye, further west; he therefore lives and dies on hope, a mere gypsey in this particular."[8] The final point of settlement receded as the traveler moved west and would continue to do so, thought one observer, until terminated only by the effective barrier of the Pacific Ocean.[9]

The peace at the end of the second war with England had come with unexpected suddenness. The joyful elation over Jackson's victory at New Orleans had hardly subsided when the bells, handbills, and excited cries of citizens in New York announced "A peace! A peace!" In spite of the fact that the treaty did not mention the major causes of the war, the terms were more favorable than the military successes of the Americans would in themselves have warranted. Relatively few people, particularly in the West, saw any incongruity in Madison's declaration that the war had "been waged with a success which is the natural result of the wisdom of the Legislative Councils, of the patriotism of the people, of the public spirit of the Militia, and of the valor of the military and naval forces of the country." The spirit of nationalism forged ahead apace; America entered into adolescence. A new era was at hand.

Since the earliest years of the young republic, problems of foreign affairs had loomed large in its path of development. In 1793 war began between England and the French Republic, to continue with but one interruption to the end of the Napoleonic period in 1815. During the years following the War for Independence hard times had sent the people westward into the trans-Appalachian region, and Kentucky, Tennessee, and a broken fringe along the southern part of the Old Northwest were settled. But with the European wars of the French Revolution came the opening of the French and Dutch West Indies, the demand for American products, and high profits in the carrying trade. Sailors, merchants, farmers,, and artisans found attractive markets for their goods and services, and emigration to the West slumped, especially to the region north of the Ohio. Kentucky and Tennessee continued to gain, for the prosperity of wartimes affected less the regions of Virginia and the Carolinas than New England and the Middle States. The Harrison Land Act of 1800, which permitted installment payments over a period of five years, and temporary peace in Europe brought enough settlers into that part of the Northwest Territory still bearing the name to justify the admission of Ohio as a state under Republican auspices in 1803.[10] War again checked the movement, however, and soon blockades, orders in council, decrees, impressment, and rights of neutrals became problems of national concern. Non-importation, embargo, and nonintercourse produced disastrous effects on American prosperity and threatened ruin to commerce.[11] Napoleonic trickery, English blundering, and Republican indecision combined with the flare-up of national feeling and the desire for expansion to drag the United States into the European struggle.

The second war with England did not involve any great expenditure of life, property, and treasure. As wars go, it was a small war, but in economic effects and nationalistic influences it played a part out of proportion to its size. The Bank of the United States expired by charter limitation in 1811, and for money the country was left to rely upon notes of individuals and corporations, foreign coins which had been recognized as legal tender, cut money, the few United States coins which remained in the country and state bank notes. From 88 state banks in 1811, mostly located in the West and western sections of the older states, the number increased in two years to 288.[12] With note issues three times capital stock, and often ten times specie held, the business of the country was soon on a paper basis. Trade restrictions and the war served as a protective tariff, and much capital, especially in New England, was turned from trade and shipping into manufacturing. New England goods sold in the South and West far overbalanced purchases, and the ensuing drainage of specie from those regions forced their banks to suspend specie payment. But times were hard everywhere. The war, with the blockade, taxes, and property destruction, was exacting its toll, and by 1814 not only those who had made up their minds before the war but thousands of others turned their faces to the West.

Better times were expected with the peace, but with peace came quite the contrary. Merchants prepared for revival of commerce, ships were overhauled and rigged, and goods were advertised for. Some time was allowed to elapse for the news of the peace to reach warships at sea, but in March 1815, a great merchant fleet sailed away to Europe, still at war and hungry for American goods. Then came the fleets of English merchantmen, bearing the silks, hardware, wine, molasses, and coffee which Americans after a prolonged period of curtailed consumption were eager to get. Auction sales were held in the leading Atlantic Coast cities from Boston to Charleston, and American buyers scrambled for the importations, often at prices which domestic producers would hardly have dared to charge.[13]

Nor was this the worst. With June came Waterloo and peace in Europe, the closing of many continental markets to England, and decreased demand for American goods. At the very time that decreasing profits in the carrying trade and export business made necessary further investment opportunities for Americans in their own manufacturing, England, with no notion of losing a good market to her late offspring, saw the American market as her financial salvation. Gladly would she have sold at or below cost to overwhelm threatening competition, but at first the dumping process was not necessary. When in the autumn cash sales in American began to slacken, business was promoted by liberal credit extensions, and overbuying was the result. Importers, merchants, and manufacturers soon found themselves overstocked with goods which they could neither sell nor pay for. By the end of the year American woolen and cotton industries were in a bad way, and it was evident that neither patriotism nor prices were enough to stop the deluge of English imports.

The tariff of 1816 was supposed to save the day, but English manufacturers and exporters were wise in the ways of the business world. Disbanded armies and unemployment offered a cheap labor market. England was confronted with a colossal national debt. Sales abroad had to be made, and neither tariffs nor fine points of business ethics were permitted to interfere. Shiploads of goods, many of them unordered, were sent to the United States, and the dumping process began with a vengeance. Goods were billed to one agent at prices below cost, and tariff duties paid on false invoices. Once safely through the tariff lines, the goods were sold by the first agent to another, who knowing the real values, disposed of them at auction. When an American merchant ordered goods, manufacturers would duplicate the order, ship it through on false billing and frequently auction it off in the importing merchant's town before he had his stuff on the shelves.

By the winter of 1816 widespread distress and unemployment were common in American cities. Of the estimated 130,000 spindles in 140 mills near Providence, only those in the old Slater Mill were reported turning in 1816.[14] Shipping, upon which probably one seventh of New England's population was dependent, was almost as hard hit as industry. Ships lay idle and deteriorating, crews wandered away, and artisans and traders dependent upon coasting and foreign trade were thrown out of employment. Agriculture, too, felt the stress, for not only were the farmers deprived of the wartime markets, but many had been caught in the postwar buying spree and some in land speculation as well. The new factory economy had unsettled conditions in the villages and on the farms. The abnormally cold season of 1816-17 and ensuing crop failures made taxes more burdensome and debtors more numerous.[15]

Besides the economic disorders of the times there were evidences of social and religious discontent. The old re-

straints weighed heavily on the more individualistic and independent types, and the distant promises of liberal re-
forms hardly seemed worth waiting for. New England may
have been in transition; many New Englanders were in transit, for:

> 'Tis I can delve and plough, love,
> And you can spin and sew;
> And we'll settle on the banks
> Of the pleasant Ohio.[16]

Since the coming of the white man to America there never
had been a time when the appeal of the region beyond, whether for precious metals, furs, land speculation, or homes,
did not furnish sufficient incentive to a few bold pioneers.
Mass migration, the *volkwanderung*, which included many
of the older generation as well as the youths starting out in
life, came only when the pressure of unsatisfactory conditions back home was combined in the popular mind with a
conception of the promised land sufficiently glamorous to
break the old ties and overcome natural inertia.[17] In a growing people the problem of finding homes and opportunities
for the new generation is a constant one, hence the western
movement was ever continuous but not uniform in flow. At
times when the negative forces of expulsion operated in max-
imum conjunction with the positive forces of attraction,
then resulted the flood tide.[18]

The West had its own appeal and its own ways of being advertised. There were the writings of the foreign travelers, a
great number of whom were attracted by the uniqueness of
the American frontier. Some were merely making the cus-
tomary tour, others were professional writers and travelers,
likely to describe only that which would prove interesting
and popular. But whether they wrote from curiosity or sin-
cere interest, with their propaganda-filled accounts, good
or bad, or with their accurate description and narration,
they were advertising the West.

Thomas Hutchins, later geographer of the United States,
Gilbert Imlay, Count Volney, and John Melish,[19] among
others, had published their accounts and descriptions of the

trans-Appalachian region between 1778 and 1812. It was in the years following the War of 1812 that travel books became numerous and easily available. Between 1815 and 1825, more than a dozen travel books on the region north of the Ohio were published either in England or America, put on sale in the bookshops of eastern cities, and reviewed in literary and news periodicals.[20] All were interesting, most were favorable, and some enthusiastic.[21] Among the most optimistic and rosy hued was Morris Birkbeck's *Notes on a Journey in America*, published in 1817, which called forth letters in refutation from the prolific William Cobbett. Birkbeck, interested financially in colonization in the Illinois country, emphasized the opportunities of material gain, but did not overlook the more abstract but nonetheless important rewards of independence and "Liberty — the fair enchantress." At his best, however, he could hardly equal in style and appeal the legislator in Missouri Territory who, in 1816, wrote that in the states west of the mountains:

. . . there neither is, nor, in the nature of things can there ever be, anything like poverty there. All is ease, tranquility and comfort. Every person, however poor, may with moderate industry, become in a very short time a landholder; his substance increases from year to year; his barns are filled with abundant harvests; his cattle multiply and are sustained by his attentions rather than the expences bestowed upon them; and his children, active, vigorous and enterprising, seem destined to sustain and extend the respectability of their parentage. Truly may it be said of that fortunate and highly favored country, "A paradise of pleasure is open'd in the wild."[22]

From romantic description to prophecy was but a step:

Looking only a few years through the vista of futurity, what a sublime spectacle presents itself! Wilderness, once the chosen residence of solitude or savageness, converted into populous cities, smiling villages beautiful farms and plantations! The happy multitude, busy in their daily occupations, manifests contentment and peace, breathing their gratitude and their prayers only to the great King of Kings! The wild Indian, taught by mild persuasion and example is become an enthusiast in the cause of civilization — behold him cultivating his fields, or at his cabin door studying the Book of Life. The Mississippi rolls her proud waves as before, but her bosom is plowed by thousands of Keels, and her surface whitened by thousands of sails, bearing the produce of millions of industrious citizens, to its destined mart! What a scene — how beautiful, how grand! — yet not ideal: another century will realize it. Yes — this fine country is destined to become the finest foothold of the Genius of American Liberty — and should he ever be driven from the Atlantic shores, he will take his stand on the loftiest peak of the Alleghany and shout to his votaries — "Here is my hold — here have I erected an empire beyond the reach of despots, which will endure when the stream of time shall have been drained into the ocean of eternity."[23]

As powerful in advertising value as the fair words of the travelers and prophets, and certainly more definite, were the military campaigns in the West. From the time of the Revolution, during the Confederation period and the Indian wars in the Northwest, down through the campaigns of the second war with England, each and every expedition into the Indian country was in effect an officially conducted land-looking tour. The expeditions of Bouquet, Clark, Harmar, St. Clair, Wayne, and Harrison all led within a few years to settlements in the regions penetrated. At times officers and men seemed more interested in the land and prospective speculation or settlement than in defeat of the Indians. The horrors incidental to Indian warfare always checked further settlement for the time, and frequently brought about a recession of the frontier, but the frontiersman was essentially

CS | SKA

CREDIT SUISSE   CREDITO SVIZZERO
SCHWEIZERISCHE KREDITANSTALT

an optimist. The loss was always more than regained in the reaction following peace.

By the time military campaigns had practically ceased and the western country was no longer possessed of the mystery and romance which interested the literary traveler, the newspapers of the region took over the task of advertising. The western journalist, like the speculator, businessman, or politician, profited directly by the growth of his community. Nor was all newspaper stuff mere "puffing" or optimistic promotion. Land sales, commodity price lists, new building, new trade opportunities, crop reports, notices of the need for artisans, doctors, and teachers — the serious news of the day — were the most effective advertising. And much of such material was republished in the "exchange clippings" of the papers in the very region which suffered most from the westward migration.

Last, and probably most effective of all, was the advertising done by word of mouth and the written communications of those who had gone before. True, means of communication were not easy, and facilities neither frequent nor cheap, yet people did return to tell of the new lands and possibilities of the West, and letters did find their way back to the settled regions to be passed around until worn out or printed and copied in newspapers and read with interest. Reports of relatives and friends could be trusted, and often the settlement of whole communities was the result of the pioneering efforts and favorable reports of one or two pioneers.

Naturally the seaboard states were alarmed over the unprecedented emigration of their people. New England was particularly sensitive on the subject, and her newspapers, in their eagerness to warn of the hardships and low prices of produce in the West, frequently went so far that they were accused by western papers of propagating known falsehoods in the interests of the "mercantile nobility" of their section.[24] The governors and legislators of Massachusetts and Connecticut hinted that the "unsettled population" of their states, tempted so much by seductive tales of milder climes and richer lands, would better stay where it was than make new settlements in distant wildernesses. It was proposed that New England taxes be lightened, and the editor of the *Boston*

Gazette thought that wide distribution of attractive maps of their own country would help acquaint the people with its advantages and keep them at home. To this a western editor replied that it was land and not maps that counted. "The march of power is to the west — let our eastern brethren think of this, and cease their unworthy efforts to retard what they cannot prevent."[25] Articles on English emigration were likewise eagerly copied from the English magazines by the western editors, for young America was elated to think she could worry the old enemy by taking away her people.

To the north of the Ohio, stretching from Pennsylvania on the east to the Mississippi River, and bounded on the north by the Great Lakes, lies a region known in American history as the Old Northwest. Its area of 265,878 square miles constitutes a domain larger than France or Germany before 1918 and about twice as large as the British Isles.[26] Physiographically this section of the United States falls within the large expanse of rolling country classified as the prairie plains or Central Lowlands.[27] Climatically or zoogeographically, all except the narrow strip which borders the two northernmost lakes, lies in the upper part of the austral or southern zone.[28] For the most part, the climate is temperate, summers hot. Except for the Lower Ohio Valley, mean annual precipitation runs from thirty to forty inches. The old Ohio-Mississippi drainage systems serve the southern and western portions of the area, but the successive glacial invasions which at one time or another covered all but small portions of what are now southeastern Ohio, southern Indiana and Illinois, and southwestern Wisconsin, established new drainage systems for the northern regions, and modified the old. Not only did glaciation account to a large extent for physical features, but also for the soil distribution, and this fact, as well as the determination of lake locations and watercourses, profoundly affected the economic history of the region. From the extensive tracts of rich organic till of the corn belt of Indiana and Illinois to the sandy and infertile pine barrens of Michigan, the glacier left its mark. It accounted for the sand dunes and the swamps, for the lake plains and beach lines, the wandering boulders and the sparkling lakes.

Over all, except the grand prairie of Illinois and other openings, stretched the great forests, somber and almost unbroken. In the region south of the lakes prevailed the deciduous trees or hardwoods — elm, beech, hickory, oak, poplar; to the north were the conifers — pine, fir, and spruce. In these forests wandered and lived bands of Indians, mostly of the Algonquin group.

> The unshorn forest o'er them waved
> Dark, dense as at Creation's birth, —
> The free winds round them wildly rav'd —
> Their tents the boughs — their couch the earth.[29]

Into the Great Lakes — Upper Mississippi country in the seventeenth century had penetrated the French explorers, fur traders, and missionaries — the pioneers of New France in America. But both La Salle's vision of western empire and the Jesuit dream of a Christian nation of Indians were destined to give way before English conquest and the westward expansion of the English colonies. The two colonial empires came together in the final struggle over the valley of the Upper Ohio, and the compact and numerous English took the heart of the continent from the more highly militarized but more widely scattered French and their Indian allies. France withdrew almost completely from North America; the French had left little of the mark of empire on the Northwest.

Under the English from 1763 to 1783, the inhabitants of the Northwest felt but lightly the rule of the mother country; a few hundred French *habitants*, a few thousand Indians, neither was much disturbed. Colonial plans and British politics, however, were influenced by problems of this vast area to the west of the settled colonies.[30] When, in 1774, for administrative purposes the region north of the Ohio was annexed to Quebec, Virginia, who claimed the land by charter grant, as well as other colonies who felt they were being cut off from westward expansion, regarded the act as one of the "Intolerable Acts." During the Revolution, George Rogers Clark, acting under the authority of the Commonwealth of Virginia, seized the southern part of the territory and broke up British military plans in the West. At the peace in 1783 the western boundary of the United States was fixed at the Mississippi River.

The ratification of the Articles of Confederation had been held up by the states without western land claims and by land company speculation and politics until 1781, when New York offered to cede her uncertain claims to the United States. Virginia generously gave over her lands north of the Ohio to the General Government on condition that when settled they should be organized into new states and admitted into the Union on an equal footing with the old. By the Ordinance of 1785 a Congressional land survey was provided for; the Ordinance of 1787 set up a territorial government, and established a colonial policy not only for the Northwest, but for all of the public domain of the future.

Aggressive Pennsylvania and Virginia squatters, largely Scotch-Irish, had pushed over into the lands north of the Ohio during the Revolution, but were ordered out by United States troops when the land was surveyed. Revolutionary soldiers who had accompanied George Rogers Clark on his campaign of 1778-79 were awarded Virginia lands north of the Ohio at the Falls in 1784, where Clarksville was founded. A still larger American settlement in the Northwest Territory was made in 1788 by New Englanders of the Ohio Company of Associates at Marietta, on their land grant along the Muskingum.[3l] The closely related Scioto Company of speculators inveigled some settlers, among them some Frenchmen who had believed the attractive descriptions of Joel Barlow, on to their lands immediately to the west. Judge Symmes and his associates speculated and promoted settlements, largely of Middle States men, in the region between the Miami rivers, and people from the South infiltrated into the Virginia military lands just to the east of the Miami Purchase. With the addition of Pennsylvania Germans and Carolina Quakers, the population of this section of the Northwest presented from the beginning a mixed make-up, a fact which was destined to play an important part in the political and social history of the future state of Ohio.

The Indian problem was imminent during the early years of the Territory. Generals Harmar and St. Clair struggled unsuccessfully with it, but after Gen. Anthony Wayne's victory over the confederated tribes at Fallen Timbers in August, 1794, peace and a boundary line were agreed upon. By the Treaty of Greenville in 1795 the Indians were restrained to the region north and west of a line running from the mouth of the Cuyahoga River through Fort Recovery to the mouth of the Kentucky River. The following year Moses Cleaveland and more New Englanders settled on the Connecticut Reserve up in the northeast corner of the Territory. A zone of settlement fifty to seventy-five miles wide now paralleled the Ohio River from Pennsylvania on past Cincinnati, with scattered settlements to the west. People continued to come in. In 1800 Indiana Territory was set off by the line running from the mouth of the Kentucky River to Fort Recovery and thence due north to the international boundary. The eastern part of the region, which still bore the name of Territory of the United States Northwest of the Ohio, was expecting redivision and early admission into the Union as the state of Ohio. William Henry Harrison, governor of Indiana Territory, by a series of treaties between 1803 and 1809, cleared the lands well back from the Ohio and up the Wabash and Mississippi valleys from any Indian claim, and the eve of the War of 1812 found the frontier line of settlement moved north and west in Ohio, looping up the Whitewater, Wabash, and Mississippi valleys, but swinging back near the Ohio River in between.[32]

Settlement did not cease during the war. In February, 1812, the Ohio legislature located the new capital site on the Scioto, on "the East High Bank, opposite the town of Franklinton."[33] On the day that Congress was declaring war the sale of town lots in the thick woods took place, and in the autumn of 1816 the government was moved to Columbus.[34] Land sales fell off, but two new counties were organized during the war, and from a population of 230,000 in 1810 Ohio had grown to about 400,000 by 1815. In Indiana Territory settlements advanced deeper into the forests as danger of Indian hostilities lessened, and the border settlements in modern Lawrence, Monroe, and Jackson counties were consolidated, while the eastern wing of advance crept up the Whitewater and into present-day Fayette, Ripley, and Jennings counties. After a temporary setback, the Wabash-White River Valley advance swept on to Spencer and Gosport. Land sales at the Jeffersonville and Vincennes offices showed a decided increase in 1813 over the preceding year. "Indiana, notwithstanding the war, is peopling very fast. Its settlements are bursting forth on the right hand and on the left. . . . Settlers will now begin to flock in, especially if the war should soon terminate."[35] The population of 24,520 in 1810 had increased to 63,897 in 1815.[36] The outposts of the invading army of settlers, mostly from Kentucky and the South, had pushed northward almost to the limits of the Indian cessions.

Across the Wabash from Vincennes were the prairies. These rich lands were at first not desirable in the eyes of the pioneers. Land which would not grow tall trees was considered infertile; besides the settlers were dependent upon the timber for homes and outbuildings, for fires and fences. Malaria and other lowland ailments also acted as deterrents. By 1809, when Illinois Territory was organized, the people were on the edge of the prairies and they did not push back from the river valley and into the open until 1814. The Indian troubles and the impossibility of getting legal land titles to any but the lands in the hands of the French settlers held down immigration into the Illinois country, and only about 3,000 people were added during the war years.[37]

In the Great Lakes — Upper Mississippi country were the old French settlements of Detroit, Mackinac, Green Bay, and Prairie du Chien. Of this country the Americans knew little. James Monroe in 1786 had written that most of it was miserably poor, "especially that near lakes Michigan and Erie and that upon the Mississippi and the Illinois consists of extensive plains which have not had from appearances and will not have a single bush on them, for ages." At the close of the war, when Edward Tiffin was sent to survey two million acres of Congressional military lands, he reported that the whole tract in Michigan Territory did not contain one hundredth of that amount in tillable land, and was not worth the expense of surveying. He said the land was low and wet, covered with swamp grass, bush, and slime. "Taking the country altogether . . . there would be not more than one acre in a hundred, if there were one out of a thousand, that would in any case admit of cultivation."[38] As for the Upper Mississippi country, the account of Zebulon Montgomery Pike's expedition of 1806 and vague reports of hunters and boatmen constituted about all the information available. It was thought to be a wild region, filled with savages — and it was.

ENDNOTES

1. The original spelling for the town at the forks of the Ohio, as used by Gen. John Forbes, was "Pittsburgh." This is also the spelling used in the act of incorporation, 1816. The more usual spelling, however, in the early nineteenth century was "Pittsburg." Travelers, newspapers, journals, etc., generally so spelled it. Late in the century the Post Office Department ruled in favor of this spelling, but the decision was reversed in 1908. Any deviations from the "official" spelling in these volumes are in keeping with the sources used.

2. Charles Fenno Hoffman, *A Winter in the West* (2 volumes. New York, 1835), I, 49-50, 57, 59-60.

So much had been written in praise of the Ohio that by 1838 a New England traveler, like the Athenian citizen who tired of hearing of Aristides the Just, was almost prepared to be prejudiced against it. "I had often heard the praises of this majestic river sung, and had curbed my expectations lest I should be disappointed. The Ohio *is* a beautiful river. There are points on the Hudson and Connecticut, and other rivers of the East, which equal any thing I saw on the Ohio; but its peculiarity is that it is *all* beautiful. There are no points bare of beauty; but every mile is as rich in scenery as it was in verdure at the time of my passage down its 'winding way.'" Abner Dumont Jones, *Illinois and the West* . . . (Boston and Philadelphia, 1838), 23.

The scenery on the Upper Ohio was best depicted in colors by the English engraver-artist, Lefevre J. Cranstone, who in 1859 made some 312 pen-and-water-color drawings largely of western Virginia, Ohio, and Indiana. To no subject did he turn more frequently than the Ohio. Originals in Indiana University Library.

3. Among the travelers' descriptions of Pittsburgh in the period from 1800 to 1820 are those in John Melish, *Travels in the United States of America, in the Years 1806, & 1807, and 1809, 1810, & 1811* . . . (2 volumes. Philadelphia, 1812); Morris Birkbeck, *Notes on a Journey in America, from the Coast of Virginia to the Territory of Illinois* . . . (3d ed. London, 1818); Henry Bradshaw Fearon, *Sketches of*

America . . . (2d ed. London, 1818); Estwick Evans, *A Pedestrious Tour of Four Thousand Miles, through the Western States and Territories, during the Winter and Spring of 1818* . . . (Concord, N. H., 1819), reprinted in Reuben Gold Thwaites (ed.), *Early Western Travels* . . . (32 volumes. Cleveland, 1904-7), VIII; Elias Pym Fordham, *Personal Narrative of Travels in Virginia, Maryland, Pennsylvania, Ohio, Indiana, Kentucky; and of a Residence in the Illinois Territory: 1817-1818*, edited by Frederic A. Ogg (Cleveland, 1906); James Flint, *Letters from America, containing Observations on the Climate and Agriculture of the Western States, the Manners of the People, the Prospects of Emigrants* . . . (Edinburgh, 1822); John Woods, *Two Years' Residence in the Settlement on the English Prairie, in the Illinois Country* . . . (London, 1822), reprinted in *Early Western Travels*, X; William Tell Harris, *Remarks Made During a Tour through the United States of America, in the Years, 1817, 1818, and 1819* . . . (London, 1821).

4. James Kirke Paulding, *The Backwoodsman* (Philadelphia, 1818), 65-66.

5. For a discussion of river boats and navigation, see Chapter VII.

6. C. P. C., "To the River Ohio," in *The Hesperian*, II (1839), 217.

7. Copied in *Zanesville Express*, December 12, 1816. Ohio roads were described as intolerable, shocking, wretched, and devilish, in fact, the worst in the world. Horses expired on them, axles snapped, and coaches of Kentucky notables upset. *Ibid.*, November 30, 1814. "Emigration to this state is almost immense: The road leading through this town seems to be covered with wagons and carriages of all descriptions." *Ibid.*, October 5, 1815. "We are induced to believe that in no year since the adoption of the Federal Constitution, has the tide of emigration set so strongly westward as the last." Chillicothe *Supporter*, June 24, 1817. From Philadelphia an observer wrote: "I can scarcely walk a square without meeting with Irish, Dutch, English and Scotch emigrants, whose destination is principally Ohio and Indiana." He predicted that in twenty years the bulk of the population would be west of the Allegheny Mountains. Letter in the Mount Pleasant (Ohio) *Philanthropist*, November 14, 1817.

8. Birkbeck, *Notes on a Journey in America*, 31; William Faux, *Memorable Days in America* . . . (London, 1823), 179.

9. Fearon, *Sketches of America*, 234.

10. Indiana Territory was set off in 1800, and only that part east of the Indiana line from the mouth of the Kentucky River to Fort Recovery and due north to Canada was left as the Territory Northwest of the Ohio. See Chapter ll and map, 62.

11. For views on the comparative results in New England and the South, see Edward Channing, *A History of the United States* (6 volumes. New York, 1905-1925), IV, 387; Henry Adams, *History of the United States . . .* (9 volumes. New York, 1891-1911), IV, 280; James Truslow Adams, *New England in the Republic, 1776-1850* (Boston, 1926), 250.

12. John Bach McMaster, *A History of the People of the United States from the Revolution to the Civil War* (8 volumes. New York, 1883-1913), IV, 290.

13. "New Goods at Peace Prices — Just Received from Philadelphia!" and similar notices were published in Ohio papers as early as May. See Chillicothe *Supporter*, May 30, 1815.

14. Adams, *New England in the Republic*, 309.

15. In May, 1816, ice froze an inch thick, June brought heavy snows in New England and New York, and ice continued to form in July and August. It was truly a "year without a summer."

16. "New-England Ballad," in *Edinburgh Review*, I.V, 480 (July, 1832).

17. Lois Kimball Mathews, in *The Expansion of New England . . .* (New York, 1909), gives a general account of the emigration from that section, with maps. Richard J. Purcell, *Connecticut in Transition, 1775-1818* (Washington, D. C., 1918), 139 ff., speaks of the movement in 1815 as "almost a migratory furor." See also passages reprinted in Louis B. Schmidt and Earle D. Ross (eds.), *Readings in the Economic History of American Agriculture* (New York, 1925), 137 ff.

The thesis that hard times back East stimulated emigration to the West is decisively contested by Murray Kane in "Some Considerations on the Safety Valve Doctrine," in *Mississippi Valley Historical Review*, XXIII (1936-37), 169-88, and by Carter Goodrich and Sol Davison in "The Wage-Earner in the Westward Movement," in *Political Science Quarterly*, L (1935), 161-85, LI (1936), 61-116. On the other side: Leifur Magnusson, *Disposition of the Public Lands of the United States with Particular Reference to Wage-Earning Labor* (U. S. Department of Labor, Washington, D. C., 1919); Frederic Logan Paxson, *History of the American Frontier, 1763-1893* (Boston, 1924), 187; McMaster, *History of the People of the United States*, IV, 38; Frederick Jackson Turner, *The Frontier in American History* (New York, 1920); Channing, *History of the United States*, V, 40.

Perhaps there is no basic issue here after all. Obviously, westward emigration diminished during the periods of national depression, such as between 1818 and 1825, and 1837 and 1841. Equally apparent, it seems, is the fact that it was increased by economic and social troubles in the Northeast between 1814 and 1818. As for the "safety valve" idea, that is, that the cheap lands offered an escape and mitigated pressing economic and social conditions back East, it all depends on the viewpoint. People who emigrated before and after the depressions helped relieve the pressure in the older regions just as certainly as if they had gone during the depression. On the other hand, it might be well argued that, since the western lands tended to stimulate speculation, build up top-heavy credit structures, encourage flimsy finance and banking, and create pressure groups, they intensified and augmented the very condition which they were supposed to relieve.

18. This has been true of European movements to America as well. Paxson, *History of the American Frontier*, Chapter XXI, treats briefly the great migration.

19. Thomas Hutchins, *A Topographical Description of Virginia, Pennsylvania, Maryland, and North Carolina* . . . (London, 1778); Gilbert Imlay, *A Topographical Description of the Western Territory of North America* (New York, 1793); Constantin François Volney, *A View of the Soil and Climate of the United States of America* (Philadelphia, 1804); Melish, *Travels in the United States*.

20. Fairly complete lists of the travelers who wrote of the West prior to 1840 may be found in Solon J. Buck, *Travel and Description 1765-1865* . . . (*Illinois Historical Collections*, IX, Springfield, 1914); Ralph Leslie Rusk, *The Literature of the Middle Western Frontier* (2 volumes. New York, 1925); R. G. Thwaites in *Early Western Travels* reprints many of the better-known accounts. Gershom Flagg, David Thomas, Estwick Evans, Henry Bradshaw Fearon, Morris Birkbeck, Elias P. Fordham, R. L. Mason, James Flint, William Faux, Thomas Hulme, John Woods, Richard Flower, Timothy Flint, William Darby, Edouard de Montulé and others, published journals, descriptions, or letters during the period from 1816 to 1826. See bibliography for titles.

21. For classification and estimate of the travelers, see Allan Nevins (comp. and ed.), *American Social History as Recorded by British Travellers* (New York, 1923).

22. Letters from Rufus Easton, House of Representatives, Missouri Territory, to Senator William Hunter, Rhode Island. *Niles' Weekly Register* (Baltimore, 1811-49), X, 428-29 (Aug. 24, 1816).

23. Quoted form the *National Intelligencer*, in the Chillicothe *Supporter*, June 24, 1817.

24. Cincinnati *Liberty Hall*, July 31, 1815, and *Liberty Hall and Cincinnati Gazette*, September 29, October 20, 1817. The Portland (Me.) *Eastern Argus* said that wheat was selling at 33 cents in Ohio and $1.25 in the Maine district. The Hamilton (Ohio) *Miami Intelligencer*, November 19, 1815, copied a long extract from the *Worceseter* (Mass.) *Gazette* of October 11, 1815, which regretted that

so many had emigrated. The *Gazette* thought the western climate was overrated and the absence of luxuries a hardship, and stated that many had returned to acknowledge the superiority of the character of New England, its well administered laws, civil liberty, security, and happiness. When the Bridgeport (Conn.) *Republican Farmer* cautioned against smallpox in the Ohio country, the editor of the *Columbus* (Ohio) *Gazette*, May 21, 1818, gave notice to all from 9 months to 999 years in the poor hills of Connecticut not to pay any attention. And when the Hartford (Conn.) *American Mercury* published what seemed "plain and unaffected simple truth" in criticism of western land speculation, the unhealthy prairies of Illinois, and the western country which was like "a great muddy hogyard," and said that western pride and distance prevented the East hearing its groans, the editor of the *Gazette* gave it vigorous and derisive treatment.

25. *Western Herald and Steubenville Gazette*, edited by James Wilson, August 1, 1817.

26. Thomas Donaldson, *The Public Domain* . . . (Washington, 1884), 161, lists the area of the states established from the Territory Northwest of the Ohio River as follows: Ohio 39,964; Indiana 33,809; Illinois 55,414; Michigan 56,451; Wisconsin 53,924; Minnesota east of the Mississippi and international boundary of 1776, 26,000 (estimated); and Erie purchase in Pennsylvania 316 — total 265,878 square miles. Later surveys have increased the figures for the region, although current statistics vary somewhat. For instance, the area of the five states, plus the 26,316 square miles of the Northwest not now included in these states is listed in the *Statesman's Year Book*, 1936, at 271,880, but in the *Rand McNally Atlas*, 1936, at 274,421. Nor will inclusion or omission of water area account for the difference. Modern surveys are constantly changing the figures. The land area of Indiana, for instance, was listed in the 1930 census as 36,045 square miles, but later official recalculations list it at 36,205 square miles. Land areas of the five states as given by the *Sixteenth Census of the United States: 1940* are Ohio 41,122; Indiana 36,205; Illinois 55,947; Michigan 57,022; and Wisconsin 54,715.

27. Of the portion of the region which is classified as Central Lowlands, the largest part (western Ohio, Indiana, Illinois) lies in the Till Plains. Eastern Ohio attaches to the Appalachian Plateau region, northern Wisconsin to the Superior Upland, and part of southern Indiana to the Interior Low Plateau region. Most of Michigan falls within the East Lake Section of the Central Plateau. Nevin W. Fenneman, "Physiographic Divisions of the United States," in *Annals of the Association of American Geographers*,

XVIII, No. 4 (Dec., 1928).

28. The northern parts of what are now Michigan and Wisconsin lie in the southern zone of the Boreal region; most of Wisconsin and southern Michigan in the transition zone of the Austral region. The rest of the area falls within the upper Austral. Isaiah Bowman, *Forest Physiography* (New York, 1911), map, 122.

29. Mrs. Hentz, in *Western Monthly Magazine*, II (1834), 147.

30. See Clarence W. Alvord, *The Mississippi Valley in British Politics* (2 volumes. Cleveland, 1917); Clarence E. Carter, *Great Britain and the Illinois Country, 1763-1774* (Washington, D. C., 1910).

31. For the scattered but important settlements already made, see Chapter III.

32. See map of Indian Land Cessions, III, and Land Surveys and Land Offices, 117.

33. E. O. Randall, "Location of Site of Ohio Capital," in *Ohio Archaeological and Historical Society Publications*, XXV (1916), 210-34.

34. *Columbus Intelligencer in Liberty Hall and Cincinnati Gazette*, October 21, 1816.

35. Samuel J. Mills and Daniel Smith, *Report of a Missionary Tour Through that Part of the United States Which Lies West of the Alleghany Mountains* . . . (Andover, Mass., 1815), 15.

36. *Executive Journal of Indiana Territory, 1800-1816 (Indiana Historical Society Publications*, 111, No. 3, Indianapolis, 1895), 82. Charles Kettleborough (ed.), *Constitution Making in Indiana* . . . (3 volumes. *Indiana Historical Collections*, I, II, XVII, Indianapolis, 1916, 1930), I, 69.

37. Clarence W. Alvord, *The Illinois Country, 1673-1818 (Centennial History of Illinois*, Volume I, Springfield, 1920), 454.

38. Until 1839 Morse's school geography printed across the interior of Michigan, "interminable swamp." Carl E. Pray, "A Historic Michigan Road," in *Michigan History Magazine*, XI (1927), 326.

I · X

Alexis de Tocqueville

THE REAL ADVANTAGES DERIVED BY AMERICAN SOCIETY FROM DEMOCRATIC GOVERNMENT

Before beginning this chapter I must remind the reader of something already mentioned several times in the course of this book.

The political constitution of the United States seems to me to be one of the forms that democracy can give to its government, but I do not think that American institutions are the only ones, or the best, that a democratic nation might adopt.

So in pointing out the blessings which the Americans derive from democratic government, I am far from claiming or from thinking that such advantages can only be obtained by the same laws.

THE GENERAL TENDENCY OF LAWS UNDER
THE SWAY OF AMERICAN DEMOCRACY AND
THE INSTINCTS OF THOSE WHO APPLY THEM

The vices of democracy are immediately apparent. Its advantages only become clear in the long run. American democracy is often clumsy, but the general tendency of its laws is advantageous. Under American democracy public officials have no permanent interests differing from those of the majority. The results of this.

The vices and weaknesses of democratic government are easy to see; they can be proved by obvious facts, whereas its salutary influence is exercised in an imperceptible and almost secret way. Its defects strike one at first glance, but its good qualities are revealed only in the long run.

The laws of American democracy are often defective or incomplete; they sometimes violate acquired rights or sanction dangerous ones; even if they were good, their frequent changes would be a great evil. All this is seen at first glance.

How, then, do the American republics maintain themselves and prosper?

In laws one should make a careful distinction between the aim sought and the way in which they progress toward that aim, and between their absolute and their relative excellence.

Suppose that the lawgiver's aim is to favor the interests of the few at the expense of the many; his measures are so combined as to accomplish the proposed aim in the shortest time and with least possible effort. The law will be well contrived, but its object bad; its very efficiency will make it the more dangerous.

In general, the laws of a democracy tend toward the good of the greatest number, for they spring from the majority of all the citizens, which may be mistaken but which cannot have an interest contrary to its own.

But those of an aristocracy do tend to monopolize power and wealth in the hands of a few, because in the nature of things an aristocracy is a minority.

One can therefore say in general terms that democracy's aim in its legislation is more beneficial to humanity than that of aristocracy in its lawmaking.

But there its advantages end.

An aristocracy is infinitely more skillful in the science of legislation than democracy can ever be. Being master of itself, it is not subject to transitory impulses; it has far-sighted plans and knows how to let them mature until the favorable opportunity offers. An aristocracy moves forward intelligently; it knows how to make the collective force of all its laws converge on one point at one time.

A democracy is not like that; its laws are almost always defective or untimely.

Therefore the measures of democracy are more imperfect than those of an aristocracy; it often unintentionally works against itself; but its aim is more beneficial.

Suppose a society so organized by nature or by its constitution that it can tolerate the passing effect of bad laws and can without disaster await the result of the *general tendency* of its laws, and in such a case you will appreciate that democratic government, for all its faults, is yet the best suited of all to make society prosper.

That is just what does happen in the United States; I here repeat what I have described elsewhere: the great privilege of the Americans is to be able to make retrievable mistakes.

I would say something similar about the public officials.

It is easy to see that American democracy often makes mistakes in the choice of men to whom it entrusts power, but it is not so easy to say why the state prospers in their hands.

Notice first that in a democratic state, though the rulers be less honest or less capable, the governed are more enlightened and more alert.

In democracies the people, constantly occupied as they are with their affairs and jealous of their rights, prevent their representatives from deviating from a general line indicated by their interests.

Note also that although a democratic magistrate may use his power worse than another, he generally holds it for a shorter time.

But there is a more general and satisfactory reason than any of these.

No doubt it is important for nations that their rulers should possess virtues and talents, but perhaps it is even more important for them that the rulers should not have interests contrary to those of the mass of the governed, for in that case their virtues might become almost useless and their talents disastrous.

I have said that it was important for the rulers not to have interests contrary or different from those of the mass of the ruled. I do not say that they should have interests similar to those of *all* the governed, for I don't suppose that such a thing has ever happened.

No one has yet found a political structure that equally favors the growth and prosperity of all the classes composing society. These classes have formed something like distinct nations within the same nation, and experience has proved it almost as dangerous completely to entrust the fate of all to one of these as it is to make one nation arbiter of the destiny of another. When the rich alone rule, the interests of the poor are always in danger; and when the poor make the law, the interests of the rich run great risks. What, then, is the advantage of democracy? The real advantage of democracy is not, as some have said, to favor the prosperity of all, but only to serve the well-being of the greatest number.

In the United States those who are entrusted with the direction of public affairs are often inferior both in capacity and in morality to those whom an aristocracy might bring to power; but their interest is mingled and identified with that of the majority of their fellow citizens. Hence they may often prove untrustworthy and make great mistakes, but they will never systematically follow a tendency hostile to the majority; they will never turn the government into something exclusive and dangerous.

The bad administration of one magistrate under a democracy is, moreover, an isolated fact that has an influence only during the short period of his tenure of office. Corruption and incapacity are not common interests capable of linking men in any permanent fashion.

A corrupt or incapable magistrate will not combine his efforts with another magistrate's simply because the latter is corrupt or incapable too, and these two men will never work in concert so that corruption or incapacity may flourish among their posterity. Quite the contrary, the ambition and intrigues of the one will help to unmask the other. Generally speaking, in a democracy the vices of a magistrate are altogether personal.

But under aristocratic rule public men have a class interest which, though it sometimes agrees with that of the majority, is more often distinct therefrom. That interest forms a lasting common link between them; it invites them to unite and combine their endeavors toward an aim which is not always the happiness of the greatest number. It not only forms a link between the actual rulers but also unites them with a considerable section of the ruled, for many of the citizens, without having any office, form part of the aristocracy.

The aristocratic magistrate therefore finds constant support within society, as well as from the government.

This common objective which in aristocracies unites the magistrates with the interests of one portion of their contemporaries identifies them also, so to say, with that of future generations. They work for the future as well as for the present. Hence the aristocratic magistrate is impelled at the same time and in the same direction by the passions of the ruled, by his own, and, I might almost say, by the passions of those who come after him.

How can we be surprised if he puts up no resistance? So in aristocracies one often sees class spirit carrying away even those who are not corrupted by it and finds that they are unconsciously shaping society gradually to their convenience and that of their descendants.

I do not know if there has ever been another aristocracy as liberal as that of England or one that has uninterruptedly furnished the government with men so worthy and so enlightened.

Nevertheless, it is easy to see that in English legislation the poor man's welfare has in the end often been sacrificed to that of the rich, and the rights of the greatest number have been sacrificed to the privileges of the few; and so England now contains within herself every extreme of human fate, and one there finds wretchedness almost as great as the greatness of her power and glory.

In the United States, where public officials have no class interest to promote, the general and continuous course of the government is beneficial, although the rulers are often inept and sometimes contemptible.

There is therefore at the bottom of democratic institutions some hidden tendency which often makes men promote the general prosperity, in spite of their vices and their mistakes, whereas in aristocratic institutions there is sometimes a secret bias which, in spite of talents and virtues, leads men to contribute to the afflictions of their fellows. In this way it may come about that under aristocratic governments public men do evil without intending it, and in democracies they bring about good results of which they have never thought.

PUBLIC SPIRIT IN THE UNITED STATES

> *Instinctive patriotism. Well-considered patriotism Their different characteristics. Why nations must strive with all their strength toward the second when the first has disappeared. The efforts of the Americans to achieve this. Individual interest intimately linked to that of the country.*

There is a patriotism which mainly springs from the disinterested, undefinable, and unpondered feeling that ties a man's heart to the place where he was born. This instinctive love is mingled with a taste for old habits, respect for ancestors, and memories of the past; those who feel it love their country as one loves one's father's house. They love the peace they enjoy there; they are attached to the quiet habits they have formed; they are attached to the memories it recalls; and they even find a certain attraction in living there in obedience. This same patriotism is often also exalted by religious zeal, and then it works wonders. It is itself a sort of religion; it does not reason, but believes, feels, and acts. Some nations have in a sense personified their country and see the monarch as standing for it. Hence they have transferred some of the feelings of patriotism to him, and they boast of his triumphs and are proud of his power. There was a time under the old monarchy when the French experienced a sort of joy in surrendering themselves irrevocably to the arbitrary will of their monarch and said with pride: "We live under the most powerful king in the world."

Like all unpondered passions, this patriotism impels men to great ephemeral efforts, but not to continuous endeavor. Having saved the state in time of crisis, it often lets it decay in time of peace.

When peoples are still simple in their mores and firm in their belief, when society gently rests on an ancient order of things whose legitimacy is not contested, then that instinctive patriotism prevails.

There is also another sort of patriotism more rational than that; less generous, perhaps less ardent, but more creative and more lasting, it is engendered by enlightenment, grows by the aid of laws and the exercise of rights, and in the end becomes, in a sense, mingled with personal interest. A man understands the influence which his country's well-being has on his own; he knows the law allows him to contribute to the production of this well-being, and he takes an interest in his country's prosperity, first as a thing useful to him and then as something he has created.

But sometimes there comes a time in the life of nations when old customs are changed, mores destroyed, beliefs shaken, and the prestige of memories has vanished, but when nonetheless enlightenment has remained incomplete and political rights are ill-assured or restricted. Then men see their country only by a weak and doubtful light; their patriotism is not centered on the soil, which in their eyes is just inanimate earth, nor on the customs of their ancestors, which they have been taught to regard as a yoke, nor on religion, which they doubt, nor on the laws, which they do not make, nor on the lawgiver, whom they fear and scorn. So they find their country nowhere, recognizing neither its own nor any borrowed features, and they retreat into a narrow and unenlightened egoism. Such men escape from prejudices without recognizing the rule of reason; they have neither the instinctive patriotism of a monarchy nor the reflective patriotism of a republic, but have come to a halt between the two amid confusion and misery.

What can be done in such a condition? Retreat. But nations do not return to the feelings of their youth any more than men return to the innocent tastes of their infancy; they may regret them, but they cannot bring them back to life.

Therefore it is essential to march forward and hasten to make the people see that individual interest is linked to that of the country, for disinterested patriotism has fled beyond recall.

Certainly I am far from claiming that in order to reach this result the exercise of political rights must immediately be granted to every man; but I do say that the most powerful way, and perhaps the only remaining way, in which to interest men in their country's fate is to make them take a share in its government. In our day it seems to me that civic spirit is inseparable from the exercise of political rights, and I think that henceforward in Europe the numbers of the citizens will be found to increase or diminish in proportion to the extension of those rights.

How is it that in the United States, where the inhabitants arrived but yesterday in the land they occupy, whither they brought with them neither customs nor memories, where they meet for the first time without knowing each other, where, to say it in one word, the instinct of country can hardly exist — how does it come about that each man is as interested in the affairs of his township, of his canton, and of the whole state as he is in his own affairs? It is because each man in his sphere takes an active part in the government of society.

The common man in the United States has understood the influence of the general prosperity on his own happiness, an idea so simple but nevertheless so little understood by the people. Moreover, he is accustomed to regard that prosperity as his own work. So he sees the public fortune as his own, and he works for the good of the state, not only from duty or from pride, but, I dare almost say, from greed.

There is no need to study the institutions or the history of the Americans to recognize the truth of what has just been said, for their mores are sufficient evidence of it. The American, taking part in everything that is done in his country, feels a duty to defend anything criticized there, for it is not only his country that is being attacked, but himself; hence one finds that his national pride has recourse to every artifice and descends to every childishness of personal vanity.

Nothing is more annoying in the ordinary intercourse of life than this irritable patriotism of the Americans. A foreigner will gladly agree to praise much in their country, but he would like to be allowed to criticize something, and that he is absolutely refused.

So America is the land of freedom where, in order not to offend anybody, the foreigner may speak freely neither about individuals nor about the state, neither about the ruled nor about the rulers, neither about public undertakings nor about private ones — indeed, about nothing that one comes across, except perhaps the climate and the soil, but yet one meets Americans ready to defend both of these, as if they had a share in forming them.

In our day we must make up our minds and dare to choose between the patriotism of all and the government of the few, for one cannot combine at the same time the social strength and activity given by the first with the guarantees of tranquility sometimes provided by the second.

THE IDEA OF RIGHTS IN THE UNITED STATES

No great people is without an idea of rights. How such a conception can be imparted to a nation. Respect for rights in the United States. Source of that respect.

Next to virtue as a general idea, nothing, I think, is so beautiful as that of rights, and indeed the two ideas are mingled. The idea of rights is nothing but the conception of virtue applied to the world of politics.

By means of the idea of rights men have defined the nature of license and of tyranny. Guided by its light, we can each of us be independent without arrogance and obedient without servility. When a man submits to force, that surrender debases him; but when he accepts the recognized right of a fellow mortal to give him orders, there is a sense in which he rises above the giver of the commands. No man can be great without virtue, nor any nation great without respect for rights; one might almost say that without it there can be no society, for what is a combination of rational and intelligent beings held together by force alone?

I keep asking myself how, in our day, this conception may be taught to mankind and made, so to say, palpable to their senses; and I find one only, namely, to give them all the peaceful use of certain rights. One can see how this works among children, who are men except in strength and in experience; when a baby first begins to move among things outside himself, instinct leads him to make use of anything his hands can grasp; he has no idea of other people's property, not even that it exists; but as he is instructed in the value of things and discovers that he too may be despoiled, he becomes more circumspect, and in the end is led to respect for others that which he wishes to be respected for himself.

As for a child with his toys, so is it later for a man with all his belongings. Why is it that in America, the land par excellence of democracy, no one makes that outcry against property in general that often echoes through Europe? Is there any need to explain? It is because there are no proletarians in America. Everyone, having some possession to defend, recognizes the right to property in principle.

It is the same in the world of politics. The American man of the people has conceived a high idea of political rights because he has some; he does not attack those of others, in order that his own may not be violated. Whereas the corresponding man in Europe would be prejudiced against all authority, even the highest, the American uncomplainingly obeys the lowest of his officials.

This truth is illustrated even in the smallest details of a nation's life. In France there are few pleasures exclusively reserved for the higher classes of society; the poor man is admitted almost everywhere where the rich can go, so one finds him behaving decently and with proper consideration for pleasures in which he shares. In England, where enjoyment is the privilege of the rich, who also monopolize power, people complain that when a poor man does furtively steal into the exclusive haunts of the rich he has a taste for causing pointless damage there. Why be surprised at that? Trouble has been taken to see that he has nothing to lose.

Democratic government makes the idea of political rights penetrate right down to the least of citizens, just as the division of property puts the general idea of property rights within reach of all. That, in my view, is one of its greatest merits.

I am not asserting it to be an easy matter to teach all men to make use of political rights; I only say that when that can happen, the results are important.

And I would add that if ever there was a century in which such an attempt should be made, that century is ours.

Do you not see that religions are growing weak and that the conception of the sanctity of rights is vanishing? Do you not see that mores are changing and that the moral conception of rights is being obliterated with them? Do you not notice how on all sides beliefs are giving way to arguments, and feelings to calculations? If amid this universal collapse you do not succeed in linking the idea of rights to personal interest, which provides the only stable point in the human heart, what other means will be left to you to govern the world, if not fear?

So, then, when I am told that laws are feeble and the governed turbulent, that passions are lively and virtue powerless, and that in this situation one must not dream of increasing the rights of democracy, I answer that it is for these very reasons that one must consider doing so, and in truth, I think the governments have an even greater interest in doing this than has society, for governments perish but society cannot die. However, I do not wish to press the example of America too far.

In America the people were invested with political rights at a time when it was difficult for them to make ill use of them because the citizens were few and their mores simple. As they have grown more powerful, the Americans have not appreciably increased the powers of democracy; rather they have extended its domain.

There can be no doubt that the moment when political rights are granted to a people who have till then been deprived of them is a time of crisis, a crisis which is often necessary but always dangerous.

A child may kill when he does not understand the value of life; he carries off other people's property before he knows that his own may be snatched from him. The man of the people, at the moment when political rights are granted to him, is much in the same position with respect to those rights as is a child faced by the whole of nature, and it is then that famous phrase applies: *homo puer robustus.*

This truth can be tested even in America. Those states in which the citizens have longest enjoyed their rights are those in which they still best know how to use them.

It cannot be repeated too often: nothing is more fertile in marvels than the art of being free, but nothing is harder than freedom's apprenticeship. The same is not true of despotism. Despotism often presents itself as the repairer of all the ills suffered, the support of just rights, defender of the oppressed, and founder of order. Peoples are lulled to sleep by the temporary prosperity it engenders, and when they do wake up, they are wretched. But liberty is generally born in stormy weather, growing with difficulty amid civil discords, and only when it is already old does one see the blessings it has brought.

RESPECT FOR LAW IN THE UNITED STATES

American respect for law. Paternal affection they feel for it. Personal interest of everybody in increasing the law's strength.

It is not always feasible to call on the whole people, either directly or indirectly, to take its part in lawmaking, but no one can deny that when that can be done the law derives great authority therefrom. This popular origin, though often damaging to the wisdom and quality of legislation, gives it peculiar strength.

There is prodigious force in the expression of the wills of a whole people. When it stands out in broad daylight, even the imagination of those who would like to contest it is somehow smothered.

Parties are will aware of this truth.

For that reason, whenever possible they cast doubts on the majority's validity. Having failed to gain a majority from those who voted, they claim it among those who abstained from voting, and if that fails them, they claim a majority among those who have no right to vote.

In the United States, except for slaves, servants, and paupers fed by the township, no one is without a vote and, hence, an indirect share in lawmaking. Therefore those who would like to attack the laws are forced to adopt ostensibly one of two courses: they must either change the nation's opinion or trample its wishes under foot.

There is a second reason, too, more direct and powerful in its effect, namely, that every American feels a sort of personal interest in obeying the laws, for a man who is not today one of the majority party may be so tomorrow, and so he may soon be demanding for laws of his choosing that respect which he now professes for the lawgiver's will. Therefore, however annoying a law may be, the American will submit to it, not only as the work of the majority but also as his own doing; he regards it as a contract to which he is one of the parties.

So in the United States there is no numerous and perpetually turbulent crowd regarding the law as a natural enemy to fear and to suspect. On the contrary, one is bound to notice that all classes show great confidence in their country's legislation, feeling a sort of paternal love for it.

I am wrong in saying all classes. As in America, the European ladder of power has been turned upside down; the wealthy find themselves in a position analogous to that of the poor in Europe: it is they who often mistrust the law. As I have said elsewhere, the real advantage of democratic government is not that it guarantees the interests of all, as is sometimes claimed, but just that it does protect those of the greatest number. In the United States, where the poor man rules, the rich have always some fear that he may abuse his power against them.

This state of mind among the wealthy may produce a silent discontent, but it creates no violent trouble for society, for the same reason which prevents the rich man from trusting the lawgiver also prevents him from defying his commands. Because he is rich he does not make the law, and because of his wealth he does not dare to break it. Among civilized nations it is generally only those with nothing to lose who revolt. Hence, though democratic laws may not always deserve respect, they are almost always respected, for those who usually break the laws cannot fail to obey those they have made and from which they profit, and those citizens who might have an interest in infringing them are impelled both by character and by circumstance to submit to the lawgiver's will, whatever it may be. Moreover, in America the people obey the law not only because it is their work but also because they can change it if by any chance it does injure them; they submit to it primarily as a self-imposed evil, and secondly as a passing one.

ACTIVITY PREVAILING IN ALL PARTS OF THE
POLITICAL BODY IN THE UNITED STATES;
THE INFLUENCE THEREBY EXERTED ON SOCIETY

political activity prevailing in the United States is harder to conceive than the freedom and equality found there. The continual feverish activity of the legislatures is only an episode and an extension of a movement that is universal. How difficult an American finds it to be occupied with his own business only. Political agitation spills over into civil society. The industrial activity of the Americans is in part due to this. Indirect advantages derived by society from democratic government.

When one passes from a free country into another which is not so, the contrast is very striking: there, all is activity and bustle; here all seems calm and immobile. In the former, betterment and progress are the questions of the day; in the latter, one might suppose that society, having acquired every blessing, longs for nothing but repose in which to enjoy them. Nevertheless, the country which is in such a rush to attain happiness is generally richer and more prosperous than the one that seems contented with its lot. And considering them one by one, it is hard to understand how this one daily discovers so many new needs, while the other seems conscious of so few.

While this remark applies to free countries that have preserved the forms of monarchy and to those dominated by an aristocracy, it is even more true of democratic republics. In them it is not only one section of the people it undertakes to better the state of society, for the whole nation is concerned therewith. It is not just the necessities and comforts of one class that must be provided for, but those of all classes at once.

It is not impossible to conceive the immense freedom enjoyed by the Americans, and one can also form an idea of their extreme equality, but the political activity prevailing in the United States is something one could never understand unless one had seen it.

No sooner do you set foot on American soil than you find yourself in a sort of tumult; a confused clamor rises on every side, and a thousand voices are heard at once, each expressing some social requirements. All around you everything is on the move: here the people of a district are assembled to discuss the possibility of building a church; there they are busy choosing a representative; further on, the delegates of a district are hurrying to town to consult about some local improvements; elsewhere it's the village farmers who have left their furrows to discuss the plan for a road or a school. One group of citizens assembles for the sole object of announcing that they disapprove of the government's course, while others unite to proclaim that the men in office are the fathers of their country. And here is yet another gathering which regards drunkenness as the main source of ills in the state and has come to enter into a solemn undertaking to give an example of temperance.[1]

The great political movement which keeps American legislatures in a state of continual agitation, and which alone is noticed from outside, is only an episode and a sort of extension of the universal movement, which begins in the lowest ranks of the people and thence spreads successively through all classes of citizens. No one could work harder to be happy.

It is hard to explain the place filled by political concerns in the life of an American. To take a hand in the government of society and to talk about it is his most important business and, so to say, the only pleasure he knows. That is obvious even in the most trivial habits of his life; even the women often go to public meetings and forget household cares while they listen to political speeches. For them clubs to some extent take the place of theaters. An American does not know how to converse, but he argues; he does not talk, but expatiates. He always speaks to you as if addressing a meeting, and if he happens to get excited, he will say "Gentlemen" when addressing an audience of one.

The inhabitant in some countries shows a sort of repugnance in accepting the political rights granted to him by the law; it strikes him as a waste of time to spend it on communal interests, and he likes to shut himself up in a narrow egoism, of which four ditches with hedges on top define the precise limits.

But if an American should be reduced to occupying himself with his own affairs, at that moment half his existence would be snatched from him; he would feel it as a vast void in his life and would become incredibly unhappy.[2]

I am convinced that if despotism ever came to be established in the United States it would find it even more difficult to overcome the habits that have sprung from freedom than to conquer the love of freedom itself.

That constantly renewed agitation introduced by democratic government into political life passes, then, into civil society. Perhaps, taking everything into consideration, that is the greatest advantage of democratic government, and I praise it much more on account of what it causes to be done than for what it does.

It is incontestible that the people often manage public affairs very badly, but their concern therewith is bound to extend their mental horizon and shake them out of the rut of ordinary routine. A man of the people, when asked to share the task of governing society, acquires a certain self-esteem. Since he then has power, the brains of very enlightened people are put at his disposal. Constant efforts are made to enlist his support, and he learns from a thousand different efforts to deceive him. In politics he takes a part in undertakings he has not thought of, and they give him a general taste for enterprise. Daily new improvements to communal property are suggested to him, and that starts him wishing to improve his own. He may not be more virtuous or happier than his forebears, but he is more enlightened and active. I have no doubt that democratic institutions, combined with the physical nature of the land, are the indirect reason, and not, as is often claimed, the direct one, for the prodigious industrial expansion seen in the United States. It is not the laws' creation, but the people have learned to achieve it by making the laws.

When the enemies of democracy claim that a single man does his appointed task better than the government of all, I think they are right. There is more consistency in one man's rule than in that of a multitude, assuming equal enlightenment on either side; one man is more persevering, has more idea of the whole problem, attends more closely to details, and is a better judge of men. Anyone who denies that either has never seen a democratic republic or bases his view on too few examples. Democracy, even when local circumstances and the character of the people allow it to maintain itself, does not display a regular or methodical form of government. That is true. Democratic freedom does not carry its undertakings through as perfectly as an intelligent despotism would; it often abandons them before it has reaped the profit, or embarks on perilous ones; but in the long run it produces more; each thing is less well done, but more things are done. Under its sway it is not especially the things accomplished by the public administration that are great, but rather those things done without its help and beyond its sphere. Democracy does not provide a people with the most skillful of governments, but it does that which the most skillful government often cannot do: it spreads throughout the body social a restless activity, superabundant force, and energy never found elsewhere, which, however little favored by circumstance, can do wonders. Those are its true advantages.

In this century, when the destinies of the Christian world seem in suspense, some hasten to assail democracy as a hostile power while it is still growing; others already worship this new deity emerging from chaos. But both parties have an imperfect knowledge of the object of their hate or their desire; they fight in the dark and strike at random.

What do you expect from society and its government? We must be clear about that.

Do you wish to raise mankind to an elevated and generous view of the things of this world? Do you want to inspire men with a certain scorn of material goods? Do you hope to engender deep convictions and prepare the way for acts of profound devotion?

Are you concerned with refining mores, elevating manners, and causing the arts to blossom? Do you desire poetry, renown, and glory?

Do you set out to organize a nation so that it will have a powerful influence over all others? Do you expect it to attempt great enterprises and, whatever be the result of its efforts, to leave a great mark on history?

If in your view that should be the main object of men in society, do not support democratic government; it surely will not lead you to that goal.

But if you think it profitable to turn man's intellectual and moral activity toward the necessities of physical life and use them to produce well-being, if you think that reason is more use to men than genius, if your object is not to create heroic virtues but rather tranquil habits, if you would rather contemplate vices than crimes and prefer fewer transgressions at the cost of fewer splendid deeds, if in place of a brilliant society you are content to live in one that is prosperous, and finally, if in your view the main object of government is not to achieve the greatest strength or glory for the nation as a whole but to provide for every individual therein the utmost well-being, protecting him as far as possible from all afflictions, then it is good to make conditions equal and to establish a democratic government.

But if there is no time left to make a choice, and if a force beyond human control is already carrying you along regardless of your desires toward one of these types of government, then at least seek to derive from it all the good that it can do; understanding its good instincts as well as its evil inclinations, try to restrain the latter and promote the former.

ENDNOTES

1. Temperance societies are associations whose members undertake to abstain from strong drink. At the time of my visit temperance societies already counted more than 270,000 members, and consequently, in the state of Pennsylvania alone the consumption of strong liquors had fallen by 500,000 gallons a year.

2. The same fact was already noted at Rome under the first Caesars. Montesquieu remarks somewhere that nothing equals the despair of certain Roman citizens who after the excitements of a political existence suddenly return to the calm of private life.

X

Allan Nevins and Henry Steele Commager

THE WEST AND DEMOCRACY

THE MOVING FRONTIER

ONE OF THE forces which did most to shape American life from the beginning was the frontier, which may be defined as the border area whose sparse population (not more than six to the square mile) was engaged chiefly in clearing and breaking land and building homes. Moving across the continent as population advanced from the Atlantic to the edge of the Great Plains, it profoundly affected the American character. It was more than a line — it was a social process. It encouraged individual initiative; it made for political and economic democracy; it roughened manners; it broke down conservatism; it bred a spirit of local self-determination coupled with respect for national authority.

When we think of the frontier we think of the West. But the Atlantic coastal strip was the first frontier and long contained frontier areas; Maine, which drew forty thousand settlers from older New England in 1790-1800, was frontier country for a generation after the Revolution. The second frontier was the region about the headwaters of the coastal rivers and just over the Appalachians. The close of the Revolution found the border in western New York, where two capitalists in 1787 obtained title to six million acres of wild lands; in the Wyoming Valley of Pennsylvania, where Connecticut settlers established homes; about Pittsburgh, which in 1792 had 130 families and "36 Mechanics"; in the eastern Tennessee area, where in 1784 independent-minded pioneers organized the short-lived "State of Franklin"; and in upland Georgia. Then by 1800 the Mississippi and Ohio valleys were becoming a third great frontier region. "Hi-o, away we go, Floating down the river on the O-hi-o," became the song of thousands of emigrants. In the spring after the writing of the Constitution, Rufus Putnam had taken the first emigrants westward to found Marietta on the northern bank of the Ohio, thus opening an area of about two million acres transferred by Congress to the Ohio Company. That same year another group of land speculators founded Cincinnati. Population was meanwhile pouring into Kentucky and Tennessee with startling rapidity. The first year after peace, ten thousand settlers entered Kentucky; and the first national census in 1790 gave it and Tennessee together a population of over a hundred thousand.

Without pause the westward stream flowed over the whole Northwest and Southwest. By 1796 Kentucky and Tennessee were full-fledged states, and Ohio, with a belt of settled lands along the Pennsylvania border and Ohio River, was about to become one; by 1820 Indiana and Illinois, in the Northwest, Louisiana, Alabama, and Mississippi in the Southwest, were all states. The first frontier had been tied closely to Europe; the second was tied to the coast settlements; but the Mississippi Valley was independent, and its people looked West rather than East.

THE FRONTIER SETTLERS

Naturally the frontier settlers were a varied body of men, but early observers distinguish three main groups. In the van of emigration marched the hunter or trapper. An English traveler named Fordham pithily described the wilder sort of pioneer, usually unmarried:

196

A daring, hardy race of men, who live in miserable cabins, which they fortify in time of war with the Indians, who they hate but much resemble in dress and manners. They are unpolished but hospitable, kind to strangers, honest and trustworthy. They raise a little Indian corn, pumpkins, hogs, and sometimes have a cow or two, and two or three horses belonging to each family. But the rifle is their principal means of support.

When they heard the sound of a neighbor's gun, it was time to move on. Fenimore Cooper has given a good picture of the pioneer hunter in Natty Bumppo, and of backwoods life in *The Prairie*. These men were dexterous with the ax, rifle, snare, and fishing line; they blazed the trails, built the first log cabins, held back the Indians, and so made way for a second group.

This second body Fordham describes as the first true settlers, "a mixed set of hunters and farmers." Instead of a cabin, they built a "log house," which had glass windows, a good chimney, and partitioned rooms, and was as comfortable as an English farm cottage; instead of using a spring they sank a well. An industrious man would rapidly clear land of timber, burning the wood for potash and letting the stumps decay. Growing his own grain, vegetables and fruit, ranging the woods for venison, wild turkeys, and honey, fishing the nearest streams, looking after some cattle and hogs, he would worry little over the loneliness and roughness of his life. The more enterprising bought large tracts of the cheap land on the theory that it was wise, as a character in Edward Eggleston's *Hoosier Schoolmaster* put it, to "git a plenty while you're agittin' "; then, as land values rose, they sold their acres and moved westward. Thus they gave way to the third group, the most important of all.

The third body included not only farmers but also doctors, lawyers, storekeepers, editors, preachers, mechanics, politicians, and land speculators — all the materials to furnish the fabric of a vigorous society. The farmers were the most important. They intended to stay all their lives where they settled and hoped their children would stay after them. They built larger barns than their predecessors and then sounder brick or frame houses. They constructed better fences, brought in improved livestock, plowed the land more skillfully, and sowed more productive seed. Some of them erected flour mills, sawmills, or distilleries. They laid out good highways, built churches and schools. As towns grew up, many of this third group, as bankers, merchants, or land dealers, became men of wealth. In short, they represented the more enduring forces in American civilization. So rapidly did the West grow that almost incredible transformations were accomplished within a few years by this third wave. Chicago in 1830 was merely an unpromising trading village with a fort; before some of its first settlers died it was one of the largest and richest cities in the world.

Many different peoples mingled their blood in the new West. Farmers of the upland South were prominent, and from this stock sprang Abraham Lincoln and Jefferson Davis, born in Kentucky log cabins in the same year. Hardheaded Scotch-Irish, thrifty Pennsylvania Germans, enterprising Yankees, and men of other origins played their part. All these people had two traits in common — individualism and democracy. By 1830 more than half the Americans had been brought up in an environment in which Old World traditions and conventions were absent or very weak. Men in the West had to stand on their own feet. They were valued not for family, inherited money, or years of schooling, but, like the castaways in Barrie's *The Admirable Crichton*, for what they could do. People could get farms for a price not beyond reach of any thrifty person; government land after 1820, as we have seen, could be obtained for $1.25 an acre, and after 1862 for merely settling on it. They could easily get the tools to work it. Then, as Horace Greeley said, they could "grow up with the country." This equality of economic opportunity bred a sense of social and political equality and gave natural leaders a chance to come quickly to the front. It should be added that the sea was practically another frontier in its effect upon American character. Vessels were small and had small crews, while many fishing ships and whalers were worked on a partnership basis. Initiative, courage, individual vigor, and hard sense were the requirements of a good pioneer hunter, frontier farmer, or Eastern sailor alike.

FRONTIER VIRTUES AND VICES

By contagion and example this democracy and individualism became marked traits on the cities of the young republic. The upright independence that the Englishman William Cobbett lauded immediately struck European visitors to New York and Philadelphia. These observers noted that workmen did not tip their hats and say "sir" to earn a shilling. The very porters accepted a job with the attitude of men conferring a favor. Cobbett mentioned approvingly that American servants wore no livery and usually ate with the family and were called "help." He saw only two beggars in America, and both were foreigners. One of Ralph Waldo Emerson's most truly American essays is that on "Self-Reliance." He speaks of the typical Yankee of the day who, going West, was by turns farmer, storekeeper, land dealer, lawyer, Congressman, and judge, a jack-of-all-trades, always landing on his feet. It was not an overdrawn portrait. One of the ablest Civil War generals, W. T. Sherman, was in turn cadet, soldier in the Mexican War, banker in San Francisco, lawyer in Leavenworth, farm manager on the Kansas frontier, head of a military college in Louisiana, and then soldier again.

But if the frontier fostered virtues, it also bred vices. The frontier folk were in general unruly, impatient of discipline, and too aggressively self-confident — too "brash." Many of the military defeats of the War of 1812 were attributable to a frontier dislike of training and discipline. Frontier-trained Americans were inclined to do everything with hurried crudity. So many tasks needed performing that careful finish seemed a waste of time. Americans hurried up rough frame houses instead of durable stone and brick structures, they built rough roads, they made makeshift bridges, they gutted rather than cultivated the soil. New York had fire bells clanging all night because its houses burned like tinder, while in 1836 two of the city's largest business buildings actually collapsed. Railroad collisions and steamboat explosions were frequent. Naturally, little attention was paid to manners or culture; the frontier had no leisure for them. And worst of all, frontier life was marked by a deplorable amount of outright criminality. Some of the scum of society swirled out to the border. Men developed ungovernable tempers and had a taste for settling their quarrels with fists or pistols. Officers of justice had to possess iron nerve and a quick trigger finger.

THE INDIAN WARS

The undisciplined character of the frontiersmen had especially tragic consequences in their dealings with the Indians. They constantly encroached on Indian lands in defiance of treaty; they destroyed the game on which the Indians depended for food and clothing; and many were ready to slay any redskin on sight. When the Indians tried to defend themselves, war ensued. Of course, the savages were often aggressors, but the inexorable westward thrust of the whites was the principal cause of the many conflicts. The most bloodcurdling wars were with the Creeks in the South, where Andrew Jackson won a bloody victory; with the Seminoles in the Florida swamps and thickets; and with Tecumseh's followers in Indiana.

Young Abraham Lincoln was a captain in the Black Hawk War, an especially brutal affair. Some spokesmen for Black Hawk's tribe, the Sauk and Fox Indians, had ceded to the government their title to about fifty million acres. The chief and a great part of the tribe denied the validity of this cession. Before a threat of force Black Hawk withdrew from his corn lands in Illinois to the west bank of the Mississippi. But his tribe suffered from hunger, and next spring they recrossed the river in order to join the friendly Winnebagos in Wisconsin and raise corn there. They had a childlike faith that their amicable intentions would be understood. But the whites immediately attacked them; Black Hawk retreated, making offers of peace, which the two thousand militia ignored. His despairing followers were driven through southern Wisconsin to the Mississippi again, where men, women, and children were mercilessly cut to pieces as they tried to cross. "It was a horrid sight," wrote one rifleman, "to witness little children, wounded and suffering the most excruciating pain, although they were of the savage enemy." This was the frontiersman at his worst.

The idea of a general removal of the Eastern Indians to

the Great Plains beyond the Mississippi, long thought to be uninhabitable by white men, was officially adopted under Monroe and energetically pursued under Jackson. Congress authorized the President to exchange lands in the West for the older Indian holdings. An "Indian Country" was created, running at first from Canada to Texas. To this area the Northern Indians were removed without much difficulty. But in the South, where the tribes were larger and stronger, the Indians offered a stubborn resistance, and the result was tragic. The so-called Five Civilized Tribes — Creeks, Choctaws, Chickasaws, Cherokees, and Seminoles — loved their homes. Many of them, especially the Creeks and Cherokees, had learned to be thrifty farmers, had built good houses, acquired herds of cattle, erected gristmills, and educated their children in missionary schools. They clung to their lands to the last, some being driven away only by force. Traveling in great part by wagon and on foot, they suffered from hunger, disease, and exposure, and many died. By 1840, however, nearly all the Indians east of the Mississippi had been taken to their new homes in what is now Oklahoma.

This removal facilitated the complete peopling of the Mississippi Valley, the richest and most distinctive part of the country. Wisconsin, the last state east of the Mississippi, was admitted in 1848. Already a tier of states had been erected west of the river, for after Missouri's entry in 1821, Arkansas became a state in 1836 and Iowa ten years later, while Minnesota Territory was organized in 1849. The panic of 1837, in large part a product of overdevelopment in the West, checked the onward movement only briefly. Cyrus H. McCormick, inventor of the reaper, set up a factory in Chicago in 1847 and began turning out machines that made it easy to cover the Western prairies with grain. Railroad building began and soon threw a mesh of tracks over the level region. In 1854 seventy-four trains a day ran into Chicago, which already boasted itself the largest primary grain market in the world. That year saw the Galena and Chicago Railroad carrying three thousand emigrants a month to Iowa, while other thousands traveled by road. Germans, Scandinavians, and Britons helped fill the upper valley and took homes in Texas or Arkansas as well. An English observer was startled in 1854 to find St. Paul in far-off Minnesota a city of seven or eight thousand, with four or five hotels, half a dozen good churches, wharves at which three hundred steamers arrived annually, and "good streets with sidewalks, and lofty brick warehouses, and stores, and shops, as well supplied as any in the Union." New Western leaders came into prominence before 1850; such men as Stephen A. Douglas and Abraham Lincoln in Illinois, Thomas Hart Benton and David R. Atchison in Missouri, Jefferson Davis in Mississippi, and Sam Houston, the hero of the Texan War for Independence, in the Lone-Star State.

THE SETTLEMENT OF THE NEARER WEST

A major part was played in the development of the Mississippi Valley by several great avenues of transportation. The first main artery to the West was the Cumberland Road, begun in 1811 and built for the most part with Federal money. Running from Cumberland, Maryland, over the mountains to Zanesville and Columbus in Ohio, and Terre Haute in Indiana, it was finally pushed on to Vandalia in Illinois. When completed its length was about six hundred miles; sixty feet wide, it had in the center a paved strip of twenty feet constructed on McAdam's principles.

Over this "National Pike" ran the Western mails, with special postage. Inns sprang up at convenient distances. The stream of colonists swelled until in summer passengers were never out of sight. "Hundreds of families are seen migrating to the West with ease and comfort," wrote one observer in 1824. "Drovers from the West with their cattle of almost every description are seen passing eastward seeking a market. Indeed, this great thoroughfare may be compared to a street through some populous city — travelers on foot, on horseback, and in carriages are seen mingling on its paved surface." The road connected at Wheeling with the Ohio River, and this also became a crowded artery of travel. At first it was navigated by flatboats, barges, and arks, which "managed to keep up with the current," and took grain, venison, peltry, pork, and flour down to New Orleans. Nicholas Roosevelt, of a family later famous, built a steamboat which in 1811 ran from Pittsburgh clear through to New Orleans and back, and he soon had many imitators.

The most famous highway to the West was the Erie Canal, which linked the Hudson River and Atlantic Ocean with the Great Lakes, thus providing a water road into the very heart of the continent. Men had dreamed of such a highway even in the eighteenth century. It would enable emigrants and trade to flank the wild Appalachian chain. But the task of digging nearly four hundred miles of canal was so formidable that leaders shied away from it. Finally, the indomitable New Yorker De Witt Clinton carried on a campaign to convert the vision into reality. He gained the governorship, began the work in 1817, and after arduous years saw "Clinton's Ditch" completed. A joyous celebration in 1825 welcomed the first procession of boats, and before an acclaiming multitude Clinton poured a kegful of Lake Erie water into the Atlantic. The canal, which made Buffalo a thriving port, and along which new towns and cities spring up, confirmed New York in her position as leader of American trade and finance.

More important than that, however, was its contribution to Western growth. New Englanders and New Yorkers traveled westward on it in a steady stream. This flood of migrants built up Cleveland, Detroit, and Chicago into bustling cities, and gave great parts of the Northwest a decidedly Yankee flavor. It was responsible in itself for a striking shift in the American population, and it did much to help save the Union, for before the Civil War broke out it had tied the upper Mississippi Valley securely to the North Atlantic states. In this it was aided by Pennsylvania's system of canals. Stung to emulation by the success of Clinton's ditch, the Pennsylvanians spent about forty million dollars upon a transportation system which linked Philadelphia with Pittsburgh, four hundred miles away. In part they used rivers and canals, while they surmounted the high Allegheny ridges by a series of inclined planes, up which boats, cargo, and passengers were hauled by steam. It was a heroic enterprise, and though it almost bankrupted the state, it did a useful work and helped make Pennsylvania one of the leading industrial states.

Population movements tended roughly to follow the parallels of latitude. Alabama and Mississippi were settled mainly by Southerners; Michigan and Wisconsin mainly by Northerners. In Ohio, Indiana, and Illinois, the two currents met, the Southern stream, crossing the Ohio, and the Northern stream, pouring along the Erie Canal and Great Lakes, peaceably mingled. Cities like Columbus, Indianapolis, and Springfield were built up by the two stocks, who intermarried with each other and with European immigrants. Thus of the five men who dominated Illinois politics in the middle period, Abraham Lincoln and Orville Browning came from Kentucky, David Davis from Maryland, Lyman Trumbull from Connecticut, and Stephen A. Douglas from Vermont; whatever their political differences, all were clearly products of this "valley of democracy."

THE TRANS-MISSISSIPPI WEST

When we turn to the vast country west of the Mississippi, we find that its settlement offers an even more colorful story. It was first made known to the nation by the exploring expedition which in l803 Jefferson sent clear to the Pacific under Meriwether Lewis and William Clark, two young Virginians with a great deal of frontier experience. This famous undertaking, which wrote an immortal chapter in geographical discovery, was financed by a Federal appropriation of only $2500! Jefferson had always been keenly interested in the wonders of the West. He had written at length about the Indians, whom he admired, and of the discovery of remains of the mammoth in the Ohio Valley. When he sent Lewis and Clark into the wilderness his object was twofold. In addition to scientific inquiry he expected these men to open up the Missouri River country to American fur traders. At that time the Indians of the area carried their furs into Canada to sell to British dealers. They would find it far easier, Jefferson thought, to send the pelts down the river to American buyers.

Both objects were accomplished. Lewis and Clark, ascending the Missouri, crossing the Rockies and descending the Columbia to the Pacific, accomplished an epic bit of exploration, which has been called "incomparably the most perfect achievement of its kind in the history of the world." They encountered little real danger, for they evaded the warlike Sioux. Covering about two thousand miles on the outward trip in eighteen months, they carefully mapped and described the country. They also laid a basis for American competition with the rich British fur-trading companies and proved the feasibility of an overland route to the Pacific. Immediately after their return Clark helped found the Missouri Fur Company, with a chain of forts on the river. It prospered and grew. And soon afterward John Jacob Astor's energetic American Fur Company entered the Northwestern field. It had hitherto traded chiefly about the Great Lakes, but Astor now resolved to plant a trading post at the mouth of the Columbia. In 1811 a ship of his, called the *Tonquin*, rounded Cape Horn, sailed north, and founded Astoria (about which Washington Irving later wrote a delightful book), while an expedition across the continent by land reached the same point the next year.

This was a good beginning. And the development of the West and its trade was hastened by three picturesque occurrences early in the 1820's. One was the opening of a brisk trade along the Santa Fe Trail to the far Southwest, then in Mexican hands. An enterprising Missourian, William Becknell, got together a trading party of about seventy men, placed goods on horses and mules, and, traveling eight hundred miles over a rough, dangerous country, sold his wares in the Mexican outpost of Santa Fe at a handsome profit. The next year he took wagons on the long journey. Other traders imitated him, and the celebrated Santa Fe Trail was fairly open. The traders who used it encountered many perils, for much of the country was semi-desert, parched by heat and drought; they had to ford difficult rivers; and they were likely to be attacked by hostile Comanche, Arapaho, and Cheyenne Indians. While large groups of eighty or a hundred men were fairly safe, small groups of ten or twenty were likely to be overwhelmed. In time the pioneers beat out an American road which did much to win the Southwest for the republic.

The second remarkable occurrence was the founding of

the Rocky Mountain Fur Company in 1822 by William Ashley, a St. Louis general of militia, who advertised for a hundred young men to ascend the Missouri and remain about its headwaters for one to three years. This was the first company which depended primarily upon trapping by its employees rather than upon trading with the Indians. Among its men were some of the greatest figures in Western exploration, including Kit Carson, who as trapper, hunter, Indian fighter, scout, and guide was to meet a series of adventures which make his life read like a romance, and Jedediah Smith, who was unsurpassed as an explorer. The third occurrence was a military expedition up the Missouri in 1823 to frighten the Arikaras and other fierce Indians into submission. This "Missouri Legion," fitted out by the national government and the St. Louis fur traders combined, made it clear that the United States would protect the fur seekers.

Missionary activity also helped greatly in the penetration of the Far West. The churches had long been active in frontier work, but a curious incident in 1831 gave new stimulus to their zeal. The Indian tribes on the upper Columbia had learned from British traders some rudiments of religion and wished to obtain further information. The Nez Percé sent four leading men to William Clark in St. Louis to ask for the Book of Heaven. When church journals published the story, keen interest was aroused. The Protestants sent several clergymen, with supporting parties, into the far Northwest, and they established a mission in the Willamette Valley and another near the junction of the Snake and Columbia. The leading figure in this effort was the devoted Dr. Marcus Whitman. These missions did a good deal to Christianize the Indians. They set up model farms, showing the savage converts how to build houses, clear the fields, and grow crops. The enthusiastic letters they wrote about the scenery and climate, meanwhile, fired the interest of relatives and friends; and soon annual caravans of settlers were crossing the plains and mountains to the Oregon country.

THE OREGON TRAIL

The first explorers and fur traders who journeyed from the Missouri River to the Columbia vaguely traced a route which

in time became definite as the Oregon Trail and which by
the middle forties was a great highway. Some two thousand
miles in length, it abounded in dangers and difficulties.
Starting at Independence on the Missouri, it traversed the
rolling plains to the Rockies, crossed them by the relatively
low South Pass, and went on through barren and mountain-
ous stretches to Fort Hall on the Snake River, whence the
trail ran through the almost impassable Blue Mountains to
the Umatilla River and down to the Columbia. An alternative route beyond Great Salt Lake led to California. The first
emigrant train to set out for the Pacific was promoted by
John Bidwell and, numbering about eighty men, women,
and children, successfully wound its way through the wild
country to Oregon in 1841. This was the advance guard of an
astonishing movement. In 1843 occurred the "Great Emigration," when not fewer than two hundred families, comprising a thousand people, crossed the plains and mountains,
driving hundreds of cattle with them, and reached their
goal. At two miles an hour the oxteam caravans could make
twenty-five miles on good days, on bad days but five or ten.
In 1845 the human rivulet following the Oregon Trail rose to
a broad stream. More than three thousand people came
into the Willamette Valley that year.

It was an epic migration, this Oregon movement. "Catch
up, catch up!" would ring out the cry at dawn; and the long
lines of covered wagons, marshaled by chosen leaders
would be got into motion. At nightfall they camped in a cir-
cle, the wagons, baggage, and men on the outside, the women, children, and animals within. Sentries were carefully
posted. Food was cooked, clothes were washed, on the way.
Courtships were carried on, children were born, the feeble
died and were buried in unmarked graves. When worn oxen
and mules could no longer drag the heavy wagons, dearly
prized possessions had to be left by the trail. To some who
met Indians, grizzlies, the dreaded cholera, or bitter weather, the trip might be a prolonged agony. Others found it
exhilarating, "It was a long picnic, the changing scenes of
the journey, the animals of the prairie, the Indians, the traders and trappers of the mountain country," wrote one. This
mass movement made Oregon an American community,
doing as much as diplomacy to secure it to the United States

in 1846. It peopled that far-off country so effectively that it was organized as a territory in 1849 and became a full-fledged state only ten years later.

THE MORMONS

By far the most striking and important of the religious settlements in the West was that of the Mormons in Utah. The traditions of individualism, dissent, and evangelism in America had led to the formation of numerous curious sects. Most of them were offshoots of existing bodies. But the Mormons were a wholly new organization. The creator of this Church of Latter-Day Saints was Joseph Smith, a youth of upper New York, who asserted that one day in 1820 he retired to the woods to pray for salvation; that two glorious personages appeared to him and asked him to wait for a full restoration of the Gospel; that in time an angel named Moroni came and told him of a record, engraved on buried plates of gold, containing the sacred history of the ancient inhabitants of North America; and that with the aid of instruments presented by this angel, he translated the history. It was published in 1830 as the *Book of Mormon*. A church was organized in that year and grew rapidly. Its headquarters, after various vicissitudes, were transferred to Illinois. Here the Mormons built on the banks of the Mississippi the prosperous city of Nauvoo, founded a university, and commenced erecting a great temple. They also adopted polygamy. Antipathy to this practice and to their religion, together with economic and political jealousies, caused an outbreak of rioting. A mob took Smith and his brother from the county jail and hanged them; and soon afterward the Mormons, now led by the able Brigham Young were expelled from the state. They crossed the Mississippi, resolved to find peace and safety in the Far West.

The upshot was a remarkable exploit in the settlement of what many thought a desert region. Brigham Young led his people across the plains and into the valley of the Great Salt Lake, where, surrounded by high mountain ranges, he found fertile land, a healthful climate, and enough water for irrigation. He directed the laying out of fields, selected the site for a city, and saw to communications with the East. The first year witnessed some scarcity, but after that Utah offered a rude plenty for everyone. Farms and irrigation ditches soon extended up and down the whole valley. Brigham Young exercised a despotic power, but his wisdom and benevolence made it endurable. He and his church officers organized the marketing of Utah products; they controlled settlement, choosing sites for new towns and sending each just the craftsmen it needed; and they made Salt Lake City, with its fine broad streets, its rills of sparkling water, and its temple and tabernacle, one of the most interesting places in America. It was the first American experiment with a planned economy, and it was successful. Polygamy for a time continued, serving a sound colonizing purpose — for women were in the majority among the converts, and the frontier had little place for unmarried and childless women. By 1850 Utah was organized as a territory. But polygamy likewise delayed its organization as a state: not until almost fifty years later — and after the Mormons had given up the practice — was it admitted to statehood.

THE ANNEXATION OF TEXAS

The annexation of Texas, and the conquest of California and the Southwest from feeble Mexico, finally rounded out the American domain in the West. Within a few years in the 1840's the United States extended its boundaries over some of the richest and most scenic regions of the continent. Various writers have treated this wrestling of territory from Mexico as immoral aggression. James Russell Lowell said that the South wanted Texas just to have "bigger pens to cram slaves in." This is unjust. A natural process brought about the addition of this territory to the United States — a process well hit off by the phrase "manifest destiny."

Texas, at first a part of the Mexican Republic, was a land as large as Germany with but a few ranchers and hunters. It early attracted many Americans and some Britons, Stephen F. Austin planting the first Anglo-American settlement in 1821. Free lands, easily accessible to the Southern States, were the principal bait. The Mexican government was inefficient, corrupt, and tyrannical. In 1835 the American settlers rose in revolt and after a number of battles won their independence. One episode was the capture by the Mexicans of the Alamo, a fort in San Antonio, where every American defender was killed: "Thermopylae had its messenger of defeat; the Alamo had none." Once established, the Texan Republic flourished and attracted many fresh American settlers. For a time the United States refused to consider any proposal for annexing the country. But for a number of reasons many Americans gradually changed their minds. For one, they thought it a duty to expand over the unpeopled and undeveloped West. For another, they felt that the Texans were a kindred people whose natural place was under the American flag. For a third reason, they feared that Great Britain might intervene in Texas and try to establish a protectorate. And finally, pocket motives were at work. Northerners wished to sell farm products and manufactured goods in Texas; shipowners saw that their vessels could make profitable voyages to Galveston; Yankee mill owners wished to have cheap Texas cotton to spin. Many Southerners wanted to migrate and yet were unwilling to leave the American flag.

In the national election of 1844 a majority of the voters showed, by their support of the expansionist candidate James K. Polk, that they were ready to take the little republic into the Union, and early the next year it was annexed.

THE MEXICAN WAR AND THE
ACQUISITION OF CALIFORNIA AND NEW MEXICO

Meanwhile many Americans were equally intent upon gaining control of California by the same peaceful means. They thought this possible because of its peculiar position. In 1845 California had a meager population of but eleven or twelve thousand people, clinging tightly to the coast. They had no money, no army, no political experience. They had more Spanish blood than the Mexican masses and regarded themselves as physically and intellectually superior and they were only nominally dependent upon Mexico. Indeed, they would have thrown off the Mexican authority altogether had it not been for their family jealousies and an old feud between northern and southern California. As it was, Mexico provided no courts, no police, no regular postal facilities, and no schools. Communication between California and Mexico City was rare and uncertain. So frankly did Mexico recognize that its sovereignty was a mere shadow that by the middle forties it showed a disposition to sell the region to Great Britain. Year by year the American element in California was growing in numbers and aggressiveness. American ships had long traded on the coast, while emigrants who wished to settle in the golden climate and make money from cattle and wheat had begun crossing the mountains in the 1830's. By 1846 California had twelve hundred foreign residents, most of them Americans. No wonder that some men believed California would drop like a ripe pear into the outstretched hand of the United States — that no force would be needed.

Perhaps it would have done so had not the Mexican War broken out in the summer of 1846. The remote cause of this conflict was the increasing distrust between the two nations, while its immediate cause was a dispute over the boundary of Texas. The United States found it a short and brilliant conflict. One American army under Zachary Taylor was sent into northern Mexico, captured the fortified city of Monterey, and defeated a large Mexican force in the stubborn battle of Buena Vista. Another army under Winfield Scott, hero of the War of 1812, landed at Vera Cruz, pushed westward over the mountains, and after hard fighting took Mexico City. Here Scott hoisted the American flag in "the halls of the Montezumas." When peace was made, in February, 1848, the United States obtained not only California, whose American residents had meantime revolted and set up the "Bear-Flag Republic," but also the huge area between it and Texas called New Mexico, which included the present Nevada and Utah. Altogether, in this country and in Texas the United States gained about 918,000 square miles.

It also gained a treasure house, for even as the treaty of peace was ratified gold was discovered in the California hills. At once a host of fortune hunters poured forth, some by sea and some by overland trail, to the canyons and gulches where nuggets could be washed out in troughs and pans. The mountains filled with roaring camps; San Francisco sprang overnight into a lusty little metropolis, full of vice, luxury, and energy; and California was converted in a twinkling from a sleepy, romantic community of Spanish-American ranchers into a hustling and populous commonwealth of Anglo-Saxons. These "days of old, and the days of gold, and the days of '49" were among the most colorful in all American history. So fast did California grow that in 1850 it was added to the Union as a state.

The acquisition of these broad new stretches in the West compelled Americans to take an interest in various neglected problems — the problem of the Caribbean; the problem of the Pacific; the problem of an isthmian canal; and above all the problem of slavery, which threatened to expand into the whole area.

THE PACIFIC FRONTIER

To many Americans, obsessed with the idea of Manifest Destiny, Oregon and California were but way stations on the road to the Pacific and Asia. President Pierce announced that he did not intend to be restrained by "any timid forebodings of evil from expansion," and Senator Thomas Hart Benton asserted that it was the duty of the United States "to reanimate the torpid body of Asia." A natural steppingstone to Asia was Hawaii. When Captain Cook discovered the Hawaiian (then named Sandwich) Islands, back in 1778, he had been accompanied by a Connecticut Yankee, John Ledyard, and it was the same Ledyard who had first seen the possibilities of trade between the Northwest coast and the mainland of China. Within a few years New England ships carrying furs from the Oregon country to China were stopping at the port of Honolulu, and soon those whalers whose epic Herman Melville was to write were putting in at Hawaii for repairs and supplies. By the 1840's, what with merchantmen from Salem and Boston with rum and Yankee notions, whalemen from Nantucket, missionaries living in white frame houses behind white picket fences, Honolulu was almost an outpost of New England. In 1842 Secretary of State Webster announced that the United States would not permit the annexation of the islands by any other power, and a few years later Secretary Marcy negotiated a treaty of annexation to the United States which fell through only because of the untimely death of the reigning King Hamehameha III. Meantime American naval, economic, and missionary interest grew apace, and it became clear that annexation was only a matter of time.

It was during these years, too, that America made its first gestures of official interest in the Far East. Sailing ships from Salem and Boston had been familiar in Chinese ports and in Java and Sumatra ever since the earliest days of the republic, but not until 1844, when Caleb Cushing negotiated a treaty giving American ships access to and privileges in certain Chinese seaports, were commercial relations with China regularized. A few years later American interest in China was dramatized when a Salem adventurer, Frederick Townsend Ward, was made commander of the "Ever Victorious Army" which put down the great Taiping Rebellion. The island kingdom of Japan had been for centuries sealed against European intercourse, but in 1853 Commodore Perry — brother to the hero of Lake Erie — sailed an expedition into Tokyo Bay; the following year he returned to negotiate a treaty opening up Japan to trade with the West: this was the famous "opening of Japan" which was to have such mixed consequences a century later.

If the United States was to be a Pacific power — and after the acquisition of Oregon and California that was inevitable — something would have to be done to provide speedier and safer communications than sailing around Cape Horn. The obvious alternative was a railroad or a canal across the Isthmus of Panama. In 1846 President Polk negotiated a treaty with Colombia guaranteeing the neutrality of the province of Panama in return for the assurance of free transit across the isthmus. To deal with the substantial British interests in Central America, Secretary Clayton negotiated, in 1850, the Clayton-Bulwer Treaty, whereby the United States agreed to joint control of any canal that was constructed across the isthmus, and Britain gave up her territorial rights in Central America. It was to be another half-century before American engineers built the canal — and then only after the abrogation of the Clayton-Bulwer Treaty. Meantime

American businessmen hurriedly constructed a railroad across the narrow but dangerous isthmus to meet the needs of the thousands of fortune-hunters hurrying to the gold fields of California. In 1855 the soldier of fortune William Walker led a filibustering expedition into Nicaragua, and from the presidential chair of that tentative republic tried to revolutionize the whole of Central America. He was frustrated by Commodore Vanderbilt, who headed up a rival gang of operators; in 1860 he was captured and executed by a Honduran army.

X · I

Samuel Eliot Morison

EXPANSION AND DEVELOPMENT

1. RAILROADS, "ELECTRICS," AND SHIPPING

DURING THE LAST third of the nineteenth century, American society began to reflect the economic transformations that began during the Civil War or earlier, but underwent no profound change such as that which followed a general adoption of the internal combustion engine. There was merely an expansion and extension of the first industrial revolution, marked by the application of machine power, in constantly enlarged units, to new processes and in new regions.

Transportation was the key. There were 35,000 miles of steam railroad in the United States in 1865; more than five times as much in 1900, more than in all Europe. Among inventions which diminished the discomfort of long-distance travel were the Pullman sleeping car, the safety coupler and the Westinghouse air brake. In the 1870's the refrigerator car, first used to carry freshly slaughtered beef from Chicago to the eastern cities, was adapted for the carriage of fruit and vegetables, which eventually enabled the products of California to undersell those of Eastern truck gardeners. After the turn of the century the Pennsylvania Railroad built the first all-steel passenger coaches, and the American Locomotive Company brought out the magnificent Pacific type, which dominated railroading for a quarter-century.

Transcontinental railroads were the most spectacular post-war achievements. The Union Pacific thrust westerly through Nebraska and Wyoming Territory, near the line of the old Oregon and California trails and across the Wasatch Range of the Rockies into the basin of the Great Salt Lake. The Central Pacific, in the meantime, climbed eastward from Sacramento over the difficult grades of the Sierras, then through the arid valleys of Nevada. When the two joined rails with a golden spike near the Great Salt Lake on 10 May 1869, the Union Pacific was regarded as the winner; but the Central Pacific promoters had made enough to enable them to buy the state government of California.

Congress in the meantime had granted charters to three other lines: (1) the Northern Pacific — from Lake Superior across Minnesota, through the Bad Lands of Dakota, up the valley of the Yellowstone, across the continental divide at Bozeman to the headwaters of the Missouri, and by an intricate route through the Rockies to the Columbia river and Portland; (2) the Southern Pacific — from New Orleans across Texas to the Rio Grande, across the *llano estacado* to El Paso, through the territory of the Gadsden Purchase to Los Angeles, and up the San Joaquin valley to San Francisco; (3) the Santa Fe — from Atchison, Kansas, up the Arkansas river to Trinidad, Colorado, across the Raton spur of the Rockies to Santa Fe and Albuquerque, through the country of the Apache and the Navajo parallel to the Grand Canyon of the Colorado, and across the Mojave desert to San Bernardino and San Diego. All three were aided by government land grants — twenty square miles to every mile of track — and by 1884, after numerous bankruptcies and reorganizations, all three had reached the coast. At the same time the Canadian Pacific, aided by even more generous subsidies, from the Dominion, was pushing through to the Pacific and reached it on 7 November 1885.

These transcontinental lines were promoted largely with a view to profit, but the peopling of a vast region proved to be their most valuable function. In this respect they performed a work comparable with that of the Virginia Company of 1612 and the Ohio Company of 1785.

At the end of the Civil War the great plains west of eastern Kansas and Nebraska, the high plains, and the Rocky Mountain region, were uninhabited by white men excepting the mining towns in Colorado and Nevada and the Mormon settlements in Utah. Mail coaches of the Overland Stage Line required at least five days to carry passengers and mails from the Missouri river to Denver. Silver ore extracted in Nevada had to be freighted by wagon to San Francisco, thence transported around Cape Horn to the East Coast and Great Britain. Transcontinental railroads pushed out into the plains in advance of settlers, advertised for immigrants in the Eastern states and Europe, transported them at reduced rates to the prairies railhead, and sold them land on credit. Thousands of construction workers became farm hands, obtained free homesteads from the federal government, and bought tools, horses, and cattle with their savings. The termini and junction points of these lines — places like Omaha, Kansas City, Missouri, hard by Independence (old jumping-off place for the Oregon trail), Duluth the "Zenith City of the Unsalted Seas," Oakland on San Francisco Bay, Portland in Oregon, Seattle and Tacoma in Washington — places non-existent or mere villages before the Civil War, became metropolitan cities in thirty years' time.

Railroading was the biggest business of a big era, and the railway builders were of the mettle that in Europe made Napoleons and Von Moltkes. The Northwest was the domain of James J. Hill, greatest of our railroad builders. St. Paul was a small town on the edge of the frontier when he emigrated thither from eastern Canada just before the Civil War, and Minneapolis a mere village at the St. Anthony falls of the Mississippi. There, the "Twin Cities" were located at the end of a trail which connected Winnipeg with the outside world. In the winter of 1870 Donald A. Smith, the future Lord Strathcona, then resident governor of the Hudson's Bay Company, started south from Winnipeg, and James J. Hill started north from St. Paul, both in dogsleds. They met on the prairie and made camp in a storm, and from that meeting sprang the Canadian Pacific and Great Northern railways.

During the panic of 1873 the St. Paul & Pacific railroad

went bankrupt. Hill watched it as a prairie wolf watches a weakening buffalo, and in 1878, in association with Donald Smith and George Stephen (the future Lord Mount Stephen), wrested it from Dutch bondholders by floating new securities.

The day of land grants and federal subsidies was past, and Hill saw that the Great Northern Railway, as he renamed his purchase, could reach the Pacific only by developing the country as it progressed; and that took time. He struck due west across the Dakota plains, sending out branches to people the region and carry wheat to market. In the summer of 1887 his construction made a record stride, 643 miles of grading, bridging, and rail-laying from Minot, North Dakota, to the Great Falls of the Missouri. Two years later, the Rockies yielded their last secret, the Marias pass, to a young engineer, John F. Stevens. In 1893 the trains of the Great Northern reached tidewater at Tacoma. Within ten years Hill acquired partial control of the Northern Pacific Railway, purchased joint control of the Chicago, Burlington & Quincy, connecting his eastern termini with Chicago, and was running steamship lines from Duluth to Buffalo and from Seattle to Japan and China.

The Great Northern, the Northern Pacific, and the Union Pacific (which sent a taproot northwesterly) were responsible for opening the great inland empire between the Cascades and the Rockies, and for an astounding development of the entire Northwest. This once isolated Oregon country, with its rich and varied natural resources, magnificent scenery, and thriving seaports, has become as distinct and self-conscious a section of the Union as New England. The three states into which it was divided — Washington, Oregon, and Idaho — increased in population from 282,000 in 1880 to 2 million in 1910 and 5.3 million in 1960; whilst California, which contained only half a million people when the golden spike was driven in 1869, kept well in front, rising to 15.7 million in 1960. The population of Kansas, Nebraska, and the Dakotas, starting at the same level in 1870, increased sixfold in two decades; Utah and Colorado, where there was a great mining boom in the 'seventies, tripled their population in the same period. Oklahoma and the Indian Territory, where not one white man was enrolled in 1880, had over 2 million palefaces and 55,000 Indians in 1960; and Texas, with the aid of a network of railways, doubled its population of 1.5 million between 1880 and 1900, and by 1960 had almost 10 million people. By 1890 the last serious Indian outbreak had been suppressed, and the surviving redskins confined to reservations; the last great area of public lands had been thrown open to settlement.

There were still great unexplored regions in the Far West in 1865 which the railroad only reached later, if ever. Four men who combined a zest for exploration with skill as naturalists, geologists, and writers were largely responsible for the conservation of some of America's greatest natural wonders. Clarence King, who headed a congressional survey of the region between eastern Colorado and California, published the results in his seven-volume *Exploration of the Fortieth Parallel* (1870-80), which has become a classic. In 1878 King was made head of the newly established United States Geological Survey. He was largely responsible for establishing the wondrous Sequoia National Park in the high Sierras.

John Muir began in 1867 a 1000-mile walk from Wisconsin to the Gulf of Mexico, visited and studied the Yosemite valley and, aided by writing articles in Eastern magazines, labored successfully to have the Yosemite made a national park. Muir was also an apostle of conservation, and it was on the basis of reports by a national forestry commission of which he was a member that President Cleveland, just before the end of his second term, created thirteen forest reserves comprising 21 million acres. The McKinley administration threw most of them back to the loggers, but Muir captured the ear of the public in a series of brilliant articles, and aroused the interest of Theodore Roosevelt in conservation.

John Wesley Powell, who lost an arm at Shiloh and became a professor of geology after the war, led a 900-mile descent of the Colorado river in boats through the Grand Canyon in 1869. He described this and later adventurous surveys in the Southwest in his *Canyons of the Colorado*, and did effective work under King in the Geological Survey; his interest in the Indians found an outlet as head of the Smithsonian's Bureau of Ethnology. Ferdinand V. Hayden, whose career as a soldier and paleontologist paralleled that of Powell, was largely responsible for Congress's creating the Yellowstone National Park in 1872. These four men deserve to be kept in fond remembrance, and not only for their discoveries; they were the lions whose boldness and determination prevented the jackals of exploitation from consuming the whole of America's most glorious natural heritage. But after they died the jackals, armed with the bulldozer, got away with a good part of it, owing, as Bernard DeVoto wrote, to the West's "historic willingness to hold itself cheap and its eagerness to sell out." The end result almost justifies De Voto's description of the Far West as "the plundered province."

This disappearance of the frontier was hailed by Frederick J. Turner, a great American historian, as the close of a movement that began in 1607; and the Spanish-American War of 1898 was interpreted as the beginning of a new phase of imperialism. After the lapse of years, it is difficult to discern any break in the rhythm of American life in the year 1890. The settlement of the Great West had not then been completed; in areas covering thousands of square miles it had not even begun. The westward movement of population continued. Even outside the national parks and forest reserves there are still areas of virgin wilderness in the Rocky Mountains, the Sierra Nevada and the high plains. There has, to be sure, been a gradual assimilation of the West to Eastern modes of living and thinking; but that, too, had been going on since the seventeenth century. Barely two generations separate the male vigor of Bret Harte's *Roaring Camp* and *Poker Flat* (1870) from the insipid society portrayed by Sinclair Lewis's *Main Street* (1920). Yet even today there is a marked difference between East and West. The transcontinental tourist, whether by train or car, as he leaves the settled farms of Dakota or Kansas for the broad sweep of the high plains, has the feeling of a land still young to the white man's tread.

Rail penetration of the far Northwest, improved agricultural machinery, the handling of grain in carload lots, transshipment to lake or ocean steamers by grain elevators, and a new milling process which ground the Northern spring wheat into superfine flour (much too superfine), were factors which combined to move the center of wheat production north and west from Illinois and Iowa into Minnesota, the Dakotas, Montana, Oregon, and the Canadian Northwest. In this new wheat belt the "bonanza" wheat farms, veritable factories for wheat production, were well established by 1890. The wheat crop increased from 152 to 612 million bushels between 1866 and 1891. With the low prices that prevailed after the panic of 1873, this meant disaster to competing farmers in the Middle West and the Eastern states; and, even more completely, to England. The silo which enabled dairy farmers to turn corn into milk, poultry raising, and the breeding of horses and cattle, saved Eastern farming from ruin; but enormous areas within a few hours of the great industrial centers on the Atlantic coast have reverted to forest.

Wool production remained almost constant in this period; and cotton, owing to the dislocation of southern society, did not attain its high prewar figure until 1878. As the corn belt extended into Kansas and Nebraska, the crop, already 868 million bushels in 1866, passed 2000 million bushels in 1891. The greater part of the corn was converted into meat, cured at thousands of local bacon factories and at the great packing plants in Chicago. And we have yet to record the revolution in meat production which took place between 1865 and 1880.

Richmond, Virginia, has the credit of making the first successful experiment with electric streetcars in 1888, a mode of urban and suburban transportation which reached its zenith around 1920 and has since almost completely disappeared. Other cities at once began replacing horsecars by trolley cars. (Oliver Wendell Holmes saluted the "broomstick train" as the Salem witches' revenge), or cars that obtained electric power from underground conduits. Before the end of the century, interurban electric railways were taking passenger traffic away from steam railroads, and it was possible to travel from northern New England to the Middle West by "electrics," if one could spare the time — as few Americans felt they could afford to do.

Nor did rail have a monopoly of long-distance freight transportation. A large part of the nation's traffic, and all foreign trade except with Canada and Mexico, was carried by ships, sail or steam. This was the heyday of the sternwheeler on the Mississippi and its tributaries — incidentally producing a galaxy of songs, such as "Waiting on the Levee . . . for the *Robert E. Lee*," a steamboat which beat the *Natchez* in a famous river race. On the Great Lakes were fleets of ore carriers, tankers, and grain ships, with a dying fleet of local sailing craft like the *Jolie Plante* in which poor Marie, freshwater counterpart to that golden-haired damsel who perished in Longfellow's "Wreck of the Hesperus," lost her life. Hard by the "reef of Norman's Woe" lies the snug haven, Gloucester, home port for hundreds of sailing fishermen; stubby "bankers" or "hand-liners" immortalized by Kipling's *Captains Courageous* (1886), and the tall mackerel seiners, which James B. Connolly described in *Out of Gloucester*. Hundreds of schooners, two-, three-, and even six-masted, plied between ports of the Maritime Provinces, the East Coast, the Caribbean, and South America, carrying fish, coal, lumber, granite, and even general cargoes in competition with the coastal steamboats. Of these there were literally hundreds: deep-water runs several times weekly from New York to Norfolk, Baltimore, Charleston, Halifax, and New Orleans; night runs of sound steamers to Hartford, Stonington, New London, and Fall River. Every evening in Boston, weather permitting, saw departures to sundry Maine and Nova Scotia ports. Traffic "down east" as yet had no Cape Cod Canal (completed in 1914), but the inland waterways from Norfolk south were being improved for tug and barge traffic. By 1894 the Fall River Line's *Puritan* and *Priscilla*, "queen of all steamboats," were carrying 300,000 passengers annually between New York and New England. These Long Island Sound lines carried on into the great depression of the 1930's, when they were killed by the competition of trucks and the exactions of the Seamen's Union.

River and coastal traffic had been protected from foreign competition by navigation laws ever since 1789. But America's foreign trade had to meet foreign competition, and thereby suffered. Before the war, two-thirds of the value of American imports and exports had been carried in American-flag ships. By 1870 the proportion had dropped to one-third; and by 1880 to one-sixth. The initial drop has often been ascribed to the depredations of Confederate cruisers; but they could hardly be blamed for the 1870-80 slump. Captain John Codman of Boston testified before a congressional committee in 1882, "We have lost our prestige and experience; we are no longer a maritime nation; our ship-owners have been wearied and disgusted; they have gone into other business, forced by their government to abandon their old calling. Our ship-masters, the pride of the ocean in the old packet days, are dead, and they have no successors."

A congressional investigation of 1882 reported that the basic cause of this decline was the superior attraction for American investors of railroads, Western land, manufacturing, and mining, when the merchant navies of several European powers and Japan were earning only 4 or 5 per cent. Congress could have made up the difference by ship subsidies; but Congress, in contrast to its lavish support of transcontinental railroads, let the merchant marine decline nearly to the vanishing point. Almost all the sound, river, and coastal steamers of this era were built of wood, and bad fire hazards they were. Owing to the backwardness of American builders and designers in steel hulls and marine engines, and the laws against placing foreign-built vessels under the American flag, the United States never regained a place in fast transatlantic traffic until after World War II. The American line, a combine of several, was enabled to compete only by virtue of a special act of Congress allowing it to acquire two foreign-built liners, *City of Paris* and *City of New York*. These two, in 1889-92, were the first to make a transatlantic passage between New York and Queenstown, Ireland, in less than six days. *Deutschland* of the North German Lloyd captured the "blue riband of the Atlantic" in 1900 and held it for seven years, when the ill-fated *Lusitania* made the crossing in less than four days, twenty hours.

Another exception made by Congress after the Civil War was a liberal subsidy of the Pacific Mail Line to carry mail from San Francisco to Hawaii and the Orient. Pacific Mail long held its own in competition with the Canadian Pacific steamship line, and Japan's Toyo Kisen Kaisha. Its 5000-ton, iron-screw steamers *City of Peking* and *City of Tokio*, built at Chester, Pennsylvania, with auxiliary four-masted barque rig, lowered the record from San Francisco to Yokohama to sixteen days. Collis Huntington of the Southern Pacific Railroad got control of this line in 1893, and built five new ships. It carried on until 1915, when killed by a law requiring the Oriental crews to be replaced by Americans.

Despite Captain Codman, the American sailing marine did pretty well. Square-riggers, built largely in Maine or on Puget Sound, officered by Americans and manned by sailors of every nation, race, and color, continued to carry bulk cargoes to European ports, around the Horn to the West Coast, Japan, China, and Hawaii, and around the Cape of Good Hope to Australia and India. As late as 1892 there was more tonnage under the American flag in sail than in steam. In this final phase of deep-water sail, the wooden square-rigger was perfected. "These splendid ships, each with her grace, her glory," as John Masefield wrote, were not so fast as the clippers, but carried more cargo for their size and, with labor-saving devices (but no auxiliary propulsion) were more economical to operate on long voyages than steamers, a large part of whose cargo space had to be given to coal bunkers. Among the famous ships of this era was Donald McKay's last creation, *Glory of the Seas*, launched in 1869, 2000 tons burthen, 240 feet long. In 1875 she hung up a record from San Francisco to Sydney, 35 days, which still stands. The slightly smaller *Grand Admiral*, also built in 1869, carried the black horse flag of the Weld family for 28 years, during which she logged 727,000 miles in 5360 sailing days — an amazing record, considering that many of those days must have been windless. Last full-rigged three-skysail yarder to be built in the United States was *Aryan*, 1939 tons, 248 feet long, designed locally and built on the Kennebec in 1893. Her owners kept her sailing out of sentiment until 1918, long after the competition of steamers had made her unprofitable. The adoption of high-pressure, triple-expansion marine engines in the 1890's, requiring less than one-tenth of the coal per horsepower of the old compound engines, doomed the sailing ship on round-the-world trading routes. They hung on for carrying bulk cargoes on protected coastal routes until the 1930's.

2. INDIANS, CATTLE, AND COWBOYS

The dismal story of relations between white Americans and the American Indian continued with little change. In contrast to the Negroes who were denied their ambition to partcipate on equal terms in American civilization, the Indians, who desired above all to continue their own way of life, were deprived of hunting grounds which would have made that possible, and were pressured to "settle down" and become "good" farmers and citizens.

Before that pressure could be exerted, the redskins had to be defeated in battle. Indians of the Great Plains and the Rocky Mountains, about 225,000 in number, presented a formidable obstacle to white settlement. The strongest and most warlike were the Sioux, Blackfoot, Crow, Cheyenne, Arapaho, and Nez Percé in the north; the Comanche, Apache, Ute, Kiowa, Southern Cheyenne, and Southern Arapaho in the south and center. Mounted on swift horses, well armed for plains warfare, and living on the herds of buffalo that roamed the open range, these tribes long maintained a stubborn resistance to white penetration of their hunting grounds.

The first serious invasion of these hunting grounds came with the great migration of the 1840's. In 1850 there were approximately 100,000 Indians in California; in 1860 there were barely 35,000 "despoiled by irresistible forces of the land of their fathers; with no country on earth to which they can migrate; in the midst of a people with whom they cannot assimilate," as Congress's committee on Indian affairs reported. The advance of miners into the mountains, the building of transcontinental railroads, and the invasion of the grasslands by cattlemen, threatened every other Indian nation of the West with the same fate. Wanton destruction of the buffalo, indispensible not only for food but for housing, bowstrings, lariats, and fuel; the Colt six-shooter, fearfully efficient in the hands of palefaces, and the spread of white men's diseases among the Indians; all were lethal.

Until 1861 the Indians of the Great Plains had been relatively peaceful, but in that year the invasion of Colorado by thousands of miners, and the advance of white settlers along the upper Mississippi and Missouri, began a series of armed clashes. Sioux of the Dakotas went on the warpath in 1862, devastated the Minnesota frontier, and massacred or captured almost 1000 white people. Retribution was swift and terrible, but for the next 25 years Indian warfare was a constant of Western history. Each new influx of settlers and of railroad gangs who carelessly destroyed the buffalo, drove the redskins to raid settlements in search of food, and to acts of desperation which brought on punitive expeditions by the United States Army. There were some 200 pitched battles between soldiers and Indians in the years 1869-76. The contest was not unequal, for the Indians had become excellent shots. They could attack or flee from the heavy United States cavalry at will, and they were not troubled by logistic problems. Had they been able to unite, they might have tired out the United States (as white resistance to reconstruction was doing in the South); but no Tecumseh, no Prophet appeared. The army could always recruit Indian scouts, and the redskins were defeated piecemeal.

It was not that nobody did anything about it. Congress in 1867 set up an Indian Peace Commission, which included Generals Sherman and Terry, to stop the fighting, and it did that for about two years. This commission recommended an end to the farce of making treaties with Indian nations — there were roughly 370 of them in the archives — and in 1871 Congress did so. General Francis A. Walker (future president of M.I.T.), whom Grant appointed commissioner of Indian affairs that year, did his best to carry out a paternalistic policy. He placed defeated tribes on new reservations, set up schools for their children, and issued rations to those who had no more game; but his best was not good enough. In his report of 1872 he remarked cogently, "Every year's advance of our frontier takes in a territory as large as some of the kingdoms of Europe. We are richer by hundreds of millions, the Indian is poorer by a large part of the little that he has. This growth is bringing imperial greatness to the nation; to the Indian it brings wretchedness, destitution, beggary."

For ten years after the Civil War the Sioux, in particular, fought desperately to preserve their hunting grounds on the Great Plains. In December 1866 Captain William J. Fetterman USA, stationed at Fort Phil Kearny, Wyoming, was ambushed by Red Cloud, and his command of eighty men were killed. Fort Buford, on the Missouri just across the Montana line, was sniped at by Sioux in 1867. The American public was stirred up by a report of a "horrible massacre" there which actually never took place, a report which the commissioner of Indian affairs attributed to "the rapacity and rascality of frontier settlers, whose interests are to bring on a war and supply our armies . . . at exorbitant prices." For several years there were occasional skirmishes with the Sioux, but their knell of doom struck in 1875 when prospectors discovered gold in the Black Hills — "them thar hills" — of South Dakota and founded fabulous Deadwood, where "Wild Bill" Hickok, hero of many a border brawl, died with his boots on. These hills, to the Sioux, were holy ground which the government had promised to retain for them inviolate. For one summer General Sheridan was able to hold back the greedy gold seekers, but in the following spring they broke through. Under Sitting Bull and Crazy Horse the Sioux struck back.

Colonel George A. Custer of the 7th Cavalry, a distinguished veteran of the Civil War who had been fighting Indians off and on for the last nine years, had come to like and respect them. "If I were an Indian," he wrote in an article about an earlier battle with the Sioux, "I would certainly prefer to cast my lot . . . to the free open plains rather than submit to the confined limits of a reservation, there to be the recipient of the blessed benefits of civilization with its vices thrown in." In June of 1876 he led a column west from Bismarck to disperse the Sioux and Northern Cheyenne, who had left their Black Hills reservation. Custer found them encamped by the Little Big Horn river in Montana. Rashly the officer in tactical command, Brigadier General Alfred Terry, divided the regiment into three columns, one of which, Custer's, was surrounded by some 2500 braves under

Crazy Horse. Custer and his entire command of 265 officers and men were killed. Colonel Nelson A. Miles in January 1877 caught up with and defeated Crazy Horse, whose enemies gave him the compliment of calling him "one of the bravest of the brave and one of the subtlest and most capable of captains." Custer became a hero to the boys who grew up in that era, and his bright and joyous figure, his long yellow locks, and trooper's swagger shine through the murk of controversy over who was to blame for the massacre on the Little Big Horn.

More Indians were now driven from their ancient homes. In Montana the Crow and Blackfoot were ejected from their reservations; in Colorado the vast holdings of the Ute were confiscated and opened to settlement. The discovery of gold on the Salmon river in western Idaho precipitated an invasion of the peaceful Nez Percé. They refused to surrender lands guaranteed to them, and the federal government in 1877 decided to drive them out. Chief Joseph struck back, but in vain, and then conducted 200 braves and 600 squaws and papooses on a fighting retreat over 1500 miles of mountain and plain, a memorable feat in the annals of Indian warfare; and for strategic and tactical skill in a class with Marshal Kesselring's Italian campaigns of 1944-45. In the end, when just short of asylum in Canada, Chief Joseph surrendered (5 October 1877), saying, "Hear me, my chiefs. I am tired; my heart is sick and sad. From where the sun now stands I will fight no more, forever." Joseph then devoted himself to the peaceful betterment of his people, part of whom returned to their ancestral lands, and part settled in Oklahoma.

In the Southwest, twenty years of intermittent warfare with various branches of the Apache ended in 1886 with the surrender of their chief Geronimo and the subjugation of his tribe. Geronimo became a Christian convert and lived both to write his autobiography and to take part in the inaugural procession of President Roosevelt in 1905.

In 1881 President Arthur declared, "We have to deal with the appalling fact that though thousands of lives have been sacrificed and hundreds of millions of dollars expended in the attempt to solve the Indian problem, it has until within the past few years seemed scarcely nearer a solution than it was half a century ago." Federal authority over Indian affairs was divided between the war and interior departments, both of which pursued a vacillating and uncertain policy, and each failed to live up to treaty obligations or to protect the Indians on their reservations from white settlers' aggressions. These aggressions often took the form of alienating by fraud and chicanery large areas of Indian lands to railroads and other speculators. One railroad acquired 800,000 acres of Cherokee land in southern Kansas, an operation that the governor of that state denounced as "a cheat and a fraud in every particular," but nothing was done to cancel it, and the railroad resold the lands to settlers at a vast profit. Only the intervention of the secretary of the interior prevented a particularly crass deal whereby the Osage were to sell 8 million acres to a railroad for 20 cents an acre.

American frontiersmen in general still subscribed to their traditional feeling that the only good Indian was a dead Indian; but in the East, churchmen and reformers urged a humane policy toward the nation's wards. Statesmen like Carl Schurz, religious leaders like Bishop Henry B. Whipple, literary figures like Helen Hunt Jackson, whose *Century of Dishonor* (1881) stirred the nation's conscience, were loud in their criticism of the government's treatment of the Indian, and their attitude was effective in bringing about important changes in policy.

Paternalism culminated in the passage of the Dawes Act of 1887, which established the policy of breaking up reservations into individual homesteads. This was an attempt to "civilize" the Indian by folding him into the body politic of the nation. Passage of this law was promoted by Indian Rights and other societies who wished the redskins well; it was based on the "Protestant ethic" premise that ownership of real estate was a moral good, fostering thrift, industry, and providing the spark of energy of ambition that leads to wealth and prestige. But the "do-gooders" overlooked the fact that the Western Indian, by habit and heredity, was a hunter rather than a cultivator; that his ideas of land ownership were communal, not individual; that the last thing he wanted was to become a homesteader. By persuading Indians to be individual land-owners as an alternative to living on government rations on a reservation, pressuring them to try homesteading before they had acquired the technique and values that alone make "the American way of life" viable, the Dawes Act was certain to be a very partial success. It overlooked a trait of the Indian character: that he literally takes "no thought for the morrow," and is easily tempted to sell his birthright to go on a big binge. Thus, it was taken advantage of by landgrabbers and speculators.

The act, in general, provided that the President of the United States should direct that a reservation be broken up when and if he had evidence that the Indians wanted it; then a homestead of 160 acres would be granted to each family, and the unallotted remainder of the reservation would be purchased by the government for sale to white men, the money to be put in trust for the tribe. After allotment began, in 1891, the acreage of Indian reservations was reduced 12 per cent in a single year. Congress then speeded up the process by passing another law which allowed the allottees to lease their lands. That really doomed the system. Indians living on a reservation lapped about by white men's farms, faced with the alternative of becoming a tribal slum on the prairie or unwilling homesteaders, snapped hungrily at the allotment bait, knowing that individual farms could now be leased, and hoping to live well on the rent. In 1894 it was ascertained that the Omaha and Winnebago in Nebraska had leased lands to a real estate syndicate for 8 to 10 cents an acre, which the syndicate released to white farmers for $1 to $2 an acre, per annum. Out of 140,000 acres allotted by 1898 to these two nations, 112,000 had been leased, mostly illegally, and the wretched lessors were living in squalor on their meager rents, drifting into the towns and cities, unable to fit into the white man's civilization. The Indian allottee did not know what to do with his land. Now for the first time he was subject to state taxes, and if he did not succumb to the temptation to lease, and held his allotment for the required 25 years, he generally sold it as soon as a fee simple patent was issued, squandered the proceeds, and became a pauper. In the half-century after 1887, Indian holdings decreased from 138 to 48 million acres. Indian timberlands, too, were acquired by speculators; the Indian commissioner blandly declared in 1917 that "as the Indian tribes were being liquidated anyway, it was only sensible to liquidate their forest holdings as well." Tribal funds amounting to more than $100 million were diverted from their proper use to meet the costs of the Indian Bureau — including the costs of despoiling the Indians of their lands.

Fortunately for the Five Civilized Tribes, the Dawes Act did not apply to them, or to a few others such as the Osage, Miami, Sauk and Fox who had located in the Indian Territory. These were given special treatment. As punishment for their support of the Confederacy, the Five Civilized Tribes were compelled in 1866 to accept new treaties relinquishing the western half of the Indian Territory, where some twenty tribes from Kansas and Nebraska were settled in thirteen new reservations. Two million acres of this western half, called Oklahoma Territory, were bought from the Indians and thrown open to settlement in 1889, with the consequent land rush which is well described in Edna Ferber's *Cimarron*. It was an extraordinary spectacle, a *reductio ad absurdum* of laissez-faire. Some 12,000 prospective settlers camped along the railroad between the Canadian and Cimarron rivers. Here, wrote an eyewitness, James Morgan, was the chronically moving family in its covered wagon, beaten on a dozen frontiers for half a century but always hopeful that the next would prove a bonanza; Texans who were finding Texas too tame; lawyers and doctors with their diplomas and instruments; gamblers and fancy men, "all the elements of western life — a wonderful mixture of thrift and unthrift, of innocence and guile, of lambs and wolves." Shepherded by United States cavalry, they lined up along the border in wagons, on horseback, and afoot, and at the shot of a pistol, raced to grab one of the 6000 free homestead lots. In many instances these men found the "sooners," those who had jumped the gun, ahead of them; claims staked out had to be defended — or lost — by gunfire, and it took years to straighten out the mess of land titles. Altogether the most inefficient and wasteful way of settling a new country that anyone could have imagined.

The Five Civilized Tribes, who numbered over 51,000 in the census of 1890, were made American citizens in 1901.

Allotments under the Dawes Act were now extended to the Cherokee, and the United States Court of Claims awarded $1.1 million to that nation as indemnity for the hardships of their removal in 1838. In 1907 Oklahoma, including Indian Territory, was admitted as a state of the Union, and from that time on the Indians in that state have been not only their own masters, but an element that no politician can ignore.

Hitherto all the world had obtained fresh meat from local butchers; beef could be exported only on the hoof or in pickle. After the Civil War thousands of young Texans came home from army service, to find the grassy plains in the southern part of the state glutted with millions of fat, mature cattle, descendants of the longhorns turned loose by Spaniards a century or more earlier. They were then bringing only $1 to $5 a head, but were worth twenty times as much in the Eastern cities. Stretching north through Texas and across the Indian Territory of Kansas, and even into Wyoming, were millions of acres of natural grass which supported the buffalo; but these beasts were rapidly being exterminated by hunters and railroad section gangs, and were practically extinct by 1884. There had been some long-distance cattle driving from Texas before the war, but now the Texans — especially Richard King whose vast ranch covered most of the territory between the Nueces and the Rio Grande — saw an opportunity to reach Eastern markets by driving herds to the western termini of railroads. Joseph G. McCoy persuaded the Kansas Pacific to build out to Abilene, Kansas, which became a famous "cow town" thirty years before it fathered a famous general and President; in 1871 the Santa Fe established another railhead at Dodge City, Kansas, and about the same time the Union Pacific established a third at Ogalalla, Nebraska. The chance discovery that beeves could winter on the Wyoming plains and come out fat and sleek in the spring, led to other shipping points on the Northern railways. Thus, by 1875 there was a belt of free pasturage extending from southern Texas to the Canadian border. The refrigerator car, in common use by that date, made it possible to sell dressed beef, slaughtered at Chicago or Kansas City, in the Eastern centers of the population. These factors, with the invention of artificial ice and a canning machine, brought even European markets within reach of the Far West.

This new industry of raising beef cattle on the Great Plains produced the last phase of the Wild West, and the most picturesque development of the ancient art of cattle-droving. Texans, who had ridden from childhood and fought in the Confederate army, and Mexican bucaroos (*vaqueros*) were the first and best cowboys. Every spring they rounded up the herds from eight to ten ranches, identified ownership by the brands, branded the calves, and divided *pro rata* the mavericks and "dogies," the motherless calves. The breeding cattle were set free for another year, while the likely three- and four-year-olds were conducted on the long drive. There were three principal trails, all of which crossed the Indian Territory; but the Indians did not object to palefaces and cattle who passed through instead of settling down; the Cherokee even issued grazier licenses for a small fee. In 1871, peak year of the long drive, some 600,000 head were driven north.

A typical herd on the long drive of 1200 to 1500 miles consisted of 2500 longhorns. This required about twelve cowboys with a *remuda* (remount) of from five to six horses each, controlled by a "horse wrangler," and a "chuck wagon" drawn by mules for the men's food and camp equipment. The cattle walked slowly, making ten to twenty miles a day, swam rivers, and, if properly driven and prevented from stampeding, would even gain weight en route. They were allowed to browse all night, for an hour or two every morning, and again at noon. At the end of the drive the cattle were sold to buyers from Chicago and Kansas City, and the cowboys, after being paid off and "blowing in" most of their wages in the cow town, returned by the same trail.

While the long line of cattle moved slowly, the cowboys were continually riding up and down, urging stragglers along, and on the lookout for raiding "bad men," wild Indians, or prairie-grass fires. They had to continue riding around the herd at night lest it be stampeded by a thunderstorm or by steers simply getting the notion to bolt. The cowboy's high-horned Mexican saddle, lariat, broad-brimmed sombrero, high-heeled boots, and leather "chaps" and six-shooter were perfectly adapted to his work. His bronco — a short-legged, varicolored mustang of Spanish origin, hardy as a donkey and fleet as an Arab, and which he broke with unnecessary cruelty — made an ideal cow pony. The authentic cowboy was spare of frame, pithy and profane in speech, a superb rider although a bowlegged walker; alert with the sort of courage needed to rope steers, fight cattle rustlers, or stop a stampede; hardworking and enduring, asking no better end than to die with his boots on. His life is recorded in ballads which are now nation-wide favorites. These ballads record the freedom and discipline, the violence and friendship of the Far West; one can almost smell the odor of sun on saddle leather, and of the buffalo-chip fire over which cookie prepared the evening meal; a hard, challenging open-air life that attracted young men, knights of the long trail. The cowboy of the long drive flourished for a brief score of years, fading into legend with the passing of the open range.

By 1885 the range had become too heavily pastured to support the long drive, and was beginning to be crisscrossed by railroads and by the barbed-wire fences of homesteaders. Then came the terrible winter of 1886-87, when thousands of animals perished in the open. Cattle owners began to stake out homestead claims in the names of their employees and to fence off areas to which they had no claim. Almost in a moment cattle and sheep ranches replaced the open range, and the cowboy of the long drive became a domesticated ranch hand.

So much for the cowboy of history. But why did this ephemeral type capture the nation's, almost the world's, imagination rather than the earlier trapper of the Far West, the lumberjack of the northern forests, the river man who rode logs down rapids, or the sailor in blue water? These, too, had their ballads or chanties; their lives were not lacking in beauty, and they too experienced the same violent contrast between long periods of exceedingly hard, dangerous work and brief, bawdy blowouts. One answer is that the cowboy was a horseman, and since the dawn of history the

rider has seemed more glamorous than the sailor or foot-
man — witness the gay cavalcade of Athenian knights on the
frieze of the Parthenon. And the cowboy was rendered famous by three gifted "tenderfeet" or "dudes,"[1] Eastern college graduates who sojourned briefly in the Far West produced souped-up versions in prose, painting, and sculpture
of Life in the Raw for the effete East. Frederic Remington, after playing football with Walter Camp at Yale, became a cowboy and rancher in Kansas for about two years but devoted
the rest of his life (at New Rochelle, New York) to drawing,
painting, and sculpturing cowpunchers, Indians, and trappers in action, partly as illustrations to his own books. Theodore Roosevelt invested half his patrimony in a cattle ranch
in the Bad Lands of Dakota Territory in 1883, lived there for
less than three years, doing the hardest work and acquiring a
taste for the "great open spaces" which produced the Rough
Riders of 1898, and fed the Rooseveltian conception of Stren-
uous Life. "In that land," he wrote in his *Autobiography*, "we
led a free and hardy life, with horse and with rifle. . . . We
knew toil and hardship and hunger and thirst; and we saw
men die violent deaths as they worked among the horses and
cattle, or fought in evil feuds with one another; but we felt
the beat of hardy life in our veins, and ours was the glory of
work and the joy of living."

Roosevelt's love for the Far West was deep and genuine;
but the man who contributed most to the cowboy legend was
a literary cowboy, Owen Wister, a Philadelphia patrician
who reached Wyoming in time to witness the so called
Johnson County War between cattle barons and the homesteaders. Many young Easterners and Englishmen of wealth,
eager to combine sportsmanship with profit, had begun cat-
tle-raising in Wyoming, taking advantage of the open
range.Wister found their society, which centered upon the
Cheyenne Club, as congenial as that of the Porcellian,
although the members wore a different costume. It so happened that Johnson County had been thrown open by the
Land Office to homesteaders, and many — mostly from the
Ozarks — had located there, built barbed-wire fences
around their 160-acre lots, and in other ways hindered the
operations of the gentlemen who had organized the power-

ful Wyoming Stock Growers' Association. Wister regarded the "grangers" or "nesters" as the settlers were called locally, as low fellows of the baser sort, and in several short stories, combined in the popular novel *The Virginian* (1902), glorified the cowboy and condoned the murderous onslaughts on homesteaders by the gentlemen's hired killers. Wister created the literary cliché of the gentle cowpuncher who respected virtuous womanhood (and eventually married a schoolteacher from New England), defending the free open life of the range against homesteaders and other bad men who were trying to destroy it. He was the progenitor of standardized "Western" literature, of the rodeos for which horses are trained to buck, and the so-called "horse opera" on radio and in the movies, which have made the fortunes of hundreds of hack and script writers. This distorted image of the American Far West has traveled around the world; small boys in Europe, Asia and Africa are still listening to these impossible tales of the Wild West and sporting imitations of Levi overalls, spurs, colt revolvers, and "ten gallon hats."

3. THE FARMING COUNTRY

There was no essential change in Northern farm life between the Civil War and the coming of the automobile.[2] From Maine westward through Nebraska and the Dakotas, country folk lived in wooden frame houses such as those depicted by Grant Wood and Grandma Moses. The kitchen served as family living room; the parlor, with horsehair-covered furniture, Prang chromos, and crayon enlargements of family photos on the walls, perhaps a Rogers group on the table, was used mostly for the daughters' courting, and for weddings and funerals. The carpenter who built a farmer's house differentiated it from the barn by putting scroll work under the eaves and by building at the front a porch with carved posts. These houses were heated in winter by cast-iron stoves, lighted by kerosene lamps and protected from flying insects by iron-meshed screens. The farmer's wife cooked for her own family and the hired hands on a wood or coal stove and hauled or pumped her water from a nearby well, unless she lived in a region where a windmill could do it. Fewer than 10 per cent of American farm houses before 1900 had plumbing; a wooden washtub served for the weekly bath, and the back-house, whose passing James Whitcomb Riley celebrated in a famous unpublished poem, served other basic human needs.

The cow barn, always larger than the house, doubled as horse stable and afforded plenty of storage space for root crops as well as hay; its well-worn floor of wide boards was perfect for country dances. Daily Bible reading and Sunday "goin' to meetin' " were the rule, and much of the farm family's recreation turned around church socials. The farmer did not invite neighbors to dinner — "swapping meals" made no sense to him. The horse served as pet, transportation, and sport to all country-bred Americans, and to many in the cities. It was a poor farmer who hadn't a team of Clydesdales or Percherons for heavy hauling, a fast trotter for his buggy, and a saddle horse or two for his children; nobody walked if he could help it. Breeding horses, raising and training the colts, were part of a farmer's education and afforded him and his children infinite pleasure and profit, especially in horse trading. And it was a rare farmer who did not take the time to go fishing with his boys, or to shoot quail, duck, and partridge; or, if he lived on the edge of the northern wilderness, to hunt deer and moose.

This horse-centered economy created a vast market for hay and feed grains, and supported such handicraft industries as blacksmithing, saddlery, and harness making, and the construction of wagons, carriages, buggies, and sleighs. These were generally lighter than European models, but fashioned to last; beautifully functional, with a different kind of wood for each part, as Dr. Holmes described in "The Wonderful One-Hoss Shay." Winter and snow were a blessing in those days. Roads were tramped down by pooling the community's ox teams as Whittier described in "Snow-Bound," or, later, by great wooden horse-drawn rollers. The farmer and his boys put away their wheeled vehicles and let down by tackles from the barn loft their steel-runnered pungs and sledges which had been gathering dust and rust since spring.

Heavy hauling of timber and the like now began, local sports-
men organized trotting races in their cutters (two-seater one-
horse sleighs) painted gay colors. A swain who had taken his
girl buggy-riding in the fall now tucked her into a smart cut-
ter with a buffalo robe; and away they went at a fast clip over
the snowy roads, to the merry jingle of sleigh bells.

The hired man on the average farm was not the pathetic
type whose death Robert Frost recorded, but a stout youth.
He had the right to keep a horse at his employer's expense,
and every Saturday afternoon he dressed up, slicked down
his hair, put on a derby hat, and drove to town in his own
buggy to call on a girl, or have fun generally. For in all Northern and Western farm country there was almost always a
small town within driving distance to which the farmer could
haul his cash crop for shipment by rail, and where he could
make his purchases. Here would be a new high school, several general stores, and (if the temperance movement had
not reached it) a hotel built around a bar; two or three Protestant churches, a lawyer or two, and a doctor who also
acted as dentist and veterinarian; possibly an "opera house"
where strolling actors played. The barber shop was the center for sporting intelligence and smut, where waiting customers sang close-harmony in "barber-shop chords." If Germans were about there was an amateur string orchestra,
brass band, or *Singverein*: possibly also a *Turnverein* for
the boys to practice simple gymnastics. Smart farmers' sons
went from high school or endowed academy to one of the little hilltop colleges scattered throughout the land, even to a
state university to prepare for business or the professions.
There were bleak and narrow aspects to this way of life, well
described in Edgar Howe's grim novel of Kansas, *The Story
of a Country Town* (1883), but it was active and robust. The
insipidity portrayed in Sinclair Lewis's *Main Street* (1920)
did not, in general, enter the life of the Northern American
countryside or small town until its more enterprising people
had been lured away by big industry. Many farmers' boys
grew up hating this rustic routine and drudgery; Henry Ford
and Frank Lloyd Wright admit in their autobiographies that
revulsion against life on the farm impelled them, respec-
tively, into automobile manufacture and architecture.

After this life had passed away forever, many became sentimental about it, and some of the best novels in American literature describe nostalgically the rural society of those days: — Mary E. Wilkins Freeman for northern New England; Willa Cather's *My Antonia* for Nebraska; Hamlin Garland for the Middle Border; O. E. Rolvaag (who wrote in Norwegian but whose *Giants in the Earth* was translated by Lincoln Colcord) for Scandinavian pioneers in the Dakotas. James Whitcomb Riley recorded Hoosier child life in verse; but nobody has better depicted this way of living in which most of our Presidents from Lincoln to Coolidge were raised, and the impact on it of big industry, than Sherwood Anderson in his *Poor White* (1920).

4. IRON AND STEEL, BIG BUSINESS AND POLITICS

A good index of the industrial development of the Middle West is the rise of ship tonnage passing through the "Soo" (Saulte Ste. Marie) canal between Lakes Superior and Huron. Roughly 100,000 tons in 1860, the burthen rose to half a million in 1869 and 25 million in 1901. Wheat and iron ore formed the bulk of these cargoes. The iron came from new orefields of Michigan and Minnesota, to which the application of the Bessemer converter process gave America cheap steel, an essential factor of industrial development. These orefields on Lake Superior are distant hundreds of miles from coal deposits, but cheap lake and rail transport brought them together in the smelters of Chicago, where the first American steel rails were rolled in 1865, and in Cleveland, Toledo, Ashtabula, and Milwaukee. Much ore was transported to Pittsburgh, center of the northern Appalachian coalfields where native and Irish labor, revolting against the twelve-hour shifts imposed by the iron masters, was replaced by sturdy Hungarians and Slavs. In the 1880's the iron and coal beds of the southern Appalachians began to be exploited, and Birmingham, Alabama, became a Southern rival to Pittsburgh and Cleveland. American steel production, a mere 20,000 tons in 1867, passed the British output with 6 million tons in 1895 and reached 10 million before 1900.

In world economy the United States in 1879 was still a country of extractive industries; by 1900 it had become one of the greater manufacturing nations of the world. Yet the value of farm products still greatly exceeded those of industry, and the expanding home market precluded serious competition with England and Germany for export markets. In 1869 there were two million wage earners in factories and small industries, producing goods to the value of $3,385 million; in 1899 there were 4.7 million wage earners in factories alone, producing goods to the value of $11,407 million. In 1870 there were 6.8 million workers on farms, and the value of farm productions was $2.4 billion; in 1900 the number of farm workers was 10.9 million, and the value of their products, $8.5 billion. The number of horses and mules "on farms" (apparently those in towns were not counted) rose from 7.8 million in 1867 to 25 million in 1920. Then began the long decline, as more and more farmers relied on gasoline-powered vehicles and machinery.

In New England and the North generally, small waterpower factories declined in favor of concentrated manufacturing cities such as Fall River, Bridgeport, Paterson, Scranton, Troy, Schenectady, Youngstown, and Akron. Chicago rose triumphantly from the ashes of the great fire started by Mrs. O'Leary's cow in 1871, became the most populous American city after New York, and in 1893 staged the World's Columbian Exposition.

This development was neither steady nor orderly. Overproduction of goods and raw materials, overcapitalization of railroads, and feverish speculation in securities brought financial panics in 1873 and 1893. During the hard times that followed, labor expressed its dissatisfaction by strikes of unparalleled violence, and the farmers sought solution for their troubles in political panaceas. It was a period of cutthroat competition in which the big fish swallowed the little fish and then tried to eat one another. Competing railroads cut freight rates between important points, in the hope of obtaining the lion's share of business, until dividends ceased and the bonds became a drug in the market. The downward trend of prices from 1865 to 1900, especially marked after 1873, put a premium on labor-saving machinery, on new processes of manufacture, and on greater units for mass production. "Gentlemen's agreements" between rival producers to maintain prices and divide business, or even to pro-rate profits, were characteristic of the period after 1872. But it was found so difficult to enforce these pools that a gentlemen's agreement came to mean one that was certain to be violated. About 1880 the pool began to be superseded by the trust, a form of combination in which the affiliated companies handed over their securities and their power to a central board of trustees. John D. Rockefeller organized the first and most successful, the Standard Oil Trust, in 1879. A large measure of his success was due to improvements, economies, and original methods of marketing; but his monopoly was secured by methods condemned even by the tolerant business ethics of his day, and pronounced criminal by the courts. By playing competing railroads against each other, Standard Oil obtained rebates from their published freight rates and even forced them to pay over rebates from its competitors' freight bills to Standard Oil. If competing oil companies managed to stagger along under such handicaps, they were "frozen out" by cutting prices below cost in their selling territory, until Standard had all the business.

Thomas W. Lawson, author of *Frenzied Finance* (1905), a plunger and speculator who acquired great wealth during this period, wrote of it cynically: "At this period Americans found they could, by the exercise of a daring and cunning of a peculiar, reckless and low order, so take advantage of the laws of the land and its economic customs as to create for themselves wealth, or the equivalent, money, to practically an unlimited extent, without the aid of time or labor or the possession of any unusual ability coming through birth or education."

The trust as a method of combination was outlawed by most of the states in the early 'eighties; but the holding company, a corporation owning the shares of other corporations, proved to be a legitimate and more efficient financial device. In popular usage, however, the term "trust" was applied to combinations of any structure, provided they had sufficient power to dictate prices. These were the trusts which became targets of popular indignation in the early twentieth century. Not until the late 1880's did the American public demand regulation of trusts, and that problem was greatly complicated by a federal form of government. The states, not the federal government, issue corporate charters (excepting transcontinental railways); and a corporation chartered by one state has the right to do business in every other. Gas, electric lighting, and water companies and street railways depended for their very existence on municipalities. Hence the corrupt alliance cemented after the Civil War between politics and business. Plain bribery was often practiced with municipal councils, which gave away for nothing franchises worth millions, while cities remained unpaved, ill-lit, and inadequately policed.

Greatest in power, and most notorious for their abuse of it, were the great railway corporations. The power of an American transcontinental railway over its exclusive territory approached the absolute; for until the automobile age people in the Far West had no alternate means of transportation. A railroad could make an industry or ruin a community merely by juggling freight rates. The funds at their disposal, often created by financial manipulation and stock-watering, were so colossal as to overshadow the budgets of state governments. Railway builders and owners, like James J. Hill, had the point of view of a feudal chieftain. Members of state legislatures were their vassals, to be coerced or bribed into voting "right" if persuasion would not serve. In their opinion, railroading was a private business, no more a fit subject for government regulation than a tailor's shop. They were unable to recognize any public interest distinct from their own. In many instances the despotism was benevolent; and if a few men became multimillionaires, their subjects also prospered. But Collis P. Huntington, Leland Stanford, and their associates who built the Central and controlled the Southern Pacific were indifferent to all save considerations of private gain. By distributing free passes to state representatives, paying their campaign expenses and giving "presents" to their wives, they evaded taxation as well as regulation. By discriminating freight charges between localities and individuals, they terrorized merchants, farmers, and communities "until matters had reached such a pass," states a government report of 1887, "that no man dared engage in any business in which transportation largely entered without first obtaining the permission of a railroad manager." Through the press and the professions they wielded a power over public opinion comparable to that of slave-owners over the old South. Their methods were imitated by Eastern and Midwestern railroads, so far as they dared. In New Hampshire as in California, the railroad lobby, entrenched in an office near the state capitol, acted as a third chamber of initiative and revision; and few could succeed in politics unless by grace of the railroad overlord. Winston Churchill's *Coniston* (1906) and Frank Norris's *Octopus* (1901) accurately portray the social and political effects of railroad domination in these two states.

These exactions and abuses were long tolerated by Americans, so imbued were they with laissez-faire doctrine, so proud of progress, improvement, and development, and so averse from increasing the power of government. Thus it was not until 1887 that the federal government first attempted to regulate railroads and break up trusts. Congress then passed the first Interstate Commerce Act, declaring "unreasonable" rates, pooling and other unfair practices to be illegal. Enforcement was vested in the first modern American administrative board, the Interstate Commerce Commission. But administrative regulations were so foreign to the American conception of government that the federal courts insisted on their right to review orders of the Commission, and by denying its power to fix rates, emasculated the Act. So the railroads continued to charge "all the traffic would bear." Equally futile was the Sherman Anti-trust Act of 1890, which declared illegal any monopoly or combination in restraint of interstate trade. When the Supreme Court in 1895 held that purchase by the sugar trust of a controlling interest in 98 per cent of the sugar refining business of the country was not a violation of the law because not an act of interstate commerce, the Sherman Act became temporarily dead letter.

Theodore Roosevelt well summed up this last quarter of the nineteenth century in his *Autobiography*: "A riot of individualistic materialism, under which complete freedom for the individual . . . turned out in practice to mean perfect freedom for the strong to wrong the weak. . . . The power of the mighty industrial overlords . . . had increased with giant strides, while the methods of controlling them, . . . through the Government, remained archaic and therefore practically impotent." Roosevelt also had the wit to see that merely breaking up the trusts into smaller units was no answer; that was merely a futile attempt to remedy by more individualism the evils that were the result of unfettered individualism.

ENDNOTES

1. "Tenderfoot" first meant a yard-raised cow turned out on the range; "dude" (pronounced "dood"), a word of unknown origin which appeared around 1881, was first applied to the New York "young men about town" glorified in Richard Harding Davis's *Van Bibber* books, who dressed in the latest London fashion and were caricatured as wearing a monocle and a topper and sucking the handle of a walking stick. In the Far West it meant any well-heeled Easterner, and there it survives in the term "dude ranch."

2. Alexander Graham Bell invented the telephone in 1876, and Thomas A. Edison the incandescent light bulb in 1879; but it was long before either spread to country districts. In 1885 the Bell Telephone Company had over 134,000 subscribers in the United States as compared with about 13,500 in the United Kingdom; but most of the telephones were in towns and cities.

X · I · I

Frederick J. Turner

THE SIGNIFICANCE OF THE FRONTIER IN AMERICAN HISTORY

I̤n a recent bulletin of the Superintendent of the Census for 1890 appear these significant words: "Up to and including 1880 the country had a frontier of settlement, but at present the unsettled area has been so broken into by isolated bodies of settlement that there can hardly be said to be a frontier line. In the discussion of its extent, its westward movement, etc., it can not, therefore, any longer have a place in the census reports." This brief official statement marks the closing of a great historic movement. Up to our own day American history has been in a large degree the history of the colonization of the Great West. The existence of an area of free land, its continuous recession, and the advance of American settlement westward, explain American development.

Behind institutions, behind constitutional forms and modifications, lie the vital forces that call these organs into life and shape them to meet changing conditions. The peculiarity of American institutions is, the fact that they have been compelled to adapt themselves to the changes of an expanding people — to the changes involved in crossing a continent, in winning a wilderness, and in developing at each area of this progress out of the primitive economic and political conditions of the frontier into the complexity of city life. Said Calhoun in 1817, "We are great, and rapidly — I was about to say fearfully — growing!"[2] So saying, he touched the distinguishing feature of American life. All peoples show development; the germ theory of politics has been sufficiently emphasized. In the case of most nations, however, the development has occurred in a limited area; and if the nation has expanded, it has met other growing peoples whom it has conquered. But in the case of the United States we have a different phenomenon. Limiting our attention to the Atlantic coast, we have the familiar phenomenon of the evolution of institutions in a limited area, such as the rise of representative government; the differentiation of simple colonial governments into complex organs; the progress from primitive industrial society, without division of labor, up to manufacturing civilization. But we have in addition to this a recurrence of the process of evolution in each western area reached in the process of expansion. Thus American development has exhibited not merely advance along a single line, but a return to primitive conditions on a continually advancing frontier line, and a new development for that area. American social development has been continually beginning over again on the frontier. This perennial rebirth, this fluidity of American life, this expansion westward with it new opportunities, its continuous touch with the simplicity of primitive society, furnish the forces dominating American character. The true point of view in the history of this nation is not the Atlantic coast, it is the Great West. Even the slavery struggle, which is made so exclusive an object of attention by writers like Professor von Holst, occupies its important place in American history because of its relation to westward expansion.

In this advance, the frontier is the outer edge of the wave — the meeting point between savagery and civilization. Much has been written about the frontier from the point of view of border warfare and the chase, but as a field for the serious study of the economist and the historian it has been neglected.

The American frontier is sharply distinguished from the

European frontier — a fortified boundary line running through dense populations. The most significant thing about the American frontier is, that it lies at the hither edge of free land. In the census reports it is treated as the margin of that settlement which has a density of two or more to the square mile. The term is an elastic one, and for our purposes does not need sharp definition. We shall consider the whole frontier belt, including the Indian country and the outer margin of the "settled area" of the census reports. This paper will make no attempt to treat the subject exhaustively; its aim is simply to call attention to the frontier as a fertile field for investigation, and to suggest some of the problems which arise in connection with it.

In the settlement of America we have to observe how European life entered the continent, and how America modified and developed that life and reacted on Europe. Our early history is the study of European germs developing in an Ameican environment. Too exclusive attention has been paid by institutional students to the Germanic origins, too little to the American factors. The frontier is the line of most rapid and effective Americanization. The wilderness masters the colonist. It finds him a European in dress, industries, tools, modes of travel, and thought. It takes him from the railroad car and puts him in the birch canoe. It strips off the garments of civilization and arrays him in the hunting shirt and the moccasin. It puts him in the log cabin of the Cherokee and Iroquois and runs an Indian palisade around him. Before long he has gone to planting Indian corn and plowing with a sharp stick; he shouts the war cry and takes the scalp in orthodox Indian fashion. In short, at the frontier the environment is at first too strong for the man. He must accept the conditions which it furnishes, or perish, and so he fits himself into the Indian clearings and follows the Indian trails. Little by little he transforms the wilderness, but the outcome is not the old Europe, not simply the development of Germanic germs, any more than the first phenomenon was a case of reversion to the Germanic mark. The fact is, that here is a new product that is American. At first, the frontier was the Atlantic coast. It was the frontier of Europe in a very real sense. Moving westward, the frontier became more and more American. As successive terminal moraines

247

result from successive glaciations, so each frontier leaves its traces behind it, and when it becomes a settled area the region still partakes of the frontier characteristics. Thus the advance of the frontier has meant a steady movement away from the influence of Europe, a steady growth of independence on American lines. And to study this advance, the men who grew up under these conditions, and the political, economic, and social results of it, is to study the really American part of our history.

In the course of the seventeenth century the frontier was advanced up the Atlantic river courses, just beyond the "fall line," and the tidewater became the settled area. In the first half of the eighteenth century another advance occurred. Traders followed the Delaware and Shawnese Indians to the Ohio as early as the end of the first quarter of the century.[3] Gov. Spotswood, of Virginia, made an expedition in 1714 across the Blue Ridge. The end of the first quarter of the century saw the advance of the Scotch-Irish and the Palatine Germans up the Shenandoah Valley into the western part of Virginia, and along the Piedmont region of the Carolinas.[4] The Germans in New York pushed the frontier of settlement up the Mohawk to German Flats.[5] In Pennsylvania the town of Bedford indicates the line of settlement. Settlements soon began on the New River, or the Great Kanawha, and on the sources of the Yadkin and French Broad.[6] The King attempted to arrest the advance by his proclamation of 1763,[7] forbidding settlements beyond the sources of the rivers flowing into the Atlantic; but in vain. In the period of the Revolution the frontier crossed the Alleghanies into Kentucky and Tennessee, and the upper waters of the Ohio were settled.[8] When the first census was taken in 1790, the continuous settled area was bounded by a line which ran near the coast of Maine, and included New England except a portion of Vermont and New Hampshire, New York along the Hudson and up the Mohawk about Schenectady, eastern and southern Pennsylvania, Virginia well across the Shenandoah Valley, and the Carolinas and eastern Georgia.[9] Beyond this region of continuous settlement were the small settled areas of Kentucky and Tennessee, and the Ohio, with the mountains intervening between them and the Atlantic area, thus giving a new and important character to the frontier. The isolation of the region increased its peculiarly American tendencies, and the need of transportation facilities to connect it with the East called out important schemes of internal improvement, which will be noted farther on. The "West," as a self-conscious section, began to evolve.

From decade to decade distinct advances of the frontier occurred. By the census of 1820[10] the settled area included Ohio, southern Indiana and Illinois, southeastern Missouri, and about one-half of Louisiana. This settled area had surrounded Indian areas, and the management of these tribes became an object of political concern. The frontier region of the time lay along the Great Lakes, where Astor's American Fur Company operated in the Indian trade,[11] and beyond the Mississippi, where Indian traders extended their activity even to the Rocky Mountains; Florida also furnished frontier conditions. The Mississippi River region was the scene of typical frontier settlements.[12]

The rising steam navigation[13] on western waters, the opening of the Erie Canal, and the westward extension of cotton[14] culture added five frontier states to the Union in this period. Grund, writing in 1836, declares: "It appears then that the universal disposition of Americans to emigrate to the western wilderness, in order to enlarge their dominion over inanimate nature, is the actual result of an expansive power which is inherent in them, and which by continually agitating all classes of society is constantly throwing a large portion of the whole population on the extreme confines of the State, in order to gain space for its development. Hardly is a new State or Territory formed before the same principle manifests itself again and gives rise to further emigration; and so is it destined to go on until a physical barrier must finally obstruct its progress."[15]

In the middle of this century the line indicated by the present eastern boundary of Indian Territory, Nebraska, and Kansas marked the frontier of the Indian country.[16] Minnesota and Wisconsin still exhibited frontier conditions,[17] but the distinctive frontier of the period is found in California, where the gold discoveries had sent a sudden tide of adventurous miners, and in Oregon, and the settlements in

Utah.[18] As the frontier had leaped over the Alleghanies, so now it skipped the Great Plains and the Rocky Mountains; and in the same way that the advance of the frontiersmen beyond the Alleghanies had caused the rise of important questions of transportation and internal improvement, so now the settlers beyond the Rocky Mountains needed means of communication with the East, and in the furnishing of these arose the settlement of the Great Plains and the development of still another kind of frontier life. Railroads, fostered by land grants, sent an increasing tide of immigrants into the Far West. The United States Army fought a series of Indian wars in Minnesota, Dakota, and the Indian Territory.

By 1880 the settled area had been pushed into northern Michigan, Wisconsin, and Minnesota, along Dakota rivers, and in the Black Hills region, and was ascending the rivers of Kansas and Nebraska. The development of mines in Colorado had drawn isolated frontier settlements into that region, and Montana and Idaho were receiving settlers. The frontier was found in these mining camps and the ranches of the Great Plains. The superintendent of the census for 1890 reports, as previously stated, that the settlements of the West lie so scattered over the region that there can no longer be said to be a frontier line.

In these successive frontiers we find natural boundary lines which have served to mark and to affect the characteristics of the frontiers, namely: the "fall line;" the Alleghany Mountains; the Mississippi; the Missouri where its direction approximates north and south; the line of the arid lands, approximately the ninety-ninth meridian; and the Rocky Mountains. The fall line marked the frontier of the seventeenth century; the Alleghanies that of the eighteenth; the Mississippi that of the first quarter of the nineteenth; the Missouri that of the middle of this century (omitting the California movement); and the belt of the Rocky Mountains and the arid tract, the present frontier. Each was won by a series of Indian wars.

At the Atlantic frontier one can study the germs of processes repeated at each successive frontier. We have the complex European life sharply precipitated by the wilderness into the simplicity of primitive conditions. The first frontier had to meet its Indian question, its question of the disposition of the public domain, of the means of intercourse with older settlements, of the extension of political organization, of religious and educational activity. And the settlement of these and similar questions for one frontier served as a guide for the next. The American student needs not to go to the "prim little townships of Sleswick" for illustrations of the law of continuity and development. For example, he may study the origin of our land policies in the colonial land policy; he may see how the system grew by adapting the statutes to the customs of the successive frontiers.[19] He may see how the mining experience in the lead regions of Wisconsin, Illinois, and Iowa was applied to the mining laws of the Sierras,[20] and how our Indian policy has been a series of experimentations on successive frontiers. Each tier of new States has found in the older ones material for its constitutions.[21] Each frontier has made similar contributions to American character, as will be discussed farther on.

But with all these similarities there are essential differences, due to the place element and the time element. It is evident that the farming frontier of the Mississippi Valley presents different conditions from the mining frontier of the Rocky Mountains. The frontier reached by the Pacific Railroad, surveyed into rectangles, guarded by the United States Army, and recruited by the daily immigrant ship, moves forward at a swifter pace and in a different way than the frontier reached by the birch canoe or the pack horse. The geologist traces patiently the shores of ancient seas, maps their areas, and compares the older and the newer. It would be a work worth the historian's labors to mark these various frontiers and in detail compare one with another. Not only would there result a more adequate conception of American development and characteristics, but invaluable additions would be made to the history of society.

Loria,[22] the Italian economist, has urged the study of colonial life as an aid in understanding the stages of European development, affirming that colonial settlement is for economic science what the mountain is for geology, bringing to light primitive stratifications. "America," he says, "has the key to the historical enigma which Europe has sought for centuries in vain, and the land which has no history reveals luminously the course of universal history." There is much truth in this. The United States lies like a huge page in the history of society. Line by line as we read this continental page from West to East we find the record of social evolution. It begins with the Indian and the hunter; it goes on to tell of the disintegration of savagery by the entrance of the trader, the pathfinder of civilization; we read the annals of the pastoral stage in ranch life; the exploitation of the soil by the raising of unrotated crops of corn and wheat in sparsely settled farming communities; the intensive culture of the denser farm settlement; and finally the manufacturing organization with city and factory system.[23] This page is familiar to the student of census statistics, but how little of it has been used by our historians. Particularly in eastern States this page is a palimpsest. What is now a manufacturing State was in an earlier decade an area of intensive farming. Earlier yet it had been a wheat area, and still earlier the "range" had attracted the cattleherder. Thus Wisconsin, now developing manufacture, is a State with varied agricultural interests. But earlier it was given over to almost exclusive grain-raising, like North Dakota at the present time.

Each of these areas has had an influence in our economic and political history; the evolution of each into a higher stage has worked political transformations. But what constitutional historian has made any adequate attempt to interpret political facts by the light of these social areas and changes?[24]

The Atlantic frontier was compounded of fisherman, fur-trader, miner, cattle-raiser, and farmer. Excepting the fisherman, each type of industry was on the march toward the West, impelled by an irresistible attraction. Each passed in successive waves across the continent. Stand at Cumberland Gap and watch the procession of civilization, marching single file — the buffalo following the trail to the salt springs, the Indian, the fur-trader and hunter, the cattle-raiser, the pioneer farmer — and the frontier has passed by. Stand at South Pass in the Rockies a century later and see the same procession with wider intervals between. The unequal rate of advance compels us to distinguish the frontier into the trader's frontier, the rancher's frontier, or the miner's frontier, and the farmer's frontier. When the mines and the cow pens were still near the fall line the traders' pack trains were tinkling across the Alleghanies, and the French on the Great Lakes were fortifying their posts, alarmed by the British trader's birch canoe. When the trappers scaled the Rockies, the farmer was still near the mouth of the Missouri.

Why was it that the Indian trader passed so rapidly across the continent? What effects followed from the trader's frontier? The trade was coeval with American discovery. The Norsemen, Vespuccius, Verrazani, Hudson, John Smith, all trafficked for furs. The Plymouth pilgrims settled in Indian cornfields, and their first return cargo was of beaver and lumber. The records of the various New England colonies show how steadily exploration was carried into the wilderness by this trade. What is true for New England is, as would be expected, even plainer for the rest of the colonies. All along the coast from Maine to Georgia the Indian trade opened up the river courses. Steadily the trader passed westward, utilizing the older lines of French trade. The Ohio, the Great Lakes, the Mississippi, the Missouri, and the Platte, the lines of western advance, were ascended by traders. They found the passes in the Rocky Mountains and guided Lewis and Clark,25 Frémont, and Bidwell. The explanation of the rapidity of this advance is connected with the effects of the trader on the Indian. The trading post left the unarmed tribes at the mercy of those that had purchased fire-arms — a truth which the Iroquois Indians wrote in blood, and so the remote and unvisited tribes gave eager welcome to the trader. "The savages," wrote La Salle, "take better care of us French than of their own children; from us only can they get guns and goods." This accounts for the trader's power and the rapidity of his advance. Thus the disintegrating forces of civilization entered the wilderness. Every river valley and Indian trail became a fissure in Indian society, and so that society became honeycombed. Long before the pioneer farmer appeared on the scene, primitive Indian life had passed away. The farmers met Indians armed with guns. The trading frontier, while steadily undermining Indian power by making the tribes ultimately dependent on the whites, yet, through its sale of guns, gave to the Indian increased power of resistance to the farming frontier. French colonization was dominated by its trading frontier; English colonization by its farming frontier. There was an antagonism between the two frontiers as between the two nations. Said Duquesne to the Iroquois, "Are you ignorant of the difference between the king of England and the king of France? Go see the forts that our king has established and you will see that you can still hunt under their very walls. They have been placed for your advantage in places which you frequent. The English, on the contrary, are no sooner in possession of a place than the game is driven away. The forest falls before them as they advance, and the soil is laid bare so that you can scarce find the wherewithal to erect a shelter for the night."

And yet, in spite of this opposition of the interests of the trader and the farmer, the Indian trade pioneered the way for civilization. The buffalo trail became the Indian trail, and this became the trader's "trace;" the trails widened into roads, and the roads into turnpikes, and these in turn were transformed into railroads. The same origin can be shown for the railroads of the South, the Far West, and the Dominion of Canada.[26] The trading posts reached by these trails were on the sites of Indian villages which had been placed in positions suggested by nature; and these trading posts, situated so as to command the water systems of the country, have grown into such cities as Albany, Pittsburgh, Detroit, Chicago, St. Louis, Council Bluffs, and Kansas City. Thus civilization in America has followed the arteries made by geology, pouring an ever richer tide through them, until at last the slender paths of aboriginal intercourse have been broadened and interwoven into the complex mazes of modern commercial lines; the wilderness has been interpenetrated by lines of civilization growing ever more numerous. It is like the steady growth of a complex nervous system for the originally simple, inert continent. If one would understand why we are today one nation, rather than a collection of isolated states, he must study this economic and social consolidation of the country. In this progress from savage conditions lie topics for the evolutionist.[27]

The effect of the Indian frontier as a consolidating agent in our history is important. From the close of the seventeenth century various intercolonial congresses have been called to treat with Indians and establish common measures of defense. Particularism was strongest in colonies with no Indian frontier. This frontier stretched along the western border like a cord of union. The Indian was a common danger, demanding united action. Most celebrated of these conferences.was the Albany congress of 1754, called to treat with the Six Nations, and to consider plans of union. Even a cursory reading of the plan proposed by the congress reveals the importance of the frontier. The powers of the general council and the officers were, chiefly, the determination of peace and war with the Indians, the regulation of Indian trade, the purchase of Indian lands, and the creation and government of new settlements as a security against the Indians. It is evident that the unifying tendencies of the Revolutionary period were facilitated by the previous coöperation in the regulation of the frontier. In this connection may be mentioned the importance of the frontier, from that day to this, as a military training school, keeping alive the power of resistance to aggression, and developing the stalwart and rugged qualities of the frontiersman.

It would not be possible in the limits of this paper to trace the other frontiers across the continent. Travelers of the eighteenth century found the "cowpens" among the canebrakes and peavine pastures of the South, and the "cow drivers" took their droves to Charleston, Philadelphia, and New York.[28] Travelers at the close of the War of 1812 met droves of more than a thousand cattle and swine from the interior of Ohio going to Pennsylvania to fatten for the Philadelphia market.[29] The ranges of the Great Plains, with ranch and cowboy and nomadic life, are things of yesterday and of to-day. The experience of the Carolina cowpens guided the ranchers of Texas. One element favoring the rapid extension of the rancher's frontier is the fact that in a remote country lacking transportation facilities the product must be in small bulk, or must be able to transport itself, and the cattle raiser could easily drive his product to market. The effect of these great ranches on the subsequent agrarian history of the localities in which they existed should be studied.

The maps of the census reports show an uneven advance of the farmer's frontier, with tongues of settlement pushed forward and with indentations of wilderness. In part this is due to Indian resistance, in part to the location of river valleys and passes, in part to the unequal force of the centers of frontier attraction. Among the important centers of attraction may be mentioned the following: fertile and favorably situated soils, salt springs, mines, and army posts.

The frontier army post, serving to protect the settlers from the Indians, has also acted as a wedge to open the Indian country, and has been a nucleus for settlement.[30] In this connection mention should also be made of the government military and exploring expeditions in determining the lines of settlement. But all the more important expeditions were greatly indebted to the earliest pathmakers, the Indian guides, the traders and trappers, and the French voyageurs, who were inevitable parts of governmental expeditions from the days of Lewis and Clark.[31] Each expedition was an epitome of the previous factors in western advance.

In an interesting monograph, Victor Hehn[32] has traced the effect of salt upon early European development, and has pointed out how it affected the lines of settlement and the form of administration. A similar study might be made for the salt springs of the United States. The early settlers were tied to the coast by the need of salt, without which they could not preserve their meats or live in comfort. Writing in 1752, Bishop Spangenburg says of a colony for which he was seeking lands in North Carolina, "They will require salt & other necessaries which they can neither manufacture nor raise. Either they must go to Charleston, which is 300 miles distant . . . Or else they must go to Boling's Point in V^a on a branch of the James & is also 300 miles from here . . . Or else they must go down the Roanoke — I know not how many miles — where salt is brought up from the Cape Fear."[33] This may serve as a typical illustration. An annual pilgrimage to the coast for salt thus became essential. Taking flocks or furs and ginseng root, the early settlers sent their pack trains after seeding time each year to the coast.[34] This proved to be an important educational influence, since it was almost the only way in which the pioneer learned what was going on in the East. But when discovery was made of the salt springs of the Kanawha, and the Holston, and Kentucky, and central New York, the West began to be freed from dependence on the coast. It was in part the effect of finding these salt springs that enabled settlement to cross the mountains.

From the time the mountains rose between the pioneer and the seaboard, a new order of Americanism arose. The West and the East began to get out of touch of each other. The settlements from the sea to the mountains kept connection with the rear and had a certain solidarity. But the over-mountain men grew more and more independent. The East took a narrow view of American advance, and nearly lost these men. Kentucky and Tennessee history bears abundant witness to the truth of this statement. The East began to try to hedge and limit westward expansion. Though Webster could declare that there were no Alleghanies in his politics, yet in politics in general they were a very solid factor.

The exploitation of the beasts took hunter and trader to the west, the exploitation of the grasses took the rancher west, and the exploitation of the virgin soil of the river valleys and prairies attracted the farmer. Good soils have been the most continuous attraction to the farmer's frontier. The land hunger of the Virginians drew them down the rivers into Carolina, in early colonial days; the search for soils took the Massachusetts men to Pennsylvania and to New York. As the eastern lands were taken up migration flowed across them to the west. Daniel Boone, the great backwoodsman, who combined the occupations of hunter, trader, cattle-raiser, farmer, and surveyor — learning, probably from the traders, of the fertility of the lands of the upper Yadkin, where the traders were wont to rest as they took their way to the Indians, left his Pennsylvania home with his father, and passed down the Great Valley road to that stream. Learning from a trader of the game and rich pastures of Kentucky, he pioneered the way for the farmers to that region. Thence he passed to the frontier of Missouri, where his settlement was long a landmark on the frontier. Here again he helped to open the way for civilization, finding salt licks, and trails, and land. His son was among the earliest trappers in the passes of the Rocky Mountains, and his party are said to have been the first to camp on the present site of Denver. His grandson, Col. A. J. Boone, of Colorado, was a power among the Indians of the Rocky Mountains, and was appointed an agent by the government. Kit Carson's mother was a Boone.[35] Thus this family epitomizes the backwoodsman's advance across the continent.

The farmer's advance came in a distinct series of waves. In Peck's New Guide to the West, published in Boston in 1837, occurs this suggestive passage:

> Generally, in all the western settlements, three classes, like the waves of the ocean, have rolled one after the other. First comes the pioneer, who depends for the subsistence of his family chiefly upon the natural growth of vegetation, called the "range," and the proceeds of hunting. His implements of agriculture are rude, chiefly of his own make, and his efforts directed mainly to a crop of corn and a "truck patch." The last is a rude garden for growing cabbage, beans, corn for roasting ears, cucumbers and potatoes. A log cabin, and, occasionally, a stable and corn-crib, and a field of a dozen acres, the timber girdled or "deadened," and fenced, are enough for his occupancy. It is quite immaterial whether he ever becomes the owner of the soil. He is the occupant for the time being, pays no rent, and feels as independent as the "lord of the manor." With a horse, cow, and one or two breeders of swine, he strikes into the woods with his family, and becomes the founder of a new county or perhaps state. He builds his cabin, gathers around him a few other families of similar tastes and habits, and occupies till the range is somewhat subdued, and hunting a little precarious, or, which is more frequently the case, till the neighbors crowd around, roads, bridges, and fields annoy him, and he lacks elbow room. The preemption law enables him to dispose of his cabin and cornfield to the next class of emigrants; and, to employ his

own figures, he "breaks for the high timber," "clears out for the New Purchase," or migrates to Arkansas or Texas, to work the same process over.

The next class of emigrants purchase the lands, add field to field, clear out the roads, throw rough bridges over the streams, put up hewn log houses with glass windows and brick or stone chimneys, occasionally plant orchards, build mills, schoolhouses, court-houses, etc., and exhibit the picture and forms of plain, frugal, civilized life.

Another wave rolls on. The men of capital and enterprise come. The settler is ready to sell out and take the advantage of the rise in property, push farther into the interior and become, himself, a man of capital and enterprise in turn. The small village rises to a spacious town or city; substantial edifices of brick, extensive fields, orchards, gardens, colleges, and churches are seen. Broadcloths, silks, leghorns, crapes, and all the refinements, luxuries, elegancies, frivolities, and fashions are in vogue. Thus wave after wave is rolling westward; the real Eldorado is still farther on.

A portion of the two first classes remain stationary amidst the general movement, improve their habits and condition, and rise in the scale of society.

The writer has traveled much amongst the first class, the real pioneers. He has lived many years in connection with the second grade; and now the third wave is sweeping over large districts of Indiana, Illinois, and Missouri. Migration has become almost a habit in the West. Hundreds of men can be found, not over 50 years of age, who have settled for the fourth, fifth, or sixth time on a new spot. To sell out and remove only a few hundred miles makes up a portion of the variety of backwoods life and manners.[36]

Omitting those of the pioneer farmers who move from the love of adventure, the advance of the more steady farmer is easy to understand. Obviously the immigrant was attracted by the cheap lands of the frontier, and even the native farmer felt their influence strongly. Year by year the farmers who lived on soil whose returns were diminished by unrotated crops were offered the virgin soil of the frontier at nominal prices. Their growing families demanded more lands, and these were dear. The competition of the unexhausted, cheap, and easily tilled prairie lands compelled the farmer either to go west and continue the exhaustion of the soil on a new frontier, or to adopt intensive culture. Thus the census of 1890 shows, in the Northwest, many counties in which there is an absolute or a relative decrease of population. These States have been sending farmers to advance the frontier on the plains, and have themselves begun to turn to intensive farming and to manufacture. A decade before this, Ohio had shown the same transition stage. Thus the demand for land and the love of wilderness freedom drew the frontier ever onward.

Having now roughly outlined the various kinds of frontiers, and their modes of advance, chiefly from the point of view of the frontier itself, we may next inquire what were the influences on the East and on the Old World. A rapid enumeration of some of the more noteworthy effects is all that I have time for.

First, we note that the frontier promoted the formation of a composite nationality for the American people. The coast was preponderantly English, but the later tides of continental immigration flowed across to the free lands. This was the case from the early colonial days. The Scotch-Irish and the Palatine Germans, or "Pennsylvania Dutch," furnished the dominant element in the stock of the colonial frontier. With these peoples were also the freed indented servants, or redemptioners, who at the expiration of their time of service passed to the frontier. Governor Spotswood of Virginia writes in 1717, "The inhabitants of our frontiers are composed generally of such as have been transported hither as servants, and, being out of their time, settle themselves where land is to be taken up and that will produce the necessarys of life with little labour."[37] Very generally these re-demptioners were of non-English stock. In the crucible of the frontier the immigrants were Americanized, liberated, and fused into a mixed race, English in neither nationality nor characteristics. The process has gone on from the early days to our own. Burke and other writers in the middle of the eighteenth century believed that Pennsylvania[38] was "threatened with the danger of being wholly foreign in language, manners, and perhaps even inclinations." The German and Scotch-Irish elements in the frontier of the South were only less great. In the middle of the present century the German element in Wisconsin was already so considerable that leading publicists looked to the creation of a German state out of the commonwealth by concentrating their colonization.[39] Such examples teach us to beware of misinterpreting the fact that there is a common English speech in America into a belief that the stock is also English.

In another way the advance of the frontier decreased our dependence on England. The coast, particularly of the South, lacked diversified industries, and was dependent on England for the bulk of its supplies. In the South there was even a dependence on the Northern colonies for articles of food. Governor Glenn, of South Carolina, writes in the middle of the eighteenth century: "Our trade with New York and Philadelphia was of this sort, draining us of all the little money and bills we could gather from other places for their bread, flour, beer, hams, bacon, and other things of their produce, all which, except beer, our new townships begin to supply us with, which are settled with very industrious and thriving Germans. This no doubt diminishes the number of shipping and the appearance of our trade, but it is far from being a detriment to us."[40] Before long the frontier created a demand for merchants. As it retreated from the coast it became less and less possible for England to bring her supplies directly to the consumer's wharfs, and carry away staple crops, and staple crops began to give way to diversified agriculture for a time. The effect of this phase of the frontier action upon the northern section is perceived when we realize how the advance of the frontier aroused seaboard cities like Boston, New York, and Baltimore, to engage in rivalry for what Washington called "the extensive and valuable trade of a rising empire."

The legislation which most developed the powers of the national government, and played the largest part in its activity, was conditioned on the frontier. Writers have discussed the subjects of tariff, land, and internal improvement, as subsidiary to the slavery question. But when American history comes to be rightly viewed it will be seen that the slavery question is an incident. In the period from the end of the first half of the present century to the close of the Civil War slavery rose to primary, but far from exclusive, importance. But this does not justify Dr. von Holst (to take an example) in treating our constitutional history in its formative period down to 1828 in a single volume, giving six volumes chiefly to the history of slavery from 1828 to 1861, under the title "Constitutional History of the United States." The growth of nationalism and the evolution of American political institutions were dependent on the advance of the frontier. Even so recent a writer as Rhodes, in his "History of the United States since the Compromise of 1850," has treated the legislation called out by the western advance as incidental to the slavery struggle.

This is a wrong perspective. The pioneer needed the goods of the coast, and so the grand series of internal improvement and railroad legislation began, with potent nationalizing effects. Over internal improvements occurred great debates, in which grave constitutional questions were discussed. Sectional groupings appear in the votes, profoundly significant for the historian. Loose construction increased as the nation marched westward.[41] But the West was not content with bringing the farm to the factory. Under the lead of Clay — "Harry of the West" — protective tariffs were passed, with the cry of bringing the factory to the farm. The disposition of the public lands was a third important subject of national legislation influenced by the frontier.

The public domain has been a force of profound importance in the nationalization and development of the government. The effects of the struggle of the landed and the landless States, and of the Ordinance of 1878, need no discussion.[42] Administratively the frontier called out some of the highest and most vitalizing activities of the general government. The purchase of Louisiana was perhaps the constitutional turning point in the history of the Republic, inasmuch as it afforded both a new area for national legislation and the occasion of the downfall of the policy of strict construction. But the purchase of Louisiana was called out by frontier needs and demands. As frontier States accrued to the Union the national power grew. In a speech on the dedication of the Calhoun monument Mr. Lamar explained: "In 1789 the States were the creators of the Federal Government: in 1861 the Federal Government was the creator of a large majority of the States."

When we consider the public domain from the point of view of the sale and disposal of the public lands we are again brought face to face with the frontier. The policy of the United States in dealing with its lands is in sharp contrast with the European system of scientific administration. Efforts to make this domain a source of revenue, and to withhold it from emigrants in order that settlement might be compact, were in vain. The jealousy and the fears of the East were powerless in the face of the demands of the frontiersmen. John Quincy Adams was obliged to confess: "My own system of administration, which was to make the national domain the inexhaustible fund for progressive and unceasing internal improvement, has failed." The reason is obvious; a system of administration was not what the West demanded; it wanted land. Adams states the situation as follows: "The slaveholders of the South have bought the coöperation of the western country by the bribe of the western lands, abandoning to the new Western States their own proportion of the public property and aiding them in the design of grasping all the lands into their own hands. Thomas H. Benton was the author of this system, which he brought forward as a substitute for the American system of Mr. Clay, and to supplant him as the leading statesman of the West. Mr. Clay, by his tariff compromise with Mr. Calhoun, abandoned his own American system. At the same time he brought forward a plan for distributing among all the States of the Union the proceeds of the sales of the public lands. His bill for that purpose passed both Houses of Congress, but was vetoed by

President Jackson, who, in his annual message of December, 1832, formally recommended that all public lands should be gratuitously given away to individual adventurers and to the States in which the lands are situated."[43]

"No subject," said Henry Clay, "which has presented itself to the present, or perhaps any preceding, Congress, is of greater magnitude than that of the public lands." When we consider the far-reaching effects of the government's land policy upon political, economic, and social aspects of American life, we are disposed to agree with him. But this legislation was framed under frontier influences, and under the lead of Western statesmen like Benton and Jackson. Said Senator Scott of Indiana in 1841: "I consider the preemption law merely declaratory of the custom or common law of the settlers."

It is safe to say that the legislation with regard to land, tariff and internal improvements — the American system of the nationalizing Whig party — was conditioned on frontier ideas and needs. But it was not merely in legislative action that the frontier worked against the sectionalism of the coast. The economic and social characteristics of the frontier worked against sectionalism. The men of the frontier had closer resemblances to the Middle region than to either of the other sections. Pennsylvania had been the seed-plot of frontier emigration, and, although she passed on her settlers along the Great Valley into the west of Virginia and the Carolinas, yet the industrial society of these Southern frontiersmen was always more like that of the Middle region than like that of the tide-water portion of the South, which later came to spread its industrial type throughout the South.

The Middle region, entered by New York harbor, was an open door to all Europe. The tide-water part of the South represented typical Englishmen, modified by a warm climate and servile labor, and living in baronial fashion on great plantations; New England stood for a special English movement — Puritanism. The Middle region was less English than the other sections. It had a wide mixture of nationalities, a varied society, the mixed town and country system of local government, a varied economic life, many religious sects. In short, it was a region mediating between New

England and the South, and the East and the West. It represented that composite nationality which the contemporary United States exhibits, that juxtaposition of non-English groups, occupying a valley or a little settlement, and presenting reflections of the map of Europe in their variety. It was democratic and nonsectional, if not national; "easy, tolerant, and contented;" rooted strongly in material prosperity. It was typical of the modern United States. It was least sectional, not only because it lay between North and South, but also because with no barriers to shut out its frontiers from its settled region, and with a system of connecting waterways, the Middle region mediated between East and West as well as between North and South. Thus it became the typically American region. Even the New Englander, who was shut out from the frontier by the Middle region, tarrying in New York or Pennsylvania on his westward march, lost the acuteness of the sectionalism on the way.[44]

The spread of cotton culture into the interior of the South finally broke down the contrast between the "tide-water" region and the rest of the State, and based Southern interests on slavery. Before this process revealed its results the western portion of the South, which was akin to Pennsylvania in stock, society, and industry, showed tendencies to fall away from the faith of the fathers into internal improvement legislation and nationalism. In the Virginia convention of 1829-30, called to revise the constitution, Mr. Leigh, of Chesterfield, one of the tide-water counties, declared:

> One of the main causes of discontent which led to this convention, that which had the strongest influence in overcoming our veneration for the work of our fathers, which taught us to contemn the sentiments of Henry and Mason and Pendleton, which weaned us from our reverence for the constituted authorities of the State, was an overweening passion for internal improvement. I say this with perfect knowledge, for it has been avowed to me by gentlemen from the West over and over again. And let me tell the gentleman from Albemarle (Mr. Gordon) that it has been

> another principal object of those who set this ball
> of revolution in motion, to overturn the doctrine
> of State rights, of which Virginia has been the
> very pillar, and to remove the barrier she has
> interposed to the interference of the Federal Gov-
> ernment in that same work of internal improve-
> ment, by so reorganizing the legislature that
> Virginia, too, may be hitched to the Federal car.

It was this nationalizing tendency of the West that transformed the democracy of Jefferson into the national republicanism of Monroe and the democracy of Andrew Jackson.
The West of the War of 1812, the West of Clay, and Benton
and Harrison, and Andrew Jackson, shut off by the Middle
States and the mountains from the coast sections, had a solidarity of its own with national tendencies.[45] On the tide of
the Father of Waters, North and South met and mingled into
a nation. Interstate migration went steadily on — a process
of cross-fertilization of ideas and institutions. The fierce
struggle of the sections over slavery on the western frontier
does not diminish the truth of this statement; it proves the
truth of it. Slavery was a sectional trait that would not down,
but in the West it could not remain sectional. It was the greatest of frontiersmen who declared: "I believe this Government can not endure permanently half slave and half free. It
will become all of one thing or all of the other." Nothing
works for nationalism like intercourse within the nation. Mobility of population is death to localism, and the western
frontier worked irresistibly in unsettling population. The effect reached back from the frontier and affected profoundly
the Atlantic coast and even the Old World.

But the most important effect of the frontier has been in
the promotion of democracy here and in Europe. As has
been indicated, the frontier is productive of individualism.
Complex society is precipitated by the wilderness into a kind
of primitive organization based on the family. The tendency
is anti-social. It produces antipathy to control, and particularly to any direct control. The tax-gatherer is viewed as a
representative of oppression. Prof. Osgood, in an able article,[46] has pointed out that the frontier conditions prevalent

in the colonies are important factors in the explanation of the American Revolution, where individual liberty was sometimes confused with absence of all effective government. The same conditions aid in explaining the difficulty of instituting a strong government in the period of the confederacy. The frontier individualism has from the beginning promoted democracy.

The frontier States that came into the Union in the first quarter of a century of its existence came in with democratic suffrage provisions, and had reactive effects of the highest importance upon the older States whose peoples were being attracted there. An extension of the franchise became essential. It was *western* New York that forced an extension of suffrage in the constitutional convention of that State in 1821; and it was *western* Virginia that compelled the tide-water region to put a more liberal suffrage provision in the constitution framed in 1830, and to give to the frontier region a more nearly proportionate representation with the tide-water aristocracy. The rise of democracy as an effective force in the nation came in with western preponderance under Jackson and William Henry Harrison, and it meant the triumph of the frontier — with all of its good and with all of its evil elements.[47] An interesting illustration of the tone of frontier democracy in 1830 comes from the same debates in the Virginia convention already referred to. A representative from western Virginia declared:

> But, sir, it is not the increase of population in the West which this gentleman ought to fear. It is the energy which the mountain breeze and western habits import to those emigrants. They are regenerated, politically I mean, sir. They soon become *working politicians*; and the difference, sir, between a *talking* and a *working* politician is immense. The Old Dominion has long been celebrated for producing great orators; the ablest metaphysicians in policy; men that can split hairs in all abstruse questions of political economy. But at home, or when they return from Congress, they have negroes to fan them asleep. But

a Pennsylvania, a New York, an Ohio, or a western Virginia statesman, though far inferior in logic, metaphysics, and rhetoric to an old Virginia statesman, has this advantage, that when he returns home he takes off his coat and takes hold of the plow. This gives him bone and muscle, sir, and preserves his republican principles pure and uncontaminated.

So long as free land exists, the opportunity for a competency exists, and economic power secures political power. But the democracy born of free land, strong in selfishness and individualism, intolerant of administrative experience and education, and pressing individual liberty beyond its proper bounds, has its dangers as well as its benefits. Individualism in America has allowed a laxity in regard to governmental affairs which has rendered possible the spoils system and all the manifest evils that follow from the lack of a highly developed civic spirit. In this connection may be noted also the influence of frontier conditions in permitting lax business honor, inflated paper currency and wild-cat banking. The colonial and revolutionary frontier was the region whence emanated many of the worst forms of an evil currency.[48] The West in the War of 1812 repeated the phenomenon on the frontier of that day, while the speculation and wild-cat banking of the period of the crisis of 1837 occurred on the new frontier belt of the next tier of States. Thus each one of the periods of lax financial integrity coincides with periods when a new set of frontier communities had arisen, and coincides in area with these successive frontiers, for the most part. The recent Populist agitation is a case in point. Many a State that now declines any connection with the tenets of the Populists, itself adhered to such ideas in an earlier stage of the development of the State. A primitive society can hardly be expected to show the intelligent appreciation of the complexity of business interests in a developed society. The continual recurrence of these areas of paper-money agitation is another evidence that the frontier can be isolated and studied as a factor in American history of the highest importance.[49]

The East has always feared the result of an unregulated advance of the frontier, and has tried to check and guide it. The English authorities would have checked settlement at the headwaters of the Atlantic tributaries and allowed the "savages to enjoy their deserts in quiet lest the peltry trade should decrease." This called out Burke's splendid protest:

> If you stopped your grants, what would be the consequence? The people would occupy without grants. They have already so occupied in many places. You can not station garrisons in every part of these deserts. If you drive the people from one place, they will carry on their annual tillage and remove with their flocks and herds to another. Many of the people in the back settlements are already little attached to particular situations. Already they have topped the Appalachian Mountains. From thence they behold before them an immense plain, one vast, rich, level meadow; a square of five hundred miles. Over this they would wander without a possibility of restraint; they would change their manners with their habits of life; would soon forget a government by which they were disowned; would become hordes of English Tartars; and, pouring down upon your unfortified frontiers a fierce and irresistible cavalry, become masters of your governors and your counselers, your collectors and comptrollers, and of all the slaves that adhered to them. Such would, and in no long time must, be the effect of attempting to forbid as a crime and to suppress as an evil the command and blessing of Providence, "Increase and multiply." Such would be the happy result of an endeavor to keep as a lair of wild beasts that earth which God, by an express charter, has given to the children of men.

But the English Government was not alone in its desire to limit the advance of the frontier and guide its destinies. Tidewater Virginia[50] and South Carolina[51] gerrymandered those colonies to insure the dominance of the coast in their legislatures. Washington desired to settle a State at a time in the Northwest; Jefferson would reserve from settlement the territory of his Louisiana Purchase north of the thirty-second parallel, in order to offer it to the Indians in exchange for their settlements east of the Mississippi. "When we shall be full on this side," he writes, "we may lay off a range of States on the western bank from the head to the mouth, and so range after range, advancing compactly as we multiply." Madison went so far as to argue to the French minister that the United States had no interest in seeing population extend itself on the right bank of the Mississippi, but should rather fear it. When the Oregon question was under debate, in 1824, Smyth, of Virginia, would draw an unchangeable line for the limits of the United States at the outer limit of two tiers of States beyond the Mississippi, complaining that the seaboard States were being drained of the flower of their population by the bringing of too much land into market. Even Thomas Benton, the man of widest views of the destiny of the West, at this stage of his career declared that along the ridge of the Rocky mountains "the western limits of the Republic should be drawn, and the statue of the fabled god Terminus should be raised upon its highest peak, never to be thrown down."[52] But the attempts to limit the boundaries, to restrict land sales and settlement, and to deprive the West of its share of political power were all in vain. Steadily the frontier of settlement advanced and carried with it individualism, democracy, and nationalism, and powerfully affected the East and the Old World.

The most effective efforts of the East to regulate the frontier came through its educational and religious activity, exerted by interstate migration and by organized societies. Speaking in 1835, Dr. Lyman Beecher declared: "It is equally plain that the religious and political destiny of our nation is to be decided in the West," and he pointed out that the population of the West "is assembled from all the States of the Union and from all the nations of Europe, and is rushing in like the waters of the flood, demanding for its moral preservation the immediate and universal action of those institutions which discipline the mind and arm the conscience and the heart. And so various are the opinions and habits, and so recent and imperfect is the acquaintance, and so sparse are the settlements of the West, that no homogeneous public sentiment can be formed to legislate immediately into being the requisite institutions. And yet they are all needed immediately in their utmost perfection and power. A nation is being 'born in a day.' . . . But what will become of the West if her prosperity rushes up to such a majesty of power, while those great institutions linger which are necessary to form the mind and the conscience and the heart of that vast world. It must not be permitted. . . . Let no man at the East quiet himself and dream of liberty, whatever may become of the West. . . . Her destiny is our destiny."[53]

With the appeal to the conscience of New England, he adds appeals to her fears lest other religious sects anticipate her own. The New England preacher and school-teacher left their mark in the West. The dread of Western emancipation from New England's political and economic control was paralleled by her fears lest the West cut loose from her religion. Commenting in 1850 on reports that settlement was rapidly extending northward in Wisconsin, the editor of the *Home Missionary* writes: "We scarcely know whether to rejoice or mourn over this extension of our settlements. While we sympathize in whatever tends to increase the physical resources and prosperity of our country, we can not forget that with all these dispersions into remote and still remoter corners of the land the supply of the means of grace is becoming relatively less and less." Acting in accordance with such ideas, home missions were established and Western colleges were erected. As seaboard cities like Philadelphia, New York, and Baltimore strove for the mastery of Western trade, so the various denominations strove for the possession of the West. Thus an intellectual stream from New England sources fertilized the West. Other sections sent their missionaries; but the real struggle was between sects. The contest for power and the expansive tendency furnished to the various sects by the existence of a moving frontier must have had important results on the character of religious organization in the United States. The multiplication of rival churches in the little frontier towns had deep and lasting social effects. The religious aspects of the frontier make a chapter in our history which needs study.

From the conditions of frontier life came intellectual traits of profound importance. The works of travelers along each frontier from colonial days onward describe certain common traits, and these traits have, while softening down, still persisted as survivals in the place of their origin, even when a higher social organization succeeded. The result is that to the frontier the American intellect owes its striking characteristics. That coarseness and strength combined with acuteness and inquisitiveness; that practical, inventive turn of mind, quick to find expedients; that masterful grasp of material things, lacking in the artistic but powerful to effect great ends; that restless, nervous energy;[54] that dominant individualism, working for good and for evil, and withal that buoyancy and exuberance which comes with freedom — these are traits of the frontier, or traits called out elsewhere because of the existence of the frontier. Since the days when the fleet of Columbus sailed into the waters of the New World, America has been another name for opportunity, and the people of the United States have taken their tone from the incessant expansion which has not only been open but has even been forced upon them. He would be a rash prophet who should assert that the expansive character of American life has now entirely ceased. Movement has been its dominant fact, and, unless this training has no effect upon a people, the American energy will continually demand a wider field for its exercise. But never again will such gifts of free land offer themselves. For a moment, at the frontier, the bonds of custom are broken and unrestraint is triumphant. There is not *tabula rasa*. The stubborn American environment is there with its imperious summons to accept its conditions; the inherited ways of doing things are also there; and yet, in spite of environment, and in spite of custom, each frontier did indeed furnish a new field of opportunity, a gate of escape from the bondage of the past; and freshness, and confidence, and scorn of older society, impatience of its restraints and its ideas, and indifference to its lessons, have accompanied the frontier. What the Mediterranean Sea was to the Greeks, breaking the bond of customs, offering new experiences, calling out new institutions and activities, that, and more, the ever retreating frontier has been to the United States directly, and to the nations of Europe more remotely. And now, four centuries from the discovery of America, at the end of a hundred years of life under the Constitution, the frontier has gone, and with its going has closed the first period of American history.

ENDNOTES

1. A paper read at the meeting of the American Historical Association in Chicago, July 12, 1893. It first appeared in the Proceedings of the State Historical Society of Wisconsin, December 14, 1893, with the following note: "The foundation of this paper is my article entitled 'Problems in American History,' which appeared in The Ægis, a publication of the students of the University of Wisconsin, November 4, 1892. . . . It is gratifying to find that Professor Woodrow Wilson — whose volume on 'Division and Reunion' in the Epochs of American History Series, has an appreciative estimate of the importance of the West as a factor in American history — accepts some of the views set forth in the papers above mentioned, and enhances their value by his lucid and suggestive treatment of them in his article in *The Forum*, December, 1893, reviewing Goldwin Smith's 'History of the United States.' " The present text is that of the *Report of the American Historical Association* for 1893, 199-227. It was printed with additions in the *Fifth Year Book of the National Herbart Society*, and in various other publications.

2. "Abridgment of Debates of Congress," v, p. 706.

3. Bancroft (1860 ed.), iii, pp. 344, 345, citing Logan MSS.; [Mitchell] "Contest in America," etc. (1752), p. 237.

4. Kercheval, "History of the Valley"; Bernheim, "German Settlements in the Carolinas"; Winsor, "Narrative and Critical History of America," v, p. 304; Colonial Records of North Carolina, iv, p. xx; Weston, "Documents Connected with the History of South Carolina," p. 82; Ellis and Evans, "History of Lancaster County, Pa.," chs. iii, xxvi.

5. Parkman, "Pontiac," ii; Griffis, "Sir William Johnson," p. 6; Simms's "Frontiersmen of New York."

6. Monette, "Mississippi Valley," i, p. 311.

7. Wis. Hist. Cols., xi, p. 50; Hinsdale, "Old Northwest," p. 121; Burke,"Oration on Conciliation," Works (1872 ed.), i, p. 473.

8. Roosevelt, "Winning of the West," and citations there given; Cutler's "Life of Cutler."

9. Scribner's Statistical Atlas, xxxviii, pl. 13; McMaster, "Hist. of People of U. S.," i, pp. 4, 60, 61; Imlay and Filson, "Western Terri-

tory of America" (London, 1793); Rochefoucault-Liancourt, "Travels Through the United States of North America" (London, 1799); Michaux's "Journal," in *Proceedings American Philosophical Society*, xxvi, No. 129; Forman, "Narrative of a Journey Down the Ohio and Mississippi in 1780-'90" (Cincinnati, 1888); Bartram, "Travels Through North Carolina," etc. (London, 1792); Pope, "Tour Through the Southern and Western Territories," etc. (Richmond, 1792); Weld, "Travels Through the States of North America" (London, 1799); Baily, "Journal of a Tour in the Unsettled States of North America, 1796-'97" (London, 1856); Pennsylvania Magazine of History, July, 1886; Winsor, "Narrative and Critical History of America," vii, pp. 491, 492, citations.

10. Scribner's Statistical Atlas, xxxix.

11. Turner, "Character and Influence of the Indian Trade in Wisconsin" (Johns Hopkins University Studies, Series ix), pp. 61 ff.

12. Monette, "History of the Mississippi Valley," ii; Flint, "Travels and Residence in Mississippi," Flint. "Geography and History of the Western States," "Abridgment of Debates of Congress," vii. pp. 397, 398, 404; Holmes, "Account of the U. S."; Kingdom, "America and the British Colonies" (London, 1820); Grund, "Americans," ii, chs. i, iii, vi (although writing in 1836, he treats of conditions that grew out of western advance from the era of 1820 to that time); Peck, "Guide for Emigrants" (Boston, 1831); Darby, "Emigrants' Guide to Western and Southwestern States and Territories"; Dana, "Geographical Sketches in the Western Country"; Kinzie, "Waubun"; Keating, "Narrative of Long's Expedition"; Schoolcraft, "Discovery of the Sources of the Mississippi River," "Travels in the Central Portions of the Mississippi Valley," and "Lead Mines of the Missouri"; Andreas, "History of Illinois," i, 86-99; Hurlbut, "Chicago Antiquities"; McKenney, "Tour to the Lakes"; Thomas, "Travels Through the Western Country," etc. (Auburn, N.Y., 1819).

13. Darby, "Emigrants' Guide," pp. 272 ff; Benton, "Abridgment of Debates," vii, p. 397.

14. De Bow's *Review*, iv, p. 254; xvii, p. 428.

15. Grund, "Americans," ii, p. 8.

16. Peck, "New Guide to the West" (Cincinnati, 1848), ch. iv; Parkman, "Oregon Trail"; Hall, "The West" (Cincinnati, 1848); Pierce, "Incidents of Western Travel"; Murray, "Travels in North America"; Lloyd, "Steamboat Directory" (Cincinnati, 1856); "Forty Days in a Western Hotel" (Chicago), in *Putnam's Magazine*, December, 1894; Mackay, "The Western World," ii, ch. ii, iii; Meeker, "Life in the West"; Bogen, "German in America" (Boston, 1851); Olmstead, "Texas Journey"; Greeley, "Recollections of a Busy Life"; Schouler, "History of the United States," v, 261-267; Peyton, "Over

the Alleghanies and Across the Prairies" (London, 1870); Loughborough, "The Pacific Telegraph and Railway" (St. Louis, 1849); Whitney, "Project for a Railroad to the Pacific" (New York, 1849); Peyton, "Suggestions on Railroad Communication with the Pacific, and the Trade of China and the Indian Islands"; Benton, "Highway to the Pacific" (a speech delivered in the U. S. Senate, December 16, 1850).

17. A writer in *The Home Missionary* (1850), p. 239, reporting Wisconsin conditions, exclaims: "Think of this, people of the enlightened East. What an example, to come from the very frontier of civilization!" But one of the missionaries writes: "In a few years Wisconsin will no longer be considered as the West, or as an outpost of civilization, any more than Western New York, or the Western Reserve."

18. Bancroft (H. H.), "History of California," "History of Oregon," and "Popular Tribiunals": Shinn, "Mining Camps."

19. See the suggestive paper by Prof. Jesse Macy, "The Institutional Beginnings of a Western State."

20. Shinn, "Mining Camps."

21. Compare Thorpe, in *Annals American Academy of Political and Social Science*, September, 1891; Bryce, "American Commonwealth" (1888), ii, p. 689.

22. Loria, Analisi della Proprieta Capitalista, ii, p. 15.

23. Compare "Observations on the North American Land Company," London, 1796, pp. xv, 144; Logan, "History of Upper South Carolina," i, pp. 149-151; Turner, "Character and Influence of Indian Trade in Wisconsin," p. 18; Peck, "New Guide for Emigrants" (Boston, 1837), ch. iv; "Compendium Eleventh Census," i, p. xl.

24. See *post*, for illustrations of the political accompaniments of changed industrial conditions.

25. But Lewis and Clark were the first to explore the route from the Missouri to the Columbia.

26. "Narrative and Critical History of America," viii, p. 10; Sparks' "Washington Works," ix, pp. 303, 327; Logan, "History of Upper South Carolina," i; McDonald, "Life of Kenton," p. 72; Cong. Record, xxiii, p. 57.

27. On the effect of the fur trade in opening the routes of migration, see the author's "Character and Influence of the Indian Trade in Wisconsin."

28. Lodge, "English Colonies," p. 152 and citations; Logan, "Hist. of Upper South Carolina," i, p. 151.

29. Flint, "Recollections," p. 9.

30. See Monette, "Mississippi Valley," i, p. 344.

31. Coues', "Lewis and Clark's Expedition," i, pp. 2, 253-259;

Benton, in Cong. Record, xxiii, p. 57.

32. Hehn, *Das Salz* (Berlin, 1873).

33. Col. Records of N. C., v, p. 3.

34. Findley, "History of the Insurrection in the Four Western Counties of Pennsylvania in the Year 1794" (Philadelphia, 1796), p. 35.

35. Hale, "Daniel Boone" (pamphlet).

36. Compare Baily, "Tour in the Unsettled Parts of North America" (London, 1856), pp. 217-219, where a similar analysis is made for 1796. See also Collot, "January in North America" (Paris, 1826), p. 109; "Observations on the North American Land Company" (London, 1796), pp. xv, 144; Logan, "History of Upper South Carolina."

37. "Spotswood Papers," in Collections of Virginia Historical Society, i, ii.

38. [Burke], "European Settlements" (1765 ed.), ii, p. 200.

39. Everest, in "Wisconsin Historical Collections," xii, pp. 7 ff.

40. Weston, "Documents connected with History of South Carolina," p. 61.

41. See, for example, the speech of Clay, in the House of Representatives, January 30, 1824.

42. See the admirable monograph by Prof. H. B. Adams, "Maryland's Influence on the Land Cessions"; and also President Welling, in Papers American Historical Association, iii, p. 411.

43. Adams' Memoirs, ix, pp. 247, 248.

44. Author's article in *The Ægis* (Madison, Wis.), November 4, 1892.

45. Compare Roosevelt, "Thomas Benton," ch. i.

46. *Political Science Quarterly*, ii, p. 457. Compare Sumner, "Alexander Hamilton," chs.-ii-vii.

47. Compare Wilson, "Division and Reunion," pp. 15, 24.

48. On the relation of frontier conditions to Revolutionary taxation, see Sumner, Alexander Hamilton, ch. iii.

49. I have refrained from dwelling on the lawless characteristics of the frontier, because they are sufficiently well known. The gambler and desperado, the regulators of the Carolinas and the vigilantes of California, are types of that line of scum that the waves of advancing civilization bore before them, and of the growth of spontaneous organs of authority where legal authority was absent. Compare Barrows, "United States of Yesterday and To-morrow"; Shinn, "Mining Camps"; and Bancroft, "Popular Tribunals." The humor, bravery, and rude strength, as well as the vices of the frontier in its worst aspect, have left traces on American character, language, and literature, not soon to be effaced.

50. Debates in the Constitutional Convention, 1829-1830.

51. [McCrady] Eminent and Representative Men of the Carolinas, i, p. 43; Calhoun's Works, i, pp. 401-406.

52. Speech in the Senate, March 1, 1825; Register of Debates. i, 721.

53. Plea for the West (Cincinnati, 1835), pp. 11 ff.

54. Colonial travelers agree in remarking on the phlegmatic characteristics of the colonists. It has frequently been asked how such a people could have developed that strained nervous energy now characteristic of them. Compare Sumner, "Alexander Hamilton," p. 98, and Adams, "History of the United States," i, p. 60; ix, pp. 240, 241. The transition appears to become marked at the close of the War of 1812, a period when interest centered upon the development of the West, and the West was noted for restless energy. Grund, "Americans," ii, ch. i.

About the Selections

The style of some of the excerpts in this book has been changed to reflect a uniform design and continuity throughout the anthology.

BIBLIOGRAPHY

Beard, Charles A., and Mary R. Beard. *New Basic History of the United States*. Garden City: Doubleday & Co., Inc., 1968.

Buley, R. Carlyle. *The Old Northwest Pioneer Period 1815-1840*, Volume One. Bloomington: Indiana University Press, 1951.

Catton, Bruce, and William B. Catton. *The Bold and Magnificent Dream: America's Founding Years, 1492-1815*. Garden City: Doubleday & Co., Inc., 1978.

Churchill, Winston S. *A History of the English-Speaking Peoples:* Volume Four, *The Great Democracies*. New York: Bantam Books, Inc., 1958.

Commager, Henry Steele. *The Empire of Reason: How Eu-*

rope Imagined and America Realized the Enlightenment. Garden City: Anchor Press/Doubleday, 1977.

de Tocqueville, Alexis. *Democracy in America.* Edited by J. P. Mayer. Garden City: Anchor Books/Doubleday & Co., Inc., 1969.

DeVoto, Bernard. *The Course of Empire.* Lincoln: University of Nebraska Press, 1952.

Handlin, Oscar. *The Americans: A New History of the People of the United States.* Boston: Atlantic-Little, Brown, 1963.

Morison, Samuel Eliot. *The Oxford History of The American People.* New York: Oxford University Press, 1965.

Nevins, Allan and Henry Steele Commager. *A Short History of the United States.* New York: The Modern Library, 1969.

Parkman, Francis. *A Half-Century of Conflict. France and England in North America. Part Sixth.* Boston: Little, Brown, and Company, 1910.

Turner, Frederick Jackson. *The Frontier in American History.* Tucson: University of Arizona Press, 1986.

ACKNOWLEDGEMENTS

Excerpt from *New Basic History of the United States* by Charles A. Beard and Mary R. Beard. Copyright © 1944, 1960, 1968 by Doubleday & Company, Inc. Reprinted by permission of the publisher.

From *The Old Northwest Pioneer Period, 1815-1840,* by Roscoe Carlyle Buley. Reprinted by permission of Indiana University Press.

Excerpt from *The Bold and Magnificent Dream* by Bruce and William Catton. Copyright © 1978 by Bruce Catton and